"This work offers a rare perspective of the interplay between the judiciary on one hand and institutions responsible for making decisions about healthcare investments, on the other. Studying real examples of priority setting institutions and of court rulings from Latin America and the UK, it offers valuable lessons for policy makers, legal experts and human rights advocates, demonstrating rather clearly that all decisions carry trade-offs and that in the strive to realise health as a human right, good intentions alone may result into perverse outcomes for the poorest and sickest amongst us".

Kalipso Chalkidou, *Professor of Public Health, Imperial College London and founder of NICE International, UK*

"A challenging dissection of the impact of courts on health care decision-making. Learned, well-researched and written in a clear style, this book's close scrutiny of three jurisdictions leads it to ask some very hard questions about whether judges – even well-meaning ones – might not be doing more harm than good in this vital arena".

Conor Gearty, *Professor of Human Rights Law, Department of Law, LSE, UK*

"Resource limits in health care generate agonizing dilemmas for health care providers. They also create challenges for the idea that everyone has a right to health, and difficulties in designing institutions that do justice to individuals' claims. In this book, Daniel Wang offers a clear-headed and empirically informed look at these problems and how they may be resolved. He stands apart in his ability to master and integrate theories of health care justice, legal theory and practice, and social science. The result is a landmark analysis of how to conceive of, and institutionalize, the right to health".

Alex Voorhoeve, *Professor of Philosophy, Department of Philosophy, Logic and Scientific Method, LSE, UK*

Health Technology Assessment, Courts, and the Right to Healthcare

Both developing and developed countries face an increasing mismatch between what patients expect to receive and what healthcare systems can afford to provide. In countries where the entitlement to receive healthcare is recognized in the law, the patients frustrated expectations have led to lawsuits challenging the denial of funding for health treatments by health systems.

Based on the case study of three jurisdictions – Brazil, Colombia, and England, this book analyses the impact of courts and litigation on the way health systems set priorities and make rationing decisions. In particular, it focuses on how the judicial protection of the right to healthcare can impact the institutionalization, functioning, and centrality of health technology assessment (HTA) for decisions about the funding of treatment. These case studies show the paradoxes of judicial control, which can promote accountability and impair it, demand administrative competence and undermine bureaucratic capacities. They offer a nuanced and evidence-informed understanding of these paradoxes in the context of healthcare by showing how the judicial control of priority-setting decisions can be used to require and control an explicit scheme for health technology assessment but can also limit and circumvent it.

This book will be essential for those working in the areas of Medical Law, Healthcare Policy, Human Rights Law, and Ethics.

Daniel Wei Liang Wang is Associate Professor at Fundação Getúlio Vargas (FGV) School of Law. Before joining FGV, he was a Lecturer (Assistant Professor) in Health and Human Rights at the Queen Mary University of London and a Law Fellow at the London School of Economics, where he taught Human Rights Law. Daniel holds a PhD in Law (LSE), an MSc in Philosophy and Public Policies (LSE), a Master in Law (University of São Paulo), a BA in Social Sciences (University of São Paulo), and a BA in Law (University of São Paulo). He was a member of the National Health Service (NHS) Central London Research Ethics Committee (2017–2019).

Health Technology Assessment, Courts, and the Right to Healthcare

Daniel Wei Liang Wang

Routledge
Taylor & Francis Group
LONDON AND NEW YORK

First published 2022
by Routledge
2 Park Square, Milton Park, Abingdon, Oxon OX14 4RN

and by Routledge
605 Third Avenue, New York, NY 10158

Routledge is an imprint of the Taylor & Francis Group, an informa business

British Library Cataloguing-in-Publication Data
A catalogue record for this book is available from the British Library

Library of Congress Cataloging-in-Publication Data
Names: Wang, Daniel Wei Liang, author.
Title: Health technology assessment, courts and the right to healthcare/ Daniel Wei Liang Wang.
Description: Abingdon, Oxon; New York, NY: Routledge, 2022. | Includes bibliographical references and index.
Identifiers: LCCN 2021039816 (print) | LCCN 2021039817 (ebook) | ISBN 9781138554757 (hardback) | ISBN 9781032184913 (paperback) | ISBN 9781315149165 (ebook)
Subjects: LCSH: Medical care–Lawand legislation–England. | Medical care–Lawand legislation–Brazil. | Medical care–Lawand legislation–Colombia. | Medical care–England–Decision making. | Medical care–Brazil–Decision making. | Medical care–Colombia–Decision making. | Judicial process–England. | Judicial process–Brazil. | Judicial process–Colombia. | Right to health care–Cases.
Classification: LCC K3601 .W3639 2022(print) | LCC K3601(ebook) | DDC 344.04/1–dc23
LC record available at https://lccn.loc.gov/2021039816
LC ebook record available at https://lccn.loc.gov/2021039817

ISBN: 978-1-138-55475-7 (hbk)
ISBN: 978-1-032-18491-3 (pbk)
ISBN: 978-1-315-14916-5 (ebk)

DOI: 10.4324/9781315149165

Typeset in Galliard
by Deanta Global Publishing Services, Chennai, India

For Thaysa Sarmento Pereira

Contents

Acknowledgements

This book is the result of a long-term project carried out in three institutions: The London School of Economics and Political Science (LSE), Queen Mary University of London (QMUL), and Fundação Getulio Vargas (FGV). I am immensely grateful to these institutions for hosting my research and for creating the stimulating academic environments that made this book possible.

I would like to offer my special thanks to Conor Gearty, Tom Poole, Richard Ashcroft, Ruth Fletcher, Alex Voorhoeve, Octávio Ferraz, and Virgílio Afonso da Silva for their supervision and mentorship at different stages of my career. They are my role models not only because they set the standard of academic excellence that I aim to achieve but especially because they are thoughtful, kind, and generous.

I was very lucky to have Leonardo Heck, Gabriela Vargas, and Bruno Oliveira as my research assistants at different stages of this project. They were instrumental in the production of this book. I am also indebted to Beatriz Rache and Fernando Falbel for their very competent support with data analysis and to Aurélio Mejía, Ornella Moreno-Mattar, Héctor Castro, and Iñaki Gutierrez Ibarluzea for their very insightful interviews.

I have had the privilege of having fantastic colleagues, students, and friends with whom I discussed different parts of my work. Trying to name all of them can only result in inexcusable omissions. I hope life will offer me the opportunity to show each of them my appreciation through words and actions.

An earlier version of Chapters 2 and 4 have been published in the *Human Rights Law Review* (Wang, Daniel Wei L. "Right to health litigation in Brazil: the problem and the institutional responses" *Human Rights Law Review* 15, no 4 (2015): 617–641 and Wang, Daniel Wei L. "Priority-setting and the right to health: synergies and tensions on the path to Universal Health Coverage" *Human Rights Law Review* 20, no 4 (2020): 704–724); and of Chapter 6 in the *Cambridge Law Journal* (Wang, Daniel Wei L. "From Wednesbury unreasonableness to accountability for reasonableness" *The Cambridge Law Journal* 76, no. 3 (2017): 642–670). I am grateful to these journals for their permission to update and reprint these articles as chapters in this book.

Part of the research in this book benefited from the financial support provided by the Wellcome Trust (Grant ID: 200120/Z/15/Z) and the São Paulo

Research Foundation (FAPESP) (Grant ID: 2019/15565-0). For their generosity and trust, I am truly indebted.

I also want to take this opportunity to thank my family and pay tribute to my grandparents – Wang Hu Chang (in memoriam), Fang Biau (in memoriam), Liu Kuei Jung (in memoriam), and Shieh Fu Mei. They lived through difficult times and experienced hardships and losses without ever losing their dignity and humanity. I will always carry with me their example of fortitude, hard work, frugality, and love for their family.

This book is dedicated to my beloved wife Thaysa Sarmento Pereira. My career opportunities meant difficult choices for us. Yet, she has given me nothing but trust, understanding, and unconditional support. Together we are building a lovely family. Making her, Beatriz Sarmento Wang, and Ian Sarmento Wang proud is my main motivation in life.

Daniel Wei Liang Wang

1 Introduction

Patients all over the world face the agonizing mismatch between the optimal level of care they expect to receive and what their health systems provide. One of the main reasons for this imbalance is the scarcity of resources, which forces even well-functioning and best-funded health systems to limit or deny funding for treatments that can potentially prolong and/or improve lives. This is a phenomenon known in the literature as healthcare rationing.

The fact that healthcare demand increasingly outstrips health systems' supply capacity is in part the result of important advances in health and healthcare in recent years. Poverty reduction, access to primary care, and the efforts to control transmissible diseases globally have increased life expectancy, which means people now need care for longer and for conditions that are more expensive to treat. Healthcare coverage has expanded significantly (albeit unevenly) all over the world and promoting access to the formerly unprotected, especially if the principles of equity and equality in healthcare are taken seriously, requires substantial subsidies and public spending that are not always sufficient. Knowledge and information spread fast, and patients and professionals have more access to information. They also have more channels where they can make their needs, preferences, and demands known (e.g., social media, lobbying/advocacy, and litigation), particularly when they have the support of the medical industry. Investment and progress in science have enabled the development of new health technologies at a breakneck pace, expanding the possibilities for patients – including for those with very rare conditions – while significantly increasing the costs for health systems.

Therefore, if all goes well, the demand–supply imbalance in healthcare will likely continue and be aggravated as living conditions, health coverage, access to information, public involvement, and scientific knowledge improve. Ironically, the "burden of triumph"[1] will also mean a continuous dissatisfaction with health systems even when their performance and results improve.

1 Andrew Dilnot, "The Burden of Triumph: Meeting Health and Social Care Needs," *The Lancet* 390, no. 10103 (October 2017).

DOI: 10.4324/9781315149165-1

Scarcity of resources and unmet health demands are a constant source of conflict between and among patients, health professionals, the healthcare industry, and health authorities. These conflicts play out in different institutional arenas and this book will focus on two of them that have been gaining increasing attention from policymakers and scholars: courts and health technology assessment (HTA) bodies. More importantly, it aims to offer an evidence-informed analysis of the relationship between courts and HTA bodies.

The involvement of courts in decisions about the funding of health treatments in several jurisdictions, which includes reviewing and making allocative decisions, has caught the attention of the literature in law, ethics, and health. The court cases against health systems that challenge healthcare rationing decisions will be called in this book the "right to healthcare litigation". In many countries, particularly in the global south, this phenomenon can be attributed to what Gauri and Brinks call social rights constitutionalism, that is, "the increasing inclusion of social and economic rights language in constitutions, the increasing use of that language by social actors to pursue their goals, and the increasing judicialization of political disputes under the social rights rubric".[2] The right to healthcare litigation can also be found in countries with very different legal and constitutional traditions such as Canada, Germany, the Netherlands, Switzerland, and Thailand.[3]

The impact of courts on access to healthcare, the distributive effects of judicial decisions on health systems, and the proper role of courts in issues of social policy have been widely debated and researched.[4] This book will build upon this relevant body of literature. However, *if*, *why*, and *how* courts and litigation affect the way health systems set priorities and make rationing decisions has been mostly neglected. Not much is known about changes in the processes of health systems for making funding decisions when policymakers are aware that courts

2 Daniel M. Brinks, Varun Gauri, and Kyle Shen, "Social Rights Constitutionalism: Negotiating the Tension between the Universal and the Particular," *Annual Review Law and Social Science* 11 (November 2015): 290.

3 Colleen M. Flood, "Just Medicare: The Role of Canadian Courts in Determining Health Care Rights and Access," *Journal of Law, Medicine & Ethics* 33, no. 4 (Winter 2005); Stefanie Ettelt, "Access to Treatment and the Constitutional Right to Health in Germany: A Triumph of Hope Over Evidence?" *Health Economics, Policy and Law* 15, no. 1 (January 2020); Floortje Moes et al., "Contested Evidence: A Dutch Reimbursement Decision Taken to Court," *Health Economics, Policy and Law* 12, no. 3 (July 2017); Felix Kesselring, "First Fundamental Decision of the Federal Supreme Court of Switzerland on Cost-Effectiveness in the Area of Human Healthcare," *European Journal of Risk Regulation* 2, no. 3 (September 2011); Sripen Tantivess and Viroj Tangcharoensathien, "Coverage Decisions and the Court: A Public Health Perspective on Glucosamine Reimbursement in Thailand," *Health Systems & Reform* 2, no. 2 (2016).

4 See, e.g., Andre den Exter and Martin Buijsen, eds., *Rationing Health Care: Hard Choices and Unavoidable Trade-offs* (Antwerp: Maklu, 2012); Colleen Flood and Aeyal Gross, eds., *The Right to Health at the Public/Private Divide: A Global Comparative Study* (New York: Cambridge University Press, 2014); Alicia Ely Yamin and Siri Gloppen, eds., *Litigating Health Rights: Can Courts Bring More Justice to Health?* (Harvard University Press, 2011); Jeff King, *Judging Social Rights* (Cambridge: Cambridge University Press, 2012).

may review their decisions and even oblige them to fund treatment. Yet, it is plausible to hypothesize that such changes occur as litigation and judicial rulings are potentially disruptive for policymakers working with the courts looking over their shoulders.

The specialist literature has not given much attention to the impact of litigation and courts on HTA either. This book will argue that it should. HTA is the systematic evaluation of health technologies to inform decision-making by health systems. In many countries, HTA has been institutionalized, that is, carried out by dedicated specialist bodies and through formal processes aimed at guaranteeing high scientific standards, transparency, and impartiality. Health systems adopt HTA to avoid funding technologies that will not produce significant health gains or whose cost may jeopardize their financial sustainability and negatively affect the provision of other services. HTA bodies are also institutional mechanisms to resolve disputes about the funding of treatment and thus legitimize rationing decisions that will often be contested by stakeholders and seen as controversial by the general public.

Legal issues related to HTA have been very rarely discussed in the specialist literature.[5] This is surprising given that the institutionalization of HTA is made through the law. The foundation of HTA bodies, the key details about their functioning (e.g., scope, members, procedures, and level of autonomy), and the nature of their outputs (e.g., whether mere recommendations or binding decisions) are all determined in legal norms. Moreover, HTA recommendations/decisions can be scrutinized by courts. They can also be presented in legal disputes as evidence to justify or challenge a priority-setting decision.

This book will fill these gaps in the scholarship on courts and HTA through an in-depth analysis and comparison of three jurisdictions – Brazil, Colombia, and England. In these jurisdictions, there is evidence that courts, by challenging the denial of funding for health treatments, have contributed to the institutionalization of HTA in their respective health systems.

Comparing Brazil, Colombia, and England may seem odd at first sight given the significant differences in their healthcare and legal systems. England has a long-established and world-renowned national health system (the National Health Service – NHS) founded in 1948, funded by general taxation, and generally free at the point of use. The NHS is responsible for most of the healthcare expenditure in the country. Brazil also has a national health system (the Sistema Único de Saúde – SUS) idealized in the 1988 Constitution and effectively created in 1990. Inspired by the NHS, it is funded by general taxation and offers universal coverage to services that are free at the point of use. However, due to chronic public underfunding and huge social inequalities, there is a strong private healthcare sector that outspends SUS (see Table 1.1). Colombia has a social

5 See, however, Daniel Widrig and Brigitte Tag, "HTA and Its Legal Issues: A Framework for Identifying Legal Issues in Health Technology Assessment," *International Journal of Technology Assessment in Health Care* 30, no. 6 (December 2014).

Table 1.1 Health and healthcare data in Brazil, Colombia, and the United Kingdom

	*Life expectancy at birth**		*Infant mortality (per 1,000 live births)*		*UHC effective coverage index***		*Health spending per type US$ (2018 PPP per capita)****							
							Total		*Government*		*Prepaid private*		*Out-of-pocket*	
	2018	*1990*	*2018*	*1990*	*2019*	*1990*	*2016*	*1995*	*2016*	*1995*	*2016*	*1995*	*2016*	*1995*
Brazil	76	66	12	52	65	42	1863	934	620 (33%)	257 (27%)	424 (23%)	196 (21%)	819 (43%)	478 (51%)
Colombia	77	70	12	29	74	56	853	720	555 (65%)	400 (55%)	122 (14%)	42 (6%)	176 (21%)	276 (38%)
United Kingdom	81	76	4	8	88	67	4364	1779	3490 (80%)	1559 (88%)	204 (5%)	60 (4%)	669 (15%)	160 (10%)

Sources: *The World Bank. **GBD 2019 Universal Health Coverage Collaborators, "Measuring universal health coverage based on an index of effective coverage of health services in 204 countries and territories, 1990–2019: a systematic analysis for the Global Burden of Disease Study 2019," *The Lancet* 396, no. 10258 (October 17, 2020). The UHC effective coverage index and individual effective coverage indicators are reported on a scale of 0–100. It evaluates the performance of health systems through indicators of intervention coverage or outcome-based measures, such as mortality-to-incidence ratios, to approximate access to quality care. ***Global Burden of Disease Health Financing Collaborator Network, "Past, present, and future of global health financing: a review of development assistance, government, out-of-pocket, and other private spending on health for 195 countries, 1995–2050," *The Lancet* 393, no. 10187 (June 1, 2019). Percentage in relation to the total spending in the respective year.

Note: (1) Due to the lack of disaggregated data and for the sake of comparability, the United Kingdom is being used as a proxy for England. (2) The numbers in the columns may not match the combined total because the spending from development assistance was not included in the table.

health insurance scheme, created in 1993, that has expanded over the years to cover almost the whole population. This system is funded by mandatory payroll taxes (with cross-subsidies for the poor) and the public budget. A public body distributes the funds to (mostly private) insurers that manage the resources and pay providers for services covered by a government-defined package. Colombia also has a robust voluntary private sector.

Colombia and Brazil have similar key health indicators but are below those of England.[6] In terms of effective coverage, government spending, prepaid private and out-of-pocket payment, Colombia is somewhere in between Brazil and England. These three countries have health systems that have the mandate to offer universal coverage of comprehensive healthcare services and have witnessed important improvements in key health indicators. There is also increasing convergence in having non-communicable diseases as the main causes of mortality and morbidity calculated using disability-adjusted life years (DALYs) losses (see Figure 1.1).

The legal systems and the constitutional role of courts in these countries are also very different and the differences go beyond the common law/civil law divide. England is part of the United Kingdom, which belongs to what Gardbaum called the "new Commonwealth model of constitutionalism".[7] The United Kingdom adopts a "weak form" of judicial rights review: courts cannot strike down legislation even when it is declared to be in breach of human rights and judicial interpretation on rights issues can be revised through the same process used to create ordinary legislation.[8] There is no codified constitution, although the European Convention on Human Rights (ECHR), incorporated into United Kingdom domestic law through the Human Rights Act (HRA) 1998, can be seen as the equivalent of a constitutional bill of rights. Yet, the HRA only allows courts to declare legislation incompatible with the ECHR or to interpret legislation in a way that is compatible with the ECHR but does not allow courts to invalidate legislation. Moreover, the ECHR protects civil and political rights only. Social rights, such as the right to health, are absent and courts at the domestic and European level have hesitated to interpret the ECHR as including an individual right to healthcare.[9] English courts also have a more limited role in the control of administrative decisions if compared with Brazil and Colombia. As will

6 This book uses England as a case study for reasons that will be explained in Chapter 6. Yet, for reasons of data accessibility, I will be using the data on the United Kingdom as a proxy for England in this Introduction.

7 Stephen Gardbaum, *The New Commonwealth Model of Constitutionalism: Theory and Practice* (Cambridge: Cambridge University Press, 2013).

8 Mark Tushnet, *Weak Courts, Strong Rights: Judicial Review and Social Welfare Rights in Comparative Constitutional Law* (Princeton, NJ: Princeton University Press, 2008).

9 The European Court of Human Rights, however, seems to recognize that the right to life (Article 2 of the ECHR) creates a duty for the State to have in place a sufficient regulatory framework to protect the right to life of everyone in emergency situations. See Aleydis Nissen, "A Right to Access to Emergency Health Care: The European Court of Human Rights Pushes the Envelope," *Medical Law Review* 26, no. 4 (Autumn 2018).

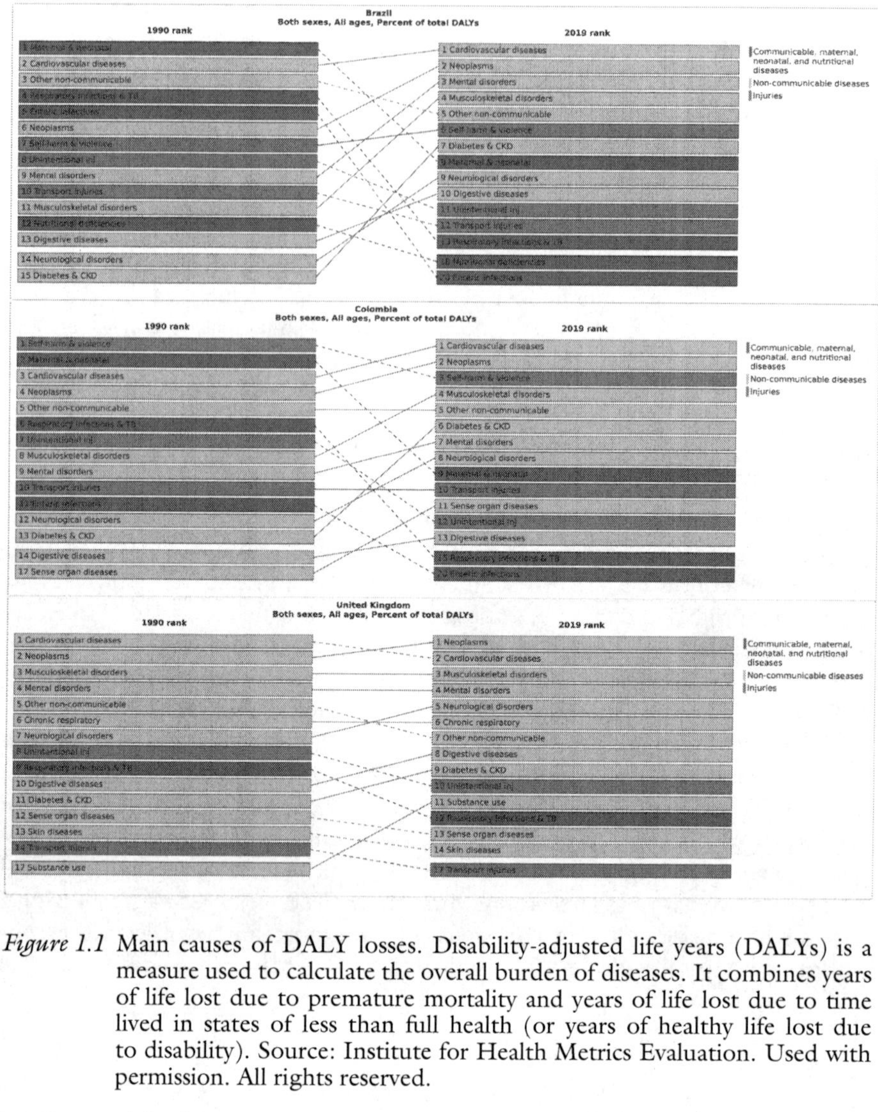

Figure 1.1 Main causes of DALY losses. Disability-adjusted life years (DALYs) is a measure used to calculate the overall burden of diseases. It combines years of life lost due to premature mortality and years of life lost due to time lived in states of less than full health (or years of healthy life lost due to disability). Source: Institute for Health Metrics Evaluation. Used with permission. All rights reserved.

be discussed further in this book, despite important changes in recent decades, English courts tend to leave a wider margin of discretion for the Executive to decide on substantive issues of policy. Moreover, courts have also avoided using rights discourse to review allocative decisions in issues of social policy.[10]

10 For a succinct but comprehensive description of the role of courts in the United Kingdom, see Peter Leyland, *The Constitution of the United Kingdom: A Contextual Analysis*, 2nd ed. (Oxford: Hart, 2012), chap. 7.

Brazil and Colombia are part of the so-called Latin American "transformative constitutionalism" or "new constitutionalism". Some of its distinctive features are worth highlighting. First, the constitutionalization of a generous and vast bill of rights via constitutional text, judicial interpretation, or the internalization of international human rights treaties. These bills include justiciable (rather than merely aspirational) social rights. Second, there is an emphasis on judicial mechanisms for the realization and enforcement of rights. The Judiciary, especially supreme and constitutional courts, has been strengthened and guaranteed more independence vis-à-vis governments. Courts' interpretative practice has also expanded their powers. Substantiating and balancing abstract constitutional principles has become a common method to adjudicate challenges against policy and legislation. Strong courts were matched by judges that are less deferential to the Executive and Legislative branches. Moreover, access to justice has expanded via the provision of legal aid, public bodies responsible for government accountability and rights protection (e.g., *Defensoría del Pueblo* in Colombia, and *Ministério Público* and *Defensoria Pública* in Brazil), and constitutional writs for expedited and unexpensive judicial remedies against rights violation (e.g., *amparos*, *tutela*, and *mandado de segurança*). The frequent recourse to rights-based judicial and constitutional review has further blurred the distinction between law, politics, and policymaking. All this has turned courts into key political players.[11]

Notwithstanding the large differences in their health and legal systems, Brazil, Colombia, and England share important similarities in key issues that make their comparison worthwhile for this book. In these jurisdictions, there have been a significant number of legal claims for health treatments and courts have engaged in issues of priority-setting and rationing in healthcare. Moreover, one of the main drivers of the right to healthcare litigation in these three countries are individual claims for new and expensive health technologies, many of them not included in the baskets of treatments that the health system in each country has selected for regular and universal provision. Therefore, despite all the differences, courts in these three countries are facing remarkably similar challenges.

In these countries, where the health systems are aware that their decisions may be scrutinized and reviewed by courts, litigation has contributed to comparable changes in the process for priority-setting. Despite the differences in the courts' approach when judging these cases, there is evidence that HTA was institutionalized, at least in part, as a response to a context of increasing litigation and

11 See Rodrigo Uprimny, "The Recent Transformation of Constitutional Law in Latin America: Trends and Challenges," *Texas Law Review* 89, no. 7 (June 2011); Oxford Research Encyclopedia of Politics, s.v. "Courts in Latin American Politics," by Ezequiel Gonzalez-Ocantos, https://doi.org/10.1093/acrefore/9780190228637.013.1680; Felipe Curcó Cobos, "The New Latin American Constitutionalism: A Critical Review in the Context of Neo-Constitutionalism," *Canadian Journal of Latin American and Caribbean Studies* 43, no. 2 (April 19, 2018). See, also, Armin von Bogdandy et al., eds., *Transformative Constitutionalism in Latin America: The Emergence of a New Ius Commune* (Oxford: Oxford University Press, 2017).

less deferential courts. It was expected that priority-setting decisions made or informed by well-functioning HTA systems would be less likely to be reviewed by courts. The institutionalization of HTA occurs through the establishment of a specialist body responsible for assessing and evaluating evidence concerning health technologies through standardized processes. Moreover, this specialist body should be formally linked to processes for making decisions about the funding of medical treatments by health systems.

I do not suggest that courts and litigation were necessary or sufficient for the creation and institutionalization of HTA systems in these jurisdictions or elsewhere. They are not necessary because other reasons may lead health authorities and politicians to adopt HTA systems.[12] HTA has been institutionalized in countries where there does not seem to be a significant volume of right to healthcare litigation. Courts and litigation are not sufficient either. Some countries have not institutionalized or given centrality to HTA despite having a high volume of healthcare judicialization. For instance, in 2015, the Department of Health of Costa Rica received funding from the Inter-American Development Bank (IDB) to create an HTA body in Costa Rica. The justifications for this agreement included the lack of "technical, systematic, consolidated, inclusive and legitimate procedure for explicit priority setting in health" in the country and the fact that litigation was diverting resources to be spent on treatments with questionable effectiveness.[13] However, according to an expert directly involved with this project, such an institution has not seen the light of the day yet, possibly due to the lack of political consensus on this topic.[14]

The in-depth analysis and comparison of cases with such important differences and similarities can offer important lessons for the scholarship on social rights adjudication, priority-setting in healthcare, and HTA systems. First, there are important differences in the courts' approach when judging complaints against rationing decisions that deny funding for health treatments. Each approach has had a different impact on the fairness of priority-setting, although they have all contributed to the institutionalization of HTA in the three case studies analysed in this book. This finding brings more nuance to the normative and doctrinal debates on how courts should judge social rights and review issues of priority-setting and distributive justice in healthcare.

Second, understanding the role of courts in the creation of HTA bodies in these countries reveals an impact of litigation and adjudication that has slipped under the radar of most analysts in law and health. This is a relevant blind spot given that this kind of impact, despite being indirect and incremental, is enduring

12 See Chapter 3.

13 Inter-American Development Bank and the Department of Health of Costa Rica, *Apoyo a la Institucionalización de la Evaluación de Tecnologías en Salud en Costa Rica - Documento de Cooperación Técnica*, CR-T1129 (Washington, DC/San José, Costa Rica: Interamerican Development Bank and the Department of Health of Costa Rica, 2015).

14 Inaki Gutierrez-Ibarluzea, interview via internet, 20 August 2020.

and has wide consequences for health systems. That court cases can have both direct and indirect effects will come as no surprise. It is also known that these effects do not necessarily depend on the outcome of the decision as the publicity of the case or the mobilization around the legal dispute can be more impactful than the court decision per se.[15] Yet, this book will analyse an impact that does not result from a specific court case, but from a large number of cases spread over a long period that has contributed to creating a context that made the case for institutionalizing HTA more compelling for health authorities and politicians.

Third, these case studies also allow the analysis of the different forms of relationship between courts and HTA once institutionalized. Courts can contribute to the creation of HTA bodies. However, they can also constrain the use of HTA for priority-setting by limiting the type of considerations that can be taken into account by health systems when making funding decisions. In Colombia, the Judiciary has implicitly ruled out the use of economic considerations for rationing decisions. Courts can also be used to circumvent priority-setting when litigation allows access to treatments that were not assessed or not recommended by HTA bodies, as in Brazil and Colombia. Lastly, courts can be used to oversee and control HTA bodies and their processes aiming at promoting quality, consistency, and procedural fairness in the assessment of health technologies, as in England. These cases show that even when courts contributed to the creation of HTA systems, this does not mean that the outcome of right to healthcare litigation is necessarily more explicit or informed priority-setting.

In sum, courts and litigation can change health systems' priority-setting processes, and the nature of this change depends on how legal entitlements to healthcare are enforced by the Judiciary in each jurisdiction. These three case studies show the paradoxes of judicial control, which can promote accountability and impair it, demand administrative competence and undermine bureaucratic capacities. These case studies offer a nuanced and evidence-informed understanding of these paradoxes by showing that the judicial control of priority-setting decisions in healthcare can be used to require and control HTA, but can also limit and circumvent it.

The approach in this book also offers a different perspective to evaluate the impact of the right to healthcare litigation on the fairness of health systems. The existing literature has mostly focused on the immediate impact of litigation on the access to the treatments that are claimed through courts. It hence tends to focus more on those who (directly or indirectly) benefit from litigation but gives less attention to the opportunity costs of funding health treatments ordered by courts that are born by other users. This book proposes a different approach by focusing on how courts and litigation impact the fairness of priority-setting

15 See, for instance, César Rodríguez-Garavito, "Beyond the Courtroom: The Impact of Judicial Activism on Socioeconomic Rights in Latin America," *Texas Law Review* 89 (2011); Daniel M. Brinks and Varun Gauri, "The 'Law's Majestic Equality? The Distributive Impact of Judicializing Social and Economic Rights," *Perspectives on Politics* 12, no. 2 (June 2014).

within a health system. If fair priority-setting is key for a health system to expand coverage and promote equality, then how courts impact the fairness of priority-setting is a good approximation for the overall impact of right to healthcare litigation on health systems and their users.

This book is divided into seven chapters, including this Introduction. Chapter 2 discusses the synergies and tensions between the right to healthcare and fair priority-setting, which are both considered central elements for achieving universal health coverage, one of the UN Sustainable Development Goals. Fair priority-setting allows efficient and just allocation of resources that are necessary for realizing the right to health. Rights can be used to demand fair priority-setting and to guarantee that priority-setting decisions are reflected in actual service provision. Yet, there can also be tension when courts apply rights to rule out economic considerations in priority-setting or order the provision of treatment to individuals or groups irrespective of the available resources and the needs of others.

Chapter 3 offers an overview of HTA. This book will discuss the relationship between courts and priority-setting in healthcare with an emphasis on HTA, an increasingly adopted tool for decisions related to the funding of health technologies and, in particular, of drugs. Drugs are the main driver of the increase in healthcare expenditure and one of the main drivers of litigation in the three countries covered in this book. HTA is one area in which health systems have put into practice principles and procedures that constitute fair priority-setting as understood by many in the contemporary literature. It thus allows us to make some concrete observations about how courts, when judging individual claims for health treatments, interact with health systems that aim to fulfil the idea of fair priority-setting.

Chapter 4 analyses the case of Brazil, where the number of judicial claims for the provision of health technologies based on the constitutional right to health has increased exponentially over recent years. The patients' high rate of success in court is, to a large extent, due to judges' lack of attention to the scientific evidence or the economic impact of their decisions, while distrusting health authorities' decisions. Explicitly in response to litigation, the Federal Law 12401/11 created a body responsible for HTA – CONITEC (National Commission for the Incorporation of Technologies at SUS) – and established a more evidence-informed and transparent administrative process for making decisions about the public funding of treatment. Yet, recent data shows that CONITEC has not changed the way courts judge claims for health treatments. Courts are being used to circumvent the HTA system they helped create as they are still ordering the provision of treatments even when they were not recommended by CONITEC.

Chapter 5 analyses the case of Colombia. Apart from the thousands of individual claims for health treatments every year, structural decisions and the constitutional control of legislation have also played an important role in forcing overarching reforms in the health system. The decision in case T-760 called for the creation of a transparent, open-for-stakeholders' participation, and an evidence-informed system for updating the basket of treatments available to users. Two of the important changes that can be traced back to this judgment are the creation of an HTA body (IETS – the Institute for Health Technology Assessment) in 2012 and Law 1751/2015. The original draft of this legislation opened the possibility for the health system to refuse funding of treatments for budget and cost-effectiveness reasons. Yet, the Constitutional Court in the case C-313 issued a decision that, in practice, ruled that the use of economic reasons for denying the funding of treatment is unconstitutional.

Chapter 6 is on England. By applying a heightened scrutiny of healthcare rationing decisions, English courts have forced health authorities to make better-informed decisions and to take procedural justice more seriously to comply with, respond to, and void judicial review. Two landmark cases – *Child B* and *Pfizer* –, coupled with several other judicial decisions, created incentives for important reforms in how the health system sets priorities, including the gradual adoption of HTA and the creation of NICE (now called National Institute for Health and Care Excellence). English courts have recognized that priority-setting is unavoidable and that these choices should be left to health authorities, which have the expertise and mandate to make them. That did not make rationing decisions non-justiciable as courts keep scrutinizing priority-setting by the health system, including by NICE, to guarantee that they are rationally justified, informed by the proper assessment of evidence, open to considering exceptional circumstances, and follow a fair procedure.

In the Conclusion, this book argues that there are many ways in which courts can strengthen and give centrality to HTA in priority-setting. However, applying the right to healthcare to limit HTA or circumvent HTA creates obstacles for fair priority-setting and rules out from the start any meaningful discussion about how the health system can, within the available resources, reduce inequalities and maximize the health benefits. If fair priority-setting is necessary for achieving universal health coverage (UHC), and UHC promotes the realization of the right to health, then right to healthcare litigation may well be pushing health systems in the opposite direction of realizing the right to health in some countries. Therefore, the expected impact of litigation on HTA is one of the main considerations to determine if, when, and how courts should be involved in the priority-setting of healthcare.

2 Priority-setting and the right to healthcare

Synergies and tensions on the path to universal health coverage

Universal health coverage and the right to healthcare

The United Nations Sustainable Development Goals (SDG) came into effect in January 2016 and set the goals that countries have committed themselves to achieve by 2030. There are 17 SDGs and within each goal there are several targets, making a total of 169 targets. Goal 3 is directly related to health ("Ensure healthy lives and promote well-being for all at all ages"). One of the targets in Goal 3 is to achieve universal health coverage (UHC), "including financial risk protection, access to quality essential healthcare services and access to safe, effective, quality and affordable essential medicines and vaccines for all" (Target 3.8). Achieving UHC has also been recognized by the World Health Organization[1] and the World Bank[2] as a fundamental goal for all countries.

There are different definitions of UHC used in the literature and by international organizations, but it is safe to affirm that UHC will necessarily encompass three elements. First, **universality**, which requires healthcare coverage for everyone without discrimination and with particular attention to the most disadvantaged groups. "No one must be left behind", as affirmed by the UN General Assembly when addressing SDG, and UHC in particular.[3] Universality can only be achieved when access to healthcare is delinked from the ability to pay and where there is extensive geographical coverage of health services, including in remote and rural areas where the neediest populations normally live. Second, healthcare coverage should allow **access to a comprehensive set of quality**

1 "World Health Assembly Concludes: Adopts Key Resolutions Affecting Global Public Health," *World Health Organization Media Centre*, May 25, 2005, https://www.who.int/mediacentre/news/releases/2005/pr_wha06/en/; "World Health Day 2018 – Key Messages for World Health Day 2018," *World Health Organization*, https://www.who.int/campaigns/world-health-day/2018/key-messages/en/.

2 World Health Organization and World Bank, *Tracking Universal Health Coverage: 2017 Global Monitoring Report* (Geneva: World Health Organization, 2017).

3 UNGA Res 70/1 "Transforming Our World: The 2030 Agenda for Sustainable Development" (September 25, 2015) UN Doc A/RES/70/1; See also, Thomas O'Connell, Kumanan Rasanathan, and Mickey Chopra, "What Does Universal Health Coverage Mean?" *The Lancet* 383, no. 9913 (January 18, 2014).

DOI: 10.4324/9781315149165-2

healthcare services. This includes access to nationally determined sets of promotive, preventive, curative, and rehabilitative health services, and of essential, safe, affordable, effective, and quality medicines and vaccines. The UN General Assembly also included public health interventions and policies to address the social determinants of health.[4] The size of each national set will vary depending on the economic circumstances of each country, but the aim is to progressively expand the coverage of health services. Third, this comprehensive set of services should offer **financial risk protection** against catastrophic healthcare expenditures. Everyone should be protected against suffering financial hardship due to the costs of medical treatment that may affect the satisfaction of other essential needs or deter the sick from accessing services because they cannot afford them.

The materialization of these three components of UHC requires a scheme based on the principle of solidarity, in which the healthy subsidize the sick and the rich subsidize the poor, and the pooling of resources to reduce or remove the need for out-of-pocket payments at the point of use.[5] The creation of such schemes will invariably require the involvement of governments through the establishment of compulsory enrolment and contribution to a health system, public funding from general government revenues, or regulatory mechanisms for risk pooling and cross-subsidies.[6] It will also require public policies that prioritize the needs of the poor.

The poor normally suffer from worse health and have more limited access to quality healthcare than the rest of the population. They are less able to afford healthcare in the market and will be particularly affected in countries where healthcare expenditure is predominantly private (out-of-pocket or through voluntary private health insurance schemes). In countries with a social insurance model, where health services are financed mainly through payroll taxes, the unemployed and those in the informal sector of the economy may not be eligible for coverage. Additionally, even if their coverage is subsidized by the government, they may not have access to the same package of services available to those in the formal sector.[7] The poor can also be disadvantaged in universal one-tier systems because they can be more severely affected by the unequal geographical distribution of professionals and facilities. In some countries, the poor may

4 UNGA Res 67/81 "Global Health and Foreign Policy" (December 12, 2012) UN Doc A/RES/67/81.

5 World Health Organization, *The World Health Report: Health Systems Financing: The Path to Universal Coverage* (Geneva: World Health Organization, 2010), xiv–xv; Dean T. Jamison et al., "Global Health 2035: A World Converging Within a Generation," *The Lancet* 382, no. 9908 (December 7, 2013): 1932; Ursula Giedion, Eduardo Andrés Alfonso, and Yadira Díaz, *The Impact of Universal Coverage Schemes in the Developing World: A Review of the Existing Evidence*, UNICO Studies Series 25 (Washington, DC: The World Bank, 2013): 1.

6 WHO, *Health Systems Financing*, 88–89; Jamison et al., 1936; Daniel Cotlear et al., *Going Universal: How 24 Developing Countries are Implementing Universal Health Coverage from the Bottom Up*, (Washington, DC: World Bank, 2015), 131.

7 Marc J. Roberts, William C. Hsiao, and Michael R. Reich, "Disaggregating the Universal Coverage Cube: Putting Equity in the Picture," *Health Systems & Reform* 1, no. 1 (2015): 23.

belong to historically disadvantaged groups and hence suffer discrimination in the access to care, whereas the better-off can use their social connections and access to information to receive healthcare in privileged conditions at the expense of other users.[8] Therefore, no matter the healthcare system model, and particularly if there is no functional health system in place, the poor have a higher probability of not receiving the care they need and are more vulnerable to catastrophic healthcare costs (depending on the level of poverty, almost any healthcare cost can be catastrophic). Unsurprisingly, the empirical evidence from the developing world shows that UHC schemes that specifically target the access of health services by the poor benefit vulnerable groups (low-income, low-assets, rural) the most, as well as producing a greater overall impact on health indicators and better value for money.[9]

The universal nature of UHC, the idea that the distribution of healthcare services should not be left to market forces and users' capacity to pay, as well as the actions required from governments for its realization for the worst-off, make the connection between UHC and human rights (and the right to health in particular) almost inevitable. This connection was explicitly made in the UN General Assembly Resolutions 67/81 (2012), 72/28 (2017), and 72/139 (2019) that propose and advocate UHC reaffirming the "right of every human being to the enjoyment of the highest attainable standard of physical and mental health", which is a direct reference to Article 12 of the UN International Covenant on Economic, Social and Cultural Rights (1966).[10] General Comment No. 14 of the United Nations Committee on Economic, Social and Cultural Rights (GC 14)[11] does not mention UHC (which is a more recent concept), but how the right to health is interpreted there reveals its proximity to the idea of UHC. According to GC14, the right to health requires, among other elements, that quality health facilities, goods, and services must be available to, accessible to, and affordable for, everyone without discrimination, especially the most vulnerable or marginalized sections of the population. In the UN Sustainable Development Goals Report (2018), it was highlighted that access to basic services, including healthcare, is a fundamental right.[12]

8 Cotlear et al., *Going Universal*, 28; Roberts, Hsiao, and Reich, 23.

9 Giedion, Alfonso, and Díaz, *Universal Coverage Schemes*, 55. See, also, Rodrigo Moreno-Serra and Peter C. Smith, "Does Progress Towards Universal Health Coverage Improve Population Health?" *The Lancet* 380, no. 9845 (September 2012).

10 "Article 12. 1. The States Parties to the Present Covenant Recognize the Right of Everyone to the Enjoyment of the Highest Attainable Standard of Physical and Mental Health."

11 ECOSOC CESCR "General Comment No. 14: The Right to the Highest Attainable Standard of Health (Art. 12 of the International Covenant on Economic, Social and Cultural Rights)" (August 11, 2000) UN Doc E/C.12/2000/4.

12 United Nations, *Sustainable Development Goals Report 2018* (New York: United Nations, 2018): 14. See, also, WHO "Shanghai Declaration on Promoting Health in the 2030 Agenda for Sustainable Development" (2016).

Other international organizations have also been vocal in defending that UHC and the right to health are conceptually close and mutually reinforcing. The World Health Organization (WHO) affirmed that UHC is the "practical expression of the concern for health equity and the right to health"[13] and that "to support the goal of universal health coverage is also to express concern for equity and for honouring everyone's right to health".[14] The association between UHC and the right to health was also made in a joint report by the World Bank and the WHO.[15] Tedros Adhanom Ghebreyesus, Director-General of the WHO, could not put it more clearly: "universal health coverage is a human right".[16]

The idea that UHC and the right to health go hand in hand has also been defended by human rights scholars who see a huge overlap between these two concepts that emphasize universality in the access to quality essential healthcare and that have a special concern for the poor and the vulnerable.[17] Indeed, it would be very difficult to achieve the right of every human being to the enjoyment of the "highest attainable standard of health" without some form of UHC that removes the financial barriers to access quality healthcare for all (and for the worst-off in particular) and which offers protection against financial risk.[18]

UHC is necessary for the realization of the right to health, but it is important to note that it is not sufficient.[19] Not all definitions of UHC will include interventions that are normally outside the responsibility of healthcare systems but that are central to the realization of the right to health because of their huge impact

13 World Health Organization, "Positioning Health in the Post-2015 Development Agenda" (WHO discussion paper, October 2012). See, also, Gorik Ooms et al., "Is Universal Health Coverage the Practical Expression of the Right to Health Care?" *BMC International Health and Human Rights* 14 (February 2014).

14 World Health Organization, *The World Health Report 2013: Research for Universal Health Coverage* (Geneva: World Health Organization, 2013), 5. See, also, WHO, *Health Systems Financing*, 13; WHO/UNICEF "Declaration of Astana" (October 25–26, 2018).

15 Cotlear et al., *Going Universal*, 21.

16 Tedros Adhanom Ghebreyesus, "All Roads Lead to Universal Health Coverage," *The Lancet Global Health* 5, no. 9 (September 1, 2017).

17 Audrey R. Chapman, "Assessing the Universal Health Coverage Target in the Sustainable Development Goals from a Human Rights Perspective," *BMC International Health and Human Rights* 16 (December 15, 2016); Lawrence O. Gostin et al., "70 Years of Human Rights in Global Health: Drawing on a Contentious Past to Secure a Hopeful Future," *The Lancet* 392, no. 10165 (December 22, 2018).

18 Alicia Ely Yamin and Allan Maleche, "Realizing Universal Health Coverage in East Africa: The Relevance of Human Rights," *BMC International Health and Human Rights* 17 (August 3, 2017); Gorik Ooms et al., "Universal Health Coverage Anchored in the Right to Health" *Bulletin of the World Health Organization* 91, no. 1 (January 2013); Tania Dmytraczenko, and Gisele Almeida, eds., *Toward Universal Health Coverage and Equity in Latin America and the Caribbean: Evidence from Selected Countries*, Directions in Development – Human Development (Washington, DC: World Bank Publications, 2015), 47; Lisa Forman et al., "What Do Core Obligations under the Right to Health Bring to Universal Health Coverage?," *Health and Human Rights Journal* 18, no. 2 (December 5, 2016): 26.

19 Susana T. Fried et al., "Universal Health Coverage: Necessary but Not Sufficient," *Reproductive Health Matters* 21, no. 42 (2013).

on health outcomes (e.g. policies related to sanitation, education, nutrition, housing, poverty reduction, and environmental protection). Even if a broader definition of UHC that encompasses the social determinants of health is adopted, the right to health can still be broader in scope as it arguably encompasses not only duties to fulfil and promote this right via the provision of services, but also duties to respect and protect it. Some interpretations of the right to health, such as the authoritative one proposed by GC14, argue that the right to health can be violated, for instance, through state violence (e.g. police brutality, torture, incarceration in inhumane conditions)[20] and through health systems that fail to protect and respect patients' autonomy, reproductive rights, bodily integrity, and privacy. In sum, UHC contributes only partially to the realization of the right to health and even the provision of health services can be a source of human rights violation when, for instance, patients' autonomy and body integrity are not respected and protected by their health systems. For reasons of scope, this book will focus exclusively on one aspect of the right to health, namely the right to healthcare.

As identified above, the right to health depends on some form of UHC for its full realization. However, the right to health, and human rights in general, can also offer important contributions for UHC. Rights can be used to inform and challenge decisions made in the context of policies for UHC. Principles familiar to those in the area of human rights, such as non-discrimination, human dignity, autonomy, accountability, and the rule of law can offer legal standards for decisions about how to achieve UHC.[21] Human rights can also guide discussions about the type of UHC a society wants to achieve. For instance, Lougarre[22] asks a very important question in the contemporary world: what is the place for asylum seekers, refugees, stateless persons, and illegal migrants in UHC given that often they are not entitled to receive, or do not receive, healthcare on an equal basis as citizens and residents? Human rights should be engaged when answering this kind of question, which should also be asked in relation to other extremely vulnerable groups, such as prisoners and discriminated-against minorities.

Another important implication of the approximation between these two concepts is that UHC has its normative status elevated when anchored in the

20 See, e.g., Jonathan M. Mann et al., "Health and Human Rights," *Health and Human Rights Journal* 1, no. 1 (Fall 1994).

21 Yamin and Maleche, "Realizing Universal Health Coverage"; Alicia Ely Yamin, "Taking the Right to Health Seriously: Implications for Health Systems, Courts, and Achieving Universal Health Coverage," *Human Rights Quarterly* 39, no. 2 (May 2017); Sofia Gruskin, Edward J. Mills, and Daniel Tarantola, "History, Principles, and Practice of Health and Human Rights," *The Lancet* 370, no. 9585 (August 4, 2007).

22 Claire Lougarre, "Using the Right to Health to Promote Universal Health Coverage: A Better Tool for Protecting Non-Nationals' Access to Affordable Health Care?" *Health and Human Rights Journal* 18, no. 2 (December 2016).

right to health.[23] UHC, apart from being a political promise and a moral commitment, also becomes a binding and enforceable legal obligation on states under international law.[24] The approximation between UHC and the right to health can also create legal duties for governments under domestic law. The right to health has been recognized in the domestic law of many jurisdictions through the constitutionalization of this right, the direct application of international human rights treaties, or the expansive interpretation by courts of other human rights such as the right to life. The legal right to healthcare may also exist even where there is no explicit recognition of the right to health in domestic law. In some jurisdictions, the legal frameworks that establish universal or expanded health coverage may create a legal mandate for authorities to provide healthcare services which have as its flip side the creation of legal entitlements to receive care.

The recognition of the legal right to healthcare, derived from human rights or from the statutory duties of authorities to provide healthcare, can enable domestic legal accountability via judicial and non-judicial means that allows rights-holders to contest governments' failures to provide care or to demand improvements in the delivery of services.[25] Legal entitlements and accountability mechanisms are frequently presented as important for achieving UHC. As argued by Alicia Yamin and Ariel Frisancho, "[u]nderstanding governments as duty bearers and health system users as claims holders have been fundamental to holding governments to account with respect to achieving aspects of universal health coverage equitably".[26] The WHO, after affirming the importance of placing the highest priority on securing the right to health, stated that "UHC secures universal entitlement to health services, which are important contributors to improving the health status of the population in all countries".[27]

In sum, UHC and the right to health are more than compatible at a conceptual level. They are mutually reinforcing. Universal access to affordable quality

23 John Tasioulas and Effy Vayena, "Getting Human Rights Right in Global Health Policy," *The Lancet* 385, no. 9978 (April 2015).

24 Gilbert Abotisem Abiiro and Manuela De Allegri, "Universal Health Coverage from Multiple Perspectives: A Synthesis of Conceptual Literature and Global Debates," *BMC International Health and Human Rights* 15 (2015); Forman et al., "What Do Core Obligations," 24; Dmytraczenko and Almeida, *Toward Universal Health Coverage*, 1; Ooms et al., "Universal Health Coverage Anchored in the Right to Health"; Dainius Puras, "Universal Health Coverage: A Return to Alma-Ata and Ottawa," *Health and Human Rights Journal* 18, no. 2 (December 2016); Lawrence O. Gostin et al., "The Legal Determinants of Health: Harnessing the Power of Law for Global Health and Sustainable Development," *The Lancet* 393, no. 10183 (May 4, 2019).

25 Audrey R. Chapman, *Global Health, Human Rights, and the Challenge of Neoliberal Policies* (Cambridge: Cambridge University Press, 2016): 288.

26 Alicia Ely Yamin and Ariel Frisancho, "Human-Rights-Based Approaches to Health in Latin America," *The Lancet* 385, no. 9975 (April 4, 2015). See, also, Cotlear et al., *Going Universal*, 179.

27 World Health Organization and World Bank, *Monitoring Progress Towards Universal Health Coverage at Country and Global Levels* (Geneva: World Health Organization, 2014): 10.

healthcare is necessary, although not sufficient, for the realization of the right to health. Human rights set standards and principles that guide and inform decisions about what sort of UHC a society should aim to achieve and how to achieve it. Last but not least, the right to health elevates the normative status of UHC and the right to healthcare (which can be derived from human rights or statutory provisions) can be used to challenge governments when they fail to fulfil their duties in the provision of healthcare.

Universal health coverage and priority-setting

As argued above, there is important proximity with, and synergies between, UHC and the right to health. However, and this is much less emphasized in the literature, there is also the potential for tension. One of the main sources of tension is the fact that UHC requires priority-setting.[28]

UHC is an aspirational objective to be progressively realized.[29] No country, no matter how well-funded their health system(s), can provide its entire population with free at-the-point-of-use access to every health intervention that can improve health or prolong life.[30] Even developed countries that already offer extensive coverage of a broad package of health services within their territories struggle to cope with the price of new technologies, the inequalities in the access to services, and the difficulties of sustaining coverage and quality in a context of budgetary constraints.[31]

The mismatch between patients' expectations and the capacity of health systems to meet them in a context of scarce resources is a reality that forces every health system to set priorities, i.e. to choose between healthcare interventions and patients competing for finite resources. Priority-setting decisions occur at many levels. Broadly speaking, there are macro-level allocations, which include decisions on the size of the budget for healthcare, which is determined by political choices regarding the level of taxation and the degree of priority given to healthcare in comparison to other policies (including those that will directly affect health, such as sanitation, education, poverty reduction etc.); meso-level allocations between different services and treatments across medical specialities, which includes choices between, for example, expanding primary care or incorporating

28 Kalipso Chalkidou et al., "Priority-Setting for Achieving Universal Health Coverage," *Bulletin of the World Health Organization* 94, no. 6 (June 2016); Sania Nishtar et al., "Time to Deliver: Report of the WHO Independent High-Level Commission on NCDs," *The Lancet* 392, no. 10143 (July 21, 2018).

29 Ties Boerma et al., "Monitoring Intervention Coverage in the Context of Universal Health Coverage," *PLoS Med* 11, no. 9 (September 22, 2014).

30 Trygve Ottersen et al., *Making Fair Choices on the Path to Universal Health Coverage – Final Report of the WHO Consultative Group on Equity and Universal Health Coverage* (Geneva: World Health Organization, 2014): 5.

31 Richard Horton, "Offline: UHC – One Promise and Two Misunderstandings," *The Lancet* 391, no. 10128 (April 7, 2018).

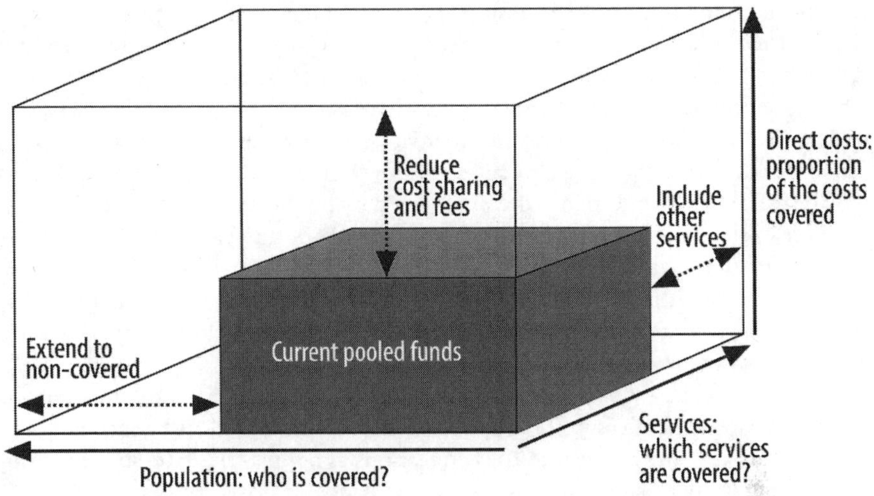

Figure 2.1 Three dimensions to consider when moving towards universal coverage. Reproduced from "The world health report: health systems financing: the path to universal coverage", World Health Organization, Executive Summary – removing financial risks and barriers to access, page xv, Copyright 2014.

high-cost cutting-edge technologies for end-of-life patients; and micro-level allocations that include decisions made by a clinician about which individuals should have priority to receive a determined service within a clinical setting.[32]

Decisions at each level are limited by what was decided at the level above, and, as will be discussed further in this chapter, in some circumstances, they can also be constrained by decisions at the level below. Macro decisions will have an obvious impact on the coverage options available for health systems. However, for reasons of scope, this chapter will not discuss macro decisions. It will rather focus on decisions directly related to the provision of services by health systems, which include choices about whether specific treatments should be covered and, if so, how they should be distributed across service users.

Countries committed to achieving UHC will need to make choices and the now-classic WHO cube (Figure 2.1) illustrates the dilemmas they will be facing. In the context of scarce resources, there are trade-offs between increasing the number of people effectively covered by a health system, expanding the list of services available for those already covered, or reducing cost-sharing and fees

32 Daniel Wei Liang Wang and Benedict Rumbold, "Priority Setting and Judicial Accountability: The Case of England," in *Philosophical Foundations of Medical Law*, eds. Andelka M. Philips, Thana C. de Campos, and Jonathan Herring (Oxford: Oxford University Press, 2020).

(where they exist) for the services provided. There are also choices to be made within each dimension. For instance, if governments want to expand coverage, should they prioritize rural areas where the population is more dispersed and difficult to reach, but suffer from poorer health and healthcare, or urban areas where the population is concentrated and there is infrastructure in place to allow quicker health gains for a larger number of people? When expanding the list of services provided, agonizing choices will have to be made about the provision of new health technologies that, when protected by intellectual property rights, can have prices that may drain resources necessary for adopting well-established interventions or the continuous provision of treatments and services already covered. Lastly, if the intention is to reduce cost-sharing and fees, choices regarding the level of reduction and which groups or what services should be exempt will have a significant impact on access.

Considering these complex trade-offs and tragic choices, which interventions or groups should be given priority and how should these choices be made? There are probably as many answers to these questions as people trying to answer them, but there is an increasing consensus on some issues and two comprehensive proposals written collectively by independent experts deserve special attention.

The Lancet Commission on Investing in Health (*Lancet CIH*) advocates the idea of progressive universalism, which can be of two types. One is a scheme that covers the whole population without co-payment or fees, but that would give preference to financing an essential set of highly cost-effective interventions that disproportionately affect the poor (e.g. infectious diseases, reproductive and child healthcare services, essential non-communicable diseases, and injury coverage). By expanding the number of people covered and removing fees and cost-sharing, this system will be very inclusive but, at least in the earlier stages, the benefit packages will be limited and will create inequality in the access to interventions outside the essential set. In such a scheme, high-cost interventions will take longer to be included,[33] as they need to be made universally available and free at the point of use, which can frustrate the UHC objective of offering financial protection against catastrophic healthcare expenditure.

The second type of progressive universalism proposed by the *Lancet CIH* would provide a larger basket of interventions to the whole population within a one-tier system, but with patient cost-sharing and fees, from which the poor would be exempt. This would allow health systems to be financed not only through general taxation but also through fees, co-payments, payroll taxes, or mandatory insurance from those who can pay for it. The disadvantage, however, is that a system to differentiate the poor from the non-poor and to manage different sources of funding can be administratively complex and costly, apart from the risk of fraud, moral hazard, stigmatization, and corruption.

No matter the type of progressive universalism adopted for achieving UHC, it will require great selectivity in the list of interventions to be included in UHC

33 Jamison et al., "Global Health 2035," 1934.

packages.[34] The need for the careful selection of interventions applies equally to developed countries with well-established and comprehensive health systems, which have also been struggling to cope with the steady increase in healthcare costs. There are many reasons why per capita health spending in recent decades has been growing around the world, but there is evidence that the diffusion and use of new health technologies is the strongest determinant of increasing healthcare spending.[35] Therefore, selecting healthcare interventions in a fair and informed way is necessary for any health system to prevent the cost escalation that may result in the underfunding and underprovision of essential healthcare and public health interventions.[36]

A WHO consultative group, building on the idea of progressive universalism, offers a framework to guide health systems' decisions about the inclusion and exclusion of interventions in UHC packages. They recommend that choices should be guided by the following considerations: (a) fair distribution: coverage and use of high-priority services should be based on need, and priority should be given to the policies benefiting the worse-off groups and that provide the highest financial risk protection; (b) benefit maximization: priority should be given to the most cost-effective interventions so as to obtain as much health benefit as possible from the available resources; and (c) fair contribution: contribution should be according to capacity to pay and not need, in particular for high-priority services.[37]

Determining services' levels of priority for a health system is central to inform choices within UHC. According to the WHO consultative group, interventions should be classified according to the level of priority: high, medium, or low. Only when the coverage of high-priority services is nearly universal should health systems expand to include medium- and, ultimately, low-priority services. It is also recommended that this classification of interventions in high, medium, and low priority should be made explicitly, through a transparent procedure that allows public participation and accountability, and according to three main criteria. First, cost-effectiveness analysis should be used to identify the interventions that can provide the largest possible sum of health benefits for a population given a certain

34 Dean T. Jamison et al., "Universal Health Coverage and Intersectoral Action for Health: Key Messages from *Disease Control Priorities*, 3rd Edition," *The Lancet* 391, no. 10125 (March 17, 2018).

35 Ursula Giedion, Ricardo Bitrán, and Ignez Tristao, eds., *Health Benefit Plans in Latin America: A Regional Comparison* (Washington, DC: Inter-American Development Bank – Social Protection and Health Division, 2014): 10; Albert A. Okunade and Vasudeva N. R. Murthy, "Technology as a 'Major Driver' of Health Care Costs: A Cointegration Analysis of the Newhouse Conjecture," *Journal of Health Economics* 21, no. 1 (January 2002); Dan Crippen and Amber E. Barnato, "The Ethical Implications of Health Spending: Death and Other Expensive Conditions," *Journal of Law, Medicine & Ethics* 39, no. 2 (Summer 2011).

36 Jamison et al., "Global Health 2035," 1937; Rebecca Masters, et al., "Return on Investment of Public Health Interventions: A Systematic Review," *Journal of Epidemiology & Community Health* 71, no. 8 (August 2017).

37 Ottersen et al., *Making Fair Choices.*

budget. As a general rule, it is unfair to cover services that are not cost-effective while people have unmet needs that could be addressed cheaply and effectively. Second, priority should be given to the worse-off, defined as those who are relatively disadvantaged with respect to health prospects, health outcomes, access to healthcare, or social and economic status.[38] Lastly, priority should also be given to services that offer substantial financial-risk protection, namely those where the costs can cause families severe financial strain if they have to pay for them. The WHO consultative group, acknowledging the complexity of this task, also recommends that countries create and strengthen institutions that can generate and use the necessary information to make these priority-setting decisions,[39] a topic that will be covered later in this book.

The two proposals discussed in this section are representative of a growing consensus among international organizations and academics on issues related to UHC and priority-setting.[40] First, priorities should be set explicitly rather than implicitly. The denial of healthcare due to budgetary limitations, known in the literature as "health care rationing", is implicit when the restrictions are not expressly laid out. Implicit rationing means that access is denied at the point of use through the withholding of information to patients about possibly beneficial treatments, undersupply or waiting lists, deflection of patients to other services or bodies, dilution through incomplete or low-standard services, or the disguise of priority-setting decisions as clinical decisions.[41] Explicit rationing, on the other hand, requires transparency and allows public accountability. It can have two forms, one meaning that there is transparency about which services will or will not be covered, for instance through clear medicine lists and health plans (*explicit about what*). The other form of explicit rationing means that there are public justifications for these decisions and that the procedure through which they are reached is transparent (*explicit about why and how*).[42]

Building on the idea of explicit rationing (in both senses), priorities should be set in a systematic way, which will allow the comparison of different policy options based on clear and fair criteria that should be coherently applied in different cases. This allows a better understanding of trade-offs and opportunity costs. This systematic comparison should be informed by robust scientific evidence to distinguish effective interventions from those of questionable value. It should also be informed by considerations over the value for money of interventions in order to maximize the impact on health that a given amount of resources can provide,

38 See Alex Voorhoeve et al., "Three Case Studies in Making Fair Choices on the Path to Universal Health Coverage," *Health and Human Rights Journal* 18, no. 2 (December 2016).

39 Ottersen et al., *Making Fair Choices*, 22.

40 See, also, Amanda Glassman and Kalipso Chalkidou, *Priority-Setting in Health Building institutions for Smarter Public Spending* (Washington, DC: Center for Global Development, 2012).

41 See Cotlear et al., *Going Universal*, 76–77; Rudolf Klein and Jo Maybin, *Thinking About Rationing* (London: The King's Fund, 2012).

42 See Chapter 6.

which can be measured using methods such as cost-effectiveness analysis. Systems that do not set priorities explicitly in the two senses explained above, and that do not consider value for money, risk undersupplying cost-effective interventions while funding those that are less cost-effective, or even wasteful.[43] They may also be jeopardizing their long-term financial sustainability. As affirmed by Glassman et al., "[a] central requirement of any system of UHC is that the services made available to the population are consistent with the funds available".[44]

Value for money, although essential, needs to be balanced against concerns about distributive justice. Health systems must go beyond the mere absence of discrimination in the access to care and should help reduce health inequalities in society by benefiting the worst-off first. The worst-off can be defined according to socio-economic criteria (e.g. the poorest, the most vulnerable, the neglected minorities, those living in rural areas, and those most deprived of public services)[45] or health criteria (e.g. those who experience the highest fatal and non-fatal health loss as a result of having an untreated health condition).[46]

Moreover, rather than a technocratic exercise, priority-setting requires mechanisms of accountability and participation so that the decision process will be informed by a plurality of views and interests, including those of service users and the general public.[47] Inclusive and deliberative processes working under scrutiny from the public and stakeholders tend to result in better informed and more thoughtful outcomes. There is evidence that health systems that are more transparent and accountable are also generally more efficient.[48] They also tend to be more legitimate. In a context of incomplete knowledge and scientific uncertainty, and where priority-setting decisions involve value judgments about which reasonable people may disagree,[49] the quality of the procedures followed by health systems is fundamental to the legitimacy of their allocative decisions.

Lastly, despite the importance of the existing guidance and recommendations advising countries on how to achieve UHC (and also despite proposals to define the actual "highest priority", "essential", or "key" interventions that all countries

43 Chalkidou et al., "Priority-Setting," 462; Amanda Glassman et al., "Defining a Health Benefits Package: What Are the Necessary Processes?" *Health Systems & Reform* 2, no. 1 (2016): 43.

44 Glassman et al., "Defining a Health Benefits Package," 40.

45 See, for instance, Jesse Bump et al., "Implementing Pro-Poor Universal Health Coverage," *The Lancet Global Health* 4, no. 1 (January 1, 2016).

46 David A. Watkins et al., "Universal Health Coverage and Essential Packages of Care," in *Disease Control Priorities: Improving Health and Reducing Poverty*, eds. Dean T. Jamison et al. (Washington, DC: The World Bank, 2017), 48.

47 See, also, Amanda Glassman, Ursula Giedion, and Peter C. Smith, *What's In, What's Out: Designing Benefits for Universal Health Coverage* (Washington, DC: Center for Global Development, 2017).

48 Alejandro Izquierdo, Carola Pessino, and Guillermo Vuletin, eds., *Better Spending for Better Lives: How Latin America and the Caribbean Can Do More with Less* (Washington, DC: Inter-American Development Bank, 2018), 328.

49 Norman Daniels, *Just Health: Meeting Health Needs Fairly* (Cambridge University Press, 2007); Wang and Rumbold, "Priority Setting and Judicial Accountability."

should include in their UHC package as a matter of priority),[50] the actual packages available will and should vary according to the circumstances of each health system (e.g. income levels, budget, epidemiological situation, demographics, existing healthcare infrastructures, social preferences, and political constraints), and to the priority-setting institutions in place to process moral disagreements and evidence that very often is complex, incomplete, and debatable.[51]

In conclusion, UHC requires priority-setting and there is now substantive academic work and policy advice offering guidance to help systems in making the necessary choices to achieve UHC fairly and efficiently. However, and even if priorities are fairly and competently set, choosing priorities in healthcare will often involve making "tragic choices"[52] that will invariably result in people who have entitlements to receive healthcare being left without the financial protection to access healthcare interventions that may potentially improve or prolong their lives. This tension between, on the one hand, the legal entitlement of people with unmet health needs to receive healthcare and, on the other, the inescapable reality of priority-setting, will be further analysed in the section that follows.

Priority-setting, right to healthcare, and courts

As discussed earlier in this chapter, the normative status of UHC is elevated when it is anchored in human rights and the right to health, in particular. Moreover, in many jurisdictions, the recognition of the right to health and the establishment of health systems with the purpose of universalizing or increasing coverage creates legal obligations for governments and legal entitlements for the population. Legal entitlements and obligations can enable accountability mechanisms that are often presented as fundamental for achieving UHC.

Although it would be a mistake to reduce accountability to judicial control, for reasons of scope this chapter will be limited to the analysis of the relationship between priority-setting and courts only. The role of courts in controlling and reviewing priority-setting decisions is a global phenomenon that has grown exponentially in the last decade. The relevance and particularities of this phenomenon justify a focused analysis, particularly in light of a general understanding that judicial accountability has a positive effect on UHC, which this book will critically analyse.

Judicially enforceable entitlements to receive healthcare, coupled with the increasing mismatch between patients' expectations and what is effectively provided by health systems, has resulted in lawsuits challenging the denial of funding for health treatments (in particular for new and expensive technologies) in several jurisdictions. This phenomenon (which I call right to healthcare litigation in this book) creates a potential tension between two central elements of UHC:

50 See, for instance, Jamison et al., "Universal Health Coverage"; Boerma et al., "Monitoring Intervention Coverage"; Forman et al., "What Do Core Obligations."

51 Watkins et al., "Universal Health Coverage," 44.

52 Guido Calabresi and Philip Bobbit, *Tragic Choices* (New York: Norton, 1978).

fair priority-setting and the legal right to healthcare. This chapter will discuss three approaches, which are not mutually exclusive, to understanding this possible tension.

The right to healthcare is compatible with and supports fair priority-setting

The first approach argues that there is no real tension between priority-setting and the right to health, or that this tension is overstated. The argument here is that the right to healthcare, as conceptualized in international law and by most human rights law scholars, is fully compatible with priority-setting.

The right to healthcare does not provide an immediate entitlement to the best healthcare available or to any treatment that can potentially benefit a patient. If interpreted in light of Art. 2(1) of the International Covenant on Economic, Social and Cultural Rights, the right to health rather creates a duty for the state to take steps with a view to progressively achieving its full realization, to the maximum of its available resources. This was reaffirmed in the UN Committee on Economic, Social and Cultural Rights General Comment n. 14 (GC 14): "[t] he notion of 'the highest attainable standard of health' in article 12.1 takes into account both the individual's biological and socio-economic preconditions and a state's available resources".[53]

Moreover, the right to health requires adequate priority-setting.[54] Health systems that do not set priorities fairly and which are not informed by sound scientific evidence and value-for-money considerations will not be able to offer the highest attainable level of physical and mental health to its population within the available resources. Resource allocations that do not result from good priority-setting processes and decisions can lead to discrimination, inequality, waste of resources, and inefficiencies in healthcare. One major risk of not taking priority-setting seriously is that health systems will end up investing disproportionately more in expensive curative services for groups with more voice, visibility, or resources, at the expense of the primary and preventive healthcare needed by a larger or more vulnerable part of the population.[55]

53 ECOSOC CESCR "General Comment No. 14" E/C.12/2000/4, 9.

54 Yamin, "Taking the Right to Health Seriously," 355.

55 ECOSOC CESCR "General Comment No. 14" E/C.12/2000/4, 19. See, also, Alicia Ely Yamin and Ole Frithjof Norheim, "Taking Equality Seriously: Applying Human Rights Frameworks to Priority Setting in Health," *Human Rights Quarterly* 36, no. 2 (May 2014); Yamin and Maleche, "Realizing Universal Health Coverage"; UNGA "Report of the Special Rapporteur on the Right of Everyone to the Enjoyment of the Highest Attainable Standard of Physical and Mental Health" (August 5, 2016) UN Doc A/71/304; Benedict Rumbold et al., "Universal Health Coverage, Priority Setting, and the Human Right to Health," *The Lancet* 390, no. 10095 (August 12, 2017).

Furthermore, the right to healthcare and judicial accountability can be instrumental to demand explicit and fair priority-setting.[56] As argued by Norman Daniels, the right to health should be understood as the right to access a health system where resources are fairly allocated.[57] The right to receive healthcare creates a burden for states to justify the non-provision of care and, when this is accompanied by adequate accountability mechanisms, it can be used to demand more inclusive, participative, deliberative, reasoned, and informed decision-making in healthcare. In other words, governments that are forced to explain the reasons for their choices will be under pressure to make priority-setting decisions with outcomes and procedures that service users and the general public will be more likely to accept as fair and legitimate.

Human rights can be used not only to demand adequate priority-setting, but they can also contribute to determining the legal limits and obligations that should be respected by decision-makers making allocative decisions. The literature on human rights has identified several human rights standards and principles for priority-setting in the context of UHC, including universality, non-discrimination, priority to disadvantaged groups, deliberation, accountability, and transparency.[58] Far from creating any sort of tension with priority-setting, these human rights standards and principles echo those that have already been recognized in other fields that justify them primarily on philosophical, policy, or public law grounds rather than human rights.[59] Rights and judicial accountability can, therefore, be an instrument for enforcing those principles that constitute good priority-setting.

Lastly, rights offer an important mechanism for enforcing the implementation of the outcomes of priority-setting processes. Decisions made at the national or regional level will not necessarily be implemented by service providers. Courts can, therefore, be used to demand the actual delivery of services established as having a high priority and that health systems have already committed themselves to providing.[60] Fair and sophisticated priority-setting would be a pointless exercise if it were not reflected in the actual provision of health services. Courts can be an institution where instances of mismatch between priority-setting decisions and actual coverage will have to be explained and, possibly, redressed. An interesting example comes from the first chairman of the National Institute for Health and

56 See, for instance, Keith Syrett, *Law, Legitimacy and the Rationing of Health Care: A Contextual and Comparative Perspective* (New York: Cambridge University Press, 2007): 146.
57 Norman Daniels, "Priority Setting and Human Rights," chap. 12 in *Just Health*.
58 See, for instance, ECOSOC CESCR "General Comment No. 14" E/C.12/2000/4; Yamin and Norheim, "Taking Equality Seriously"; Yamin and Frisancho, "Human-Rights-Based Approaches"; Yamin, "Taking the Right to Health Seriously," 355; Audrey R. Chapman, "The Contributions of Human Rights to Universal Health Coverage," *Health and Human Rights Journal* 18, no. 2 (December 2016): 2.
59 Daniels, *Just Health*; Jamison et al., "Global Health 2035"; Ottersen et al., *Making Fair Choices;* Greg Bognar and Iwao Hirose, *The Ethics of Health Care Rationing* (London: Routledge, 2014); Wang and Rumbold, "Priority Setting and Judicial Accountability."
60 See Rumbold et al., "Universal Health Coverage."

Clinical Excellence (NICE), the body responsible for health-technology assessment in England, who publicly encouraged patients to apply for judicial review against the English National Health Service when there are delays in the provision of the drugs approved by NICE.[61]

In sum, this first approach sees priority-setting as compatible with and necessary for the realization of the right to health. Priority-setting allows the efficient and fair allocation of resources necessary for the realization of the right to health. Legal entitlements to receive healthcare can be used to demand adequate priority-setting, and to enforce principles and standards recognized as constitutive of good priority-setting. Judicial accountability can also be a mechanism to guarantee that priority-setting decisions are reflected in actual service provision.

The right to healthcare creates substantive entitlements and is a driver for UHC

The second approach accepts that there are tensions between priority-setting and the right to healthcare. It also argues that this is positive because rights and adjudication can push countries to move or to move faster towards UHC. The tension between rights and priority-setting can be well illustrated using Gopal Sreenivasan's distinction between the "rationing" and the "reverse-engineered" approaches.[62] The "rationing" approach starts by determining the amount of resources available for healthcare and then applying priority-setting principles, processes, and methods to define the services that will be provided to users. The "reverse-engineered" approach, as the name says, goes the other way around: it first decides, based on an interpretation of the right to health, which services should be covered and then the priority-setting process and the budget will have to adapt to guarantee these services will be provided. The applications of the right to health that create tension with priority-setting are variations of the "reverse-engineered" approach.

Many consider that courts, when protecting rights, should not limit their scope to guaranteeing fair priority-setting within a certain budget. Courts should also identify and enforce substantive entitlements and, if necessary, promote structural changes in policies to address situations in which the underprovision of services violates the right to health. Therefore, through some sort of "reverse-engineered" approach, courts can enforce substantive rights and guarantee effective access to health treatments.

61 Michael Rawlins, "Playing Fair on Treatments," *Health Service Journal*, 26 July 2012, https://www.hsj.co.uk/comment/michael-rawlins-playing-fair-on-treatments/5047276.article/.

62 Gopal Sreenivasan, "Why Justice Requires Rationing in Health Care," in *Medicine and Social Justice: Essays on the Distribution of Health Care*, eds. Rosamond Rhodes, Margaret P. Battin, and Anita Silvers (New York: Oxford University Press, 2012).

One position within this approach is to deny that resource constraints can limit the provision of services protected by the right to health. Therefore, whenever there is a health need, there is an unqualified right to receive any medically effective (or the most effective) healthcare intervention available, irrespective of price, budget, and opportunity costs. As illustrated in the following excerpt from the Brazilian Supreme Federal Court judgment of a claim for public funding for an experimental treatment in the United States:

> [In choosing] between protecting the inviolability of the right to life, an inalienable Constitutional fundamental right, and a financial and secondary interest of the State, I believe – once this dilemma is established – ethical and legal reasons leave the judge with only one possible option: unwavering respect for life.[63]

This position would rule out the rationing of life-prolonging treatments and allow individual needs to trump financial or distributive considerations. This application of the right to health has not found much academic support, although some have pointed out that such an uncomplicated interpretation of a readily enforceable right to health that rejects trade-offs has promoted access to care for individuals and improvements in policies.[64] However, it has been explicitly endorsed by some courts in Latin America, as will be seen later in this book. The German Constitutional Court also had a similar approach and, based on the constitutional right to life and physical integrity, found in the famous *Nikolaus* case that the funding for treatment cannot be withheld if a patient suffers from a life-threatening illness, there is no available alternative treatment, and that the prospect of curing or improving the condition is not entirely remote.[65]

Even if the right to health does not mean the right to access all existing treatments, some have advanced interpretations of the right to health that identify a "basic", "essential", or "minimum" substantive content within this right that will

63 Pet 1246 MC, STF, 31/01/1997.

64 Flavia Piovesan, "Brazil: Impact and Challenges of Social Rights in the Courts," in *Social Rights Jurisprudence: Emerging Trends in International and Comparative Law*, ed. Malcolm Langford (Cambridge: Cambridge University Press, 2009); Daniel M. Brinks and Varun Gauri, "The Law's Majestic Equality? The Distributive Impact of Judicializing Social and Economic Rights," *Perspectives on Politics* 12, no. 2 (June 2014); João Biehl, Mariana P. Socal, and Joseph J. Amon, "The Judicialization of Health and the Quest for State Accountability: Evidence from 1,262 Lawsuits for Access to Medicines in Southern Brazil," *Health and Human Rights Journal* 18, no. 1 (June 2016); Leonardo Cubillos et al., "Universal Health Coverage and Litigation in Latin America," *Journal of Health Organization and Management* 26, no. 3 (June 15, 2012); Benjamin Mason Meier et al., "Employing Human Rights Frameworks to Realize Access to an HIV Cure," *Journal of the International AIDS Society* 18, no. 1 (November 13, 2015).

65 BVerfGE 115. For an analysis of the German case-law on the right health care see Stefanie Ettelt, "Access to Treatment and the Constitutional Right to Health in Germany: A Triumph of Hope Over Evidence?" *Health Economics, Policy and Law* 15, no. 1 (January 2020).

exclude or prevail over priority-setting considerations. It is the role of the courts, therefore, to guarantee that this basic, essential, or minimum level of provision is satisfied.

GC 14, for instance, identifies "core obligations" that are not subject to progressive realization within available resources and have immediate effect as "a State party cannot, under any circumstances whatsoever, justify its non-compliance with the core obligations". GC 14 includes in the "core obligations" under the right to health procedural duties (e.g. non-discrimination in the access to healthcare, equitable distribution of healthcare resources, transparency, and participation in the planning of health policies), key social determinants of health (food, water, housing, sanitation), but, interestingly, the provision of essential drugs defined by the WHO is the only example of a healthcare intervention mentioned.[66]

The concept of "core obligations" (or variations thereof) has been enthusiastically endorsed by some courts to justify heavy-handed judicial intervention on policy (e.g. Colombia)[67] but has been resisted by others unwilling to recognize core obligations as creating immediately justiciable entitlements to litigants (e.g. South Africa).[68] There is also substantial scholarly discussion about what should be part of the core obligations and how to determine its content. The GC 14, for example, has been criticized for creating more procedural obligations than substantive entitlements to the provision of services, which resulted in an arguably too limited list of healthcare interventions within the "core".[69]

It is beyond the scope of this book to offer a comprehensive analysis of the concept of "core obligations",[70] but it is important to recognize that not all applications of "core obligations" will raise the tension between rights and priority-setting. "Core obligations" are not always interpreted as non-derogable (i.e. no competing consideration, such as limited resources, can justify their non-fulfilment) or as creating an immediately justiciable right.[71]

The UN Committee on Economic, Social and Cultural Rights General Comment n. 3 (GC 3), from where GC 14 draws the idea of "core obligations", states that social rights have minimum core obligations that should have first priority and their non-fulfilment should attract higher scrutiny. However,

66 ECOSOC CESCR "General Comment No. 14" E/C.12/2000/4, 43.

67 See David Landau, "The Reality of Social Rights Enforcement," *Harvard International Law Journal* 53, no. 1 (Winter 2012).

68 See Katharine G. Young, "A Typology of Economic and Social Rights Adjudication: Exploring the Catalytic Function of Judicial Review," *International Journal of Constitutional Law* 8, no. 3 (July 1, 2010): 385–420.

69 See, for instance, Forman et al., "What Do Core Obligations."

70 For a review of the literature, see, for instance, Lisa Forman et al., "Conceptualising Minimum Core Obligations Under the Right to Health: How Should We Define and Implement the 'Morality of the Depths'," *The International Journal of Human Rights* 20, no. 4 (2016); John Tasioulas, *Minimum Core Obligations: Human Rights in the Here and Now*, Research Paper – October 2017 (Washington, DC: The World Bank, 2017).

71 See Tasioulas, 17.

GC 3 recognizes that "any assessment as to whether a State has discharged its minimum core obligation must also take account of resource constraints applying within the country concerned" (paragraph 10). Following this approach, core obligations can be seen as a principle or a framework to help identify what should receive first priority in the allocation of resources. John Tasioulas, for instance, defends an interpretation of core obligations that, according to him, has strong connections with the proposals in the "Setting Priorities Fairly in the Path Towards UHC" report by the WHO consultative group discussed earlier in this chapter.[72]

However, "core obligations" can be in tension with priority-setting when they are applied by courts to (a) determine via adjudication the policy outcomes and substantive entitlements within the "core" and (b) overrule priority-setting decisions when needs within the "core" of a right are unfulfilled in concrete situations, irrespective of the circumstances and the trade-offs involved. In sum, the doctrine of "core obligations" may be interpreted to allow substantive entitlements and obligations to be judicially determined and enforced without them being necessarily evaluated alongside other interventions through a priority-setting process, or even in opposition to priority-setting decisions made by health systems. And the larger the package of interventions within the "core obligations", and the stronger its judicial protection, the higher the tension with priority-setting.

Lastly, the right to healthcare can be interpreted to directly rule out the use of some considerations in priority-setting. In Colombia, the 1751/2015 Act brought significant changes to the Colombian health system, including a new scheme for making decisions on the selection of drugs for funding. The original draft bill proposed a negative list with the treatments that should not be provided, which included treatments for cosmetic purposes only; for which there is no evidence of effectiveness, safety or efficacy; that do not have marketing authorization; that are experimental; or that are provided abroad. It also proposed a positive list determining the treatments to be covered by the health system.

The Colombian Constitutional Court reviewed the constitutionality of this draft bill and declared the positive list unconstitutional because it would breach the right to health. Therefore, whatever is not on the negative list will have to be funded. In practice, this would rule out all other considerations – such as cost-effectiveness and budget impact – that are not considered when determining the negative list.[73] The Constitutional Court also declared that the health system's "financial sustainability cannot comprise the denial of efficient and timely provi-

72 Tasioulas, 26.

73 Redación El Tiempo, " 'Magistrados No Entendieron Ley Estatutaria Que Aprobaron': Minsalud," *El Tiempo*, November 5, 2014, https://www.eltiempo.com/archivo/documento/CMS-14793359; Semana, "Pacientes Multimillonarios," *Semana*, November 11, 2014, https://www.semana.com/nacion/articulo/las-criticas-del-ministro-gaviria-al-sistema-de-salud/407662-3.

sion of all the services owed to any service user".[74] Therefore, the right to health was interpreted to reduce the scope of priority-setting in Colombia as economic considerations are not legally acceptable justifications for rationing healthcare.

In sum, according to this approach, courts willing to ignore, limit, or override priority-setting decisions that result in the non-realization of the right to health can be a quick and effective mechanism to guarantee that the health needs of the litigants (or those they represent) will be met. This judicial role can be particularly useful when the public institution responsible for service provision is intransigent, immune from conventional political mechanisms of accountability,[75] or deliberately obstructive or hostile to protecting rights.[76]

The right to health creates substantive entitlements and is an obstacle for UHC

The third approach also recognizes the tension between rights and priority-setting but, as opposed to the second approach, has concerns that a justiciable right to healthcare can undermine fair priority-setting. Adjudication, according to this argument, can become an obstacle for the fair priority-setting necessary to achieve UHC because courts, using the language of rights, may foreclose value-for-money considerations and will end up distributing healthcare resources unfairly and inefficiently.

A justiciable right to healthcare can create horizontal inequality when courts, through adjudication, make micro-level allocations of healthcare resources that result in patients with similar conditions receiving different levels of care as a result of judicial intervention. This will occur when individual claims for treatments, coupled with courts that ignore or minimize the impact of their judgments, allow litigants to access care in a privileged condition (e.g. "jumping the queue" in a waiting list) or to access interventions that are not available for the rest of the population on a regular and universal basis, which will impact the provision of other services by the health system. The best example of courts creating horizontal inequality is the prevalent model of right to healthcare litigation in Latin America: high volumes of litigation, the prevalence of individual claims demanding high-cost curative treatments, high success rates for claimants, and courts disregarding the aggregated impact that a large number of individual remedies may cause.[77]

74 Sentencia C-313/14, CCC, 29/05/2014.

75 Charles F. Sabel and William H. Simon, "Destabilization Rights: How Public Law Litigation Succeeds," *Harvard Law Review* 117, no. 4 (2004): 1063; David Landau, "Political Institutions and Judicial Role in Comparative Constitutional Law," *Harvard International Law Journal* 51, no. 2 (Summer 2010).

76 Young, "Typology of Economic and Social Rights Adjudication," 416.

77 Octavio Luiz Motta Ferraz, "The Right to Health in the Courts of Brazil: Worsening Health Inequities?" *Health and Human Rights Journal* 11, no. 2 (December 2009); Jeff King, *Judging Social Rights* (Cambridge: Cambridge University Press, 2012), 84.

It is true that individualized litigation can benefit others apart from claimants. For instance, a great volume of individual claims for a particular treatment can create incentives for the government to accelerate its inclusion in its health system's packages. This would allow less-privileged citizens to piggyback on the gains of the normally privileged first movers.[78] By applying the same logic to all other drugs constantly claimed for in courts, the result could be the overall expansion of the pharmaceutical policy in a health system. In other words, meso-level allocations are constrained by judicial rulings at the level below, which were made without knowing or considering the trade-offs at the level above.

This is possibly what happened in Colombia, where the escalation of individual legal claims for new and high-cost drugs has been associated with a significant increase in public expenditure on pharmaceuticals. However, this coincides with stagnation in preventive health measures and the deterioration in key social determinants of health in the country.[79] Correlation is not causation so, without further data, it is not possible to affirm that litigation in Colombia is limiting preventive health measures or causing the deterioration in social determinants of health. However, it is possible to say that courts, through thousands of individual remedies, are forcing the health system to move in a certain direction and that this will have opportunity costs that will be felt elsewhere in the health system, most likely in areas with less visibility and by people who are less able to respond politically or legally.[80]

One way to avoid the problem of horizontal inequality is by tackling the issues in a structural and programmatic, rather than individualized, way. Through collective claims and structural remedies that take into consideration broader interests and perspectives, courts can address rights complaints by putting forward a far-reaching reform to avert a status quo in which the insufficient provision of a certain service breaches the right to healthcare of particular groups. Some argue that such legal actions and remedies are more likely to benefit the worst-off because they address the healthcare needs of whole groups of patients and produce broader social change.[81]

78 Daniel M. Brinks, Varun Gauri, and Kyle Shen, "Social Rights Constitutionalism: Negotiating the Tension between the Universal and the Particular," *Annual Review Law and Social Science* 11 (November 2015): 303.

79 Everaldo Lamprea, "Colombia's Right to Health Litigation in a Context of Health Care Reform," in *The Right to Health at a Public/Private Divide: A Global Comparative Study*, eds. Colleen M. Flood and Aeyal Gross (New York: Cambridge University Press, 2014).

80 See Chapter 5.

81 Brinks, Gauri, and Shen, "Social Rights Constitutionalism," 289; Landau, "Reality of Social Rights Enforcement"; Pedro Felipe de Oliveira Santos, "Beyond Minimalism and Usurpation: Designing Judicial Review to Control the Mis-Enforcement of Socio-Economic Rights," *Washington University Global Studies Law Review* 18, no. 3 (2019). There is also a growing literature on health rights and the social determinants of health, which have an intrinsically collective nature. See, for instance, Ana Ayala and Benjamin Mason Meier, "A Human Rights Approach to the Health Implications of Food and Nutrition Insecurity," *Public Health Review* 38 (March 2017); Benjamin Mason Meier et al., "Bridging Interna-

The challenge, though, is that courts granting remedies to benefit larger groups, or to address structural issues, will be making meso-level decisions and will determine the services that should be prioritized by the health system. Different groups compete for scarce healthcare resources and those able to file resource-demanding collective claims will have an advantage in this competition.

Not all forms of structural remedies will be in tension with priority-setting, as they can have different levels of strength depending on the specificity of instructions and goals set by courts for governments, the mechanisms to monitor compliance with courts order, and courts' willingness to impose sanctions if authorities fail to do so. Weaker forms of rights enforcement give governments a wider margin of discretion to make allocative choices, although the literature seems to indicate that the weaker the judicial remedy, the lower the probability that courts will promote timely material change.[82]

In both micro and meso allocations, particularly if courts are able to promote material change, policies with opportunity costs and distributive consequences will be set by an institution that has limited capacity to fully understand the broader impact of their rulings, and the trade-offs and opportunity costs for health systems. As will be seen later in this book, the aggregate financial cost of complying with judicial decisions ordering the provision of treatment can be enormous in some countries. Moreover, resources will be distributed between competing legitimate claims for healthcare resources according to service users' capacity to litigate, which is a morally arbitrary distributive principle.

tional Law and rights-based litigation: Mapping Health-Related Rights Through the Development of the Global Health and Human Rights Database," *Health and Human Rights Journal* 14 (June 2012); Audrey R. Chapman, "The Social Determinants of Health, Health Equity, and Human Rights," *Health and Human Rights Journal* 12, no. 2 (December 15, 2010); Chapman, "Globalization, Human Rights, and the Social Determinants of Health," *Bioethics* 23, no 2 (February 2009); Kristi Heather Kenyon, Lisa Forman, and Claire E. Brolan, "Deepening the Relationship between Human Rights and the Social Determinants of Health: A Focus on Indivisibility and Power," *Health Human Rights* 20, no. 2 (December 2018). For reasons of scope explained earlier in this chapter, this will not be further explored.

82 See, on this issue, Rosalind Dixon, "Creating Dialogue About Socioeconomic Rights: Strong-Form Versus Weak-Form Judicial Review Revisited," *International Journal of Constitutional Law* 5, no. 3 (July 2007); Landau, "Reality of Social Rights Enforcement"; Anashri Pillay, "Revisiting the Indian Experience of Economic and Social Rights Adjudication: The Need for Principled Approach to Judicial Activism and Restraint," *International and Comparative Law Quarterly* 63, no. 2 (April 2014); Sharanjeet Parmar and Namita Wahi, "India: Citizens, Courts and the Right to Health: Between Promise and Progress?" in *Litigating Health Rights: Can Courts Bring More Justice to Health?*, eds. Alicia Yamin and Siri Gloppen (Harvard University Press, 2011); Katherine Young, *Constituting Economic and Social Rights* (Oxford: Oxford University Press, 2012): 182; Mark Tushnet, *Weak Courts, Strong Rights: Judicial Review and Social Welfare Rights in Comparative Constitutional Law* (Princeton, NJ: Princeton University Press, 2008); César Rodríguez-Garavito, "Beyond the Courtroom: the Impact of Judicial Activism on Socioeconomic Rights in Latin America," *Texas Law Review* 89 (2011).

To deal with this problem, one could envisage the right to healthcare being used to affect macro decisions, such as the amount of resources that governments should spend on healthcare, so adjudication does not have to be a zero-sum game between individuals or groups in need of healthcare. This movement from micro to macro would be the natural consequence of the "reverse-engineered" approach discussed in the section above as decisions at a higher level will have to adapt to guarantee a certain outcome determined at the level below. However, bringing health rights disputes to the macro level will involve courts in deeply political issues regarding the importance of healthcare as opposed to all other areas of governmental activity, including those that have an enormous impact on health outcomes, such as education, employment, science, environment, housing etc.

Those who believe adjudication can promote more inclusive, deliberative, and principle-based decision-making may not see priority-setting by courts at micro, meso, or macro levels as necessarily undesirable. The idea that courts are incapable of deciding cases taking into account the broader implications of their judgments, and the complex trade-offs involved in priority-setting, has been challenged. Others, however, are less convinced that courts are well suited for deciding between competing social needs for scarce resources because, if compared with other institutions, they are less accountable, work under more severe epistemic constraints, and have fewer resources for policy-making.[83] Particularly when considering what adequate priority-setting for achieving UHC requires, as discussed earlier in this chapter and to be further analysed in the next, the inadequacy of courts for allocating healthcare resources becomes even clearer.

In sum, the third approach argues that entitlements to receive healthcare that are de-linked from resource availability, value for money, and opportunity costs limit the capacity of health systems to set priorities explicitly by systematically comparing different policy options based on clear criteria and fair principles of justice. This will not make scarcity disappear but will likely result in implicit rationing.[84] Judicial intervention that, at least to a certain extent, predetermines the result of priority-setting or excludes cost-related considerations can thus be an obstacle to achieving UHC. It forces the allocation of funding for the provision of additional services based on an arbitrary principle of justice (access to courts) and limits health systems' capacity to address health inequalities and to promote the efficient use of resources.

83 On the debate about courts' legitimacy and institutional capacity to make allocative decisions, see Daniel Wei Liang Wang, "Social Rights and the Nirvana Fallacy," *Public Law* (July 1, 2018).

84 Glassman et al., "Defining a Health Benefits Package," 43.

Conclusion

Fair priority-setting and the right to health contribute to the aim of achieving UHC. There are clear synergies between them. But there can also be tensions, particularly when the right to healthcare creates judicially enforceable entitlements to healthcare. This chapter, building on the specialist literature and the experience from different jurisdictions, identifies three approaches to understand the complex relationship between the right to healthcare and priority-setting. The first denies or minimizes the tension between them and emphasizes that the right to healthcare and judicial accountability contribute to fair priority-setting (and vice versa). The second accepts that there is tension but sustains that the right to healthcare, at least in some circumstances, should be used by courts to guarantee access to care irrespective of priority-setting decisions. The third also accepts that this tension exists but argues that the judicial protection of substantive entitlements to healthcare undermines or limits fair priority-setting.

The second approach is very attractive at first sight. Rights adjudication can be a relatively effective and quick way to meet the health needs of individuals or groups and to change the status quo of insufficient or inadequate service provision. However, one should not minimize the challenges that judicially enforceable legal entitlements to receive healthcare create for the fair priority-setting necessary to achieving UHC. Courts adjudicating rights and ordering the funding of additional treatments can limit or frustrate priority-setting by predetermining winners without having the full picture of the health systems' capacity and of other unmet health needs of the population that compete for scarce resources. Furthermore, some interpretations of the right to healthcare de-link entitlements and resource availability, ruling out from the start the use of cost-effectiveness or budget impact analysis in priority-setting. This forces priority-setting to be implicit and makes it more difficult for health systems to focus on good value-for-money interventions and on reducing inequalities.

Therefore, to understand the full impact of the right to healthcare litigation on a particular health system, it is necessary to look beyond the immediate material or symbolic effect of specific court cases. It is also important to look at how (or if) courts and litigation affect the fairness of priority-setting processes in this system. The hypothesis in this book is that courts and litigation change health systems' priority-setting processes and that the nature of this change depends on how legal entitlements to healthcare are enforced by the Judiciary in each jurisdiction. The next chapters will show that how courts decide right to healthcare cases will, to a certain extent, determine if the right to healthcare helps to promote or impairs the fair priority-setting necessary for achieving UHC.

3 Priority-setting and health technology assessment

The previous chapter discussed the relationship between UHC, right to healthcare, and priority-setting. As seen, the need to maximize health benefits, expand coverage, and prioritize the worst-off to reduce health inequalities makes priority-setting necessary. Therefore, there are economic, policy, and ethical justifications for rationing healthcare. However, these justifications will be more compelling in concrete situations if rationing is explicit "about what" and, especially, about "why and how", so that there is transparency in relation to the priority-setting decisions that are being made and to the reasons and procedures for these decisions. In other words, rationing is easier to justify if it is the result of fair priority-setting.

This chapter will focus specifically on one modality of priority-setting that aims to satisfy the requirements for explicit rationing "about what" and "about why and how": health technology assessment (HTA). There are three main reasons for focusing on HTA in this book. First, new health technologies, and in particular drugs, are the main driver for the increase in healthcare expenditure worldwide.[1] Therefore, assessing the economic and health impact of technologies is central for health systems working under the pressure to offer the benefits made possible by scientific research while maintaining equitable access and financial sustainability. Second, HTA is one of the most visible attempts by health systems to promote fair priority-setting, which includes the informed comparison of different policy options based on clear criteria that are systematically and consistently applied in different cases. Third, an important part of the right to healthcare litigation in the jurisdictions that will be analysed in this book involves claims for new health technologies. Therefore, HTA may affect and be particularly affected by litigation and judicial rulings that review rationing decisions and that order the provision of treatments grounded on patients' rights to receive healthcare.

1 Corinna Sorenson, Michael Drummond, and Beena Bhuiyan Khan, "Medical Technology as a Key Driver of Rising Health Expenditure: Disentangling the Relationship," *ClinicoEconomics and Outcomes Research* 5 (2013).

DOI: 10.4324/9781315149165-3

Health technologies, priority-setting, and HTA

Medicine has undergone a revolution since the 20th century through the systematic application of the scientific method to understand diseases and to test medical treatments. These advances were not only due to progress in our understanding of chemistry, biology, and anatomy but also because doctors, instead of relying on anecdotal evidence or mere convention, started to compare different treatments using control groups to check if a tested intervention has any impact on health.[2] As a result of scientific progress, conditions that in the past would almost inevitably have resulted in death or serious disability have now become effectively preventable, treatable, and better managed.

This science-intensive medicine, coupled with the global recognition of intellectual property rights following the Agreement on Trade-Related Aspects of Intellectual Property Rights (TRIPS), has increased the cost of healthcare. The development and testing of treatments using rigorous scientific methods is a long and expensive process with uncertain outcomes. The investment in the research and development of health technologies is currently rewarded by the recognition of patents that give their holders the monopoly over their inventions for at least 20 years. The monopoly over these technologies means that prices can be set very high, increasing the cost of healthcare for patients or for the health system under which they are covered. This helps explain why countries are globally investing more in healthcare in absolute figures and as a proportion of their GDP. In the EU, for instance, healthcare expenditure is one of the largest and fastest-growing spending items in the public budget and accounts for 7.8% of the GDP and 15% of the total government expenditure.[3]

The advent of new technologies (e.g. drugs, devices, equipment, techniques) is certainly not the only reason for the increase in healthcare costs, but it has been considered the main or one of the main drivers of cost increases.[4] Drugs play a particularly important role in this trend as they are the fastest-growing expenditure within healthcare.[5] Some examples can illustrate this phenomenon. A WHO report found a ten-fold increase in the prices of new cancer medicines during the last decade (and 20-fold over the past 20 years).[6] Another example

2 David Wootton, *Bad Medicine: Doctors Doing Harm Since Hippocrates* (Oxford: Oxford University Press, 2007): 283; David Banta, "The Development of Health Technology Assessment," *Health Policy* 63, no. 2 (February 2003).

3 European Commission, *Health Systems, European Semester Thematic Factsheet* (European Commission, 2017): 4–5.

4 Organization for Economic Co-operation and Development, *Fiscal Sustainability of Health Systems: Bridging Health and Finance Perspectives* (Paris: OECD Publishing, 2015): 33; Sorenson, Drummond and Khan, "Medical Technology."

5 Fiona M. Clement et al., "Using Effectiveness and Cost-effectiveness to Make Drug Coverage Decisions: A Comparison of Britain, Australia, and Canada," *JAMA* 302, no. 13 (October 7, 2009).

6 World Health Organization, *Access to New Medicines in Europe: Technical Review of Policy Initiatives and Opportunities for Collaboration and Research* (Copenhagen: WHO Regional Office for Europe, 2015), 104.

is the drugs for Hepatitis C – sofosbuvir and ledipasvir – the universal provision of which, immediately after its launch, would have consumed an enormous proportion of what many countries spend on drugs. In countries like New Zealand, Italy, and Spain, it would have cost more than the total amount they spend on pharmaceuticals.[7] Orphan drugs for rare diseases, despite the reduced number of potential patients, can also have a significant impact on health budgets because of their very high unitary prices. For instance, a drug called Eculizumab costs US$700,000 per patient per year in the United States and Zolgensma, for spinal muscular atrophy, costs up to US$2.1 million per patient. It has been estimated that orphan drugs may account for 20% of the worldwide pharmaceutical market for non-generic prescription drugs.[8]

The cost increase that results from the development of new technologies is not proportional to the increase in health gains for patients. Despite the record increase in medicines approval in the US, Canada, and Europe in recent years, most of the new drugs are not superior to existing alternatives from a clinical perspective, and the great majority of those which are superior offer only minor improvements.[9] The aforementioned WHO report shows that the huge increase in the price of new cancer treatments brought only minimal health benefits to patients.[10] A paper on British Columbia in Canada shows that 80% of the increase in drug expenditure between 1996 and 2003 was explained by the use of new patented drugs that did not offer substantial improvements over the existing, less expensive alternatives.[11] Drugs for severe conditions, particularly when no alternative treatment is available, may have high prices that are disconnected from the benefits provided to patients. For instance, just one out of 12 drugs for cancer approved by the US FDA in 2012 provides survival gains that exceed two months.[12]

There are multiple strategies to maintain the financial sustainability of health systems facing the increasing pressure created by high-cost technologies.[13] One strategy is to reduce population coverage, increase co-payment, or exclude the funding of high-cost treatments. In principle, this strategy is contrary to UHC and hence will not be considered in this book. One of the UHC premises is that the financial sustainability of a health system is not an end in itself, but a condition

7 Swathi Iyengar et al., "Prices, Costs, and Affordability of New Medicines for Hepatitis C in 30 Countries: An Economic Analysis," *PLoS Med* 13, no. 5 (May 2016).

8 Annalisa Belloni, David Morgan, and Valérie Paris, *Pharmaceutical Expenditure and Policies: Past Trends and Future Challenges*, OECD Health Working Papers 87 (Paris: OECD Publishing, 2016): 36.

9 Huseyin Naci, Alexander Carter, and Elias Mossialos, "Why the Drug Development Pipeline Is Not Delivering Better Medicines," *BMJ* 351 (October 2015).

10 WHO, *Access to New Medicines*, 104.

11 Steven G. Morgan et al., "'Breakthrough' Drugs and Growth in Expenditure on Prescription Drugs in Canada," *BMJ* 331 (October 2005).

12 Belloni, Morgan, and Paris, "Pharmaceutical Expenditure and Policies," 37.

13 OECD, *Fiscal Sustainability of Health Systems*, 33; Sorenson, Drummond, and Khan, "Medical Technology."

for countries to offer high-quality care and promote fair access to health services. Another alternative for reducing the financial impact of new technologies is price regulation and negotiation, incentives for the use of generics, and reviewing IP laws or making use of their flexibilities (e.g. compulsory licence). For reasons of scope, these proposals will not be discussed in much depth in this book.

This book will rather focus on strategies for health systems to carefully select the health technologies on which they spend their scarce resources. New technologies will be competing for scarce healthcare resources with other interventions, and they may drive resources away from currently provided health technologies or services (e.g. immunization, primary healthcare, hospital-care based). Even the best-funded health systems need to be selective with regard to the inclusion of new technologies. Developed countries such as Sweden, The Netherlands, and Finland had to create positive lists of drugs (which determine the medicines eligible for funding) based on cost-effectiveness criteria due to the increase in the expenditure on drugs in the last decades.[14] The need to select technologies carefully and spend wisely is even more important in low- and middle-income countries, where the pressure for funding new technologies will coexist with the lack of universal provision of basic health services.[15]

New health technologies will not always increase the cost of healthcare as some may be cost-neutral or even cost-saving. Technologies will be cost-saving when they replace costlier or less efficient services, lead to the cure of an otherwise chronic disease that would require long-term care, or have fewer side effects that would require costly care. On the other hand, the cost may be increased when a new technology expands the list of treatable conditions, replaces a cheaper intervention, or is used on top of the existing services.[16]

In the same way that it would be wrong to assess a treatment looking exclusively at the benefits to the receiving patients, it is also misguided to look at the costs of new technologies only. Increased costs can result in improvements in health outcomes (e.g. patient satisfaction, quality of life, life expectancy). Therefore, if treatment is cost-increasing, it is essential to know what extra health benefits it will bring (if any) and at what cost. In other words, it is important to consider value for money in a context of scarce resources, competing needs for public funding, and rising expectations that result, at least in part, from the development of new health technologies in the context of wide access to information.

14 Corinna Sorenson, Michael Drummond, and Panos Kanavos, *Ensuring Value for Money in Health Care: The Role of Health Technology Assessment in the European Union*, Observatory Studies Series 11 (Copenhagen: European Observatory on Health Systems and Policies, 2008).

15 Virginia Wiseman et al., "Using Economic Evidence to Set Healthcare Priorities in Low-Income and Lower-Middle-Income Countries: A Systematic Review of Methodological Frameworks," *Health Economics* 25, no. S1 (February 2016): 154.

16 Sorenson, Drummond and Khan, "Medical Technology", 227.

This sort of information to inform resource allocation decisions can be generated through HTA. *The Health Technology Assessment international (HTAi) Glossary* defines HTA as the

> A multidisciplinary process that uses explicit methods to determine the value of a health technology at different points in its lifecycle. The purpose is to inform decision-making in order to promote an equitable, efficient, and high-quality health system.[17]

HTA assessments can have many purposes (e.g. to determine the price of drugs and medical products or to inform clinical practice and the standard of service provision),[18] but the focus in this chapter is on the use of HTA to inform funding decisions, i.e. decisions about what and who should be given priority in the allocation of healthcare resources.

HTA is a mechanism to prevent waste and inefficiency by identifying high-cost and low-impact interventions, which disproportionately absorb scarce resources that could be more efficiently used elsewhere in the health system. As affirmed by WHO, the drive to achieve UHC heightens the need to choose interventions judiciously given that wasteful spending on health technologies, particularly drugs, is a major cause of inefficiencies in health services delivery.[19] The information generated through HTA can also help improve the quality of care by preventing the use of medical services that are more likely to cause harm than good and by promoting the use of high-impact interventions.

Institutionalizing HTA

The incorporation of HTA in priority-setting processes can help promote the efficient and equitable allocation of healthcare resources, which is essential for achieving UHC.[20] Moreover, given the complexity of HTA and the almost inevitable controversies around decisions that result in the rationing of care that could potentially benefit patients, there is a growing consensus among scholars and international organizations that HTA should be institutionalized.[21]

17 "Health Technology Assessment," *HtaGlossary.net*, accessed June 15, 2021, http://htaglossary.net/health-technology-assessment.

18 Sorenson, Drummond, and Kanavos, *Ensuring Value*, 6; Aris Angelis, Ansgar Lange, and Panos Kanavos, "Using Health Technology Assessment to Assess the Value of New Medicines: Results of a Systematic Review and Expert Consultation Across Eight European Countries," *European Journal of Health Economics* 19, no. 1 (January 2018).

19 WHO, "Health Intervention and Technology Assessment in Support of Universal Health Coverage," (March 14, 2014) UN Doc A67/33.

20 Kalipso Chalkidou et al., "Health Technology Assessment in Universal Health Coverage," *The Lancet* 382, no. 9910 (December 21, 2013): e48.

21 Trygve Ottersen et al., *Making Fair Choices on the Path to Universal Health Coverage – Final Report of the WHO Consultative Group on Equity and Universal Health Coverage* (Geneva: World Health Organization, 2014); Daniel Cotlear et al., *Going Universal: How 24 Develop-*

Institutionalizing HTA means the creation of a body (either a unit within the ministerial structure or an independent agency) that is primarily responsible and resourced for gathering, assessing, and evaluating evidence about medical treatments. It also means HTA is formally established and linked to processes for making decisions about the coverage or reimbursement of medical treatments by health systems, although different jurisdictions will have different rules on whether HTA is obligatory before a funding decision is made, or if the outputs of an HTA body bind health systems.[22] Another aspect of institutionalization is the creation of standardized processes for gathering evidence, analysing data, receiving inputs from experts and stakeholders, deliberating about values and ethical judgments, and making decisions/recommendations about the funding of treatments.

The institutionalization of HTA is advanced in high-income countries, and particularly in Europe, where most member states have started to introduce HTA systems at the national or regional level since the 1990s.[23] Low- and middle-income countries have also recently started to adopt HTA (or, at least, to consider adopting it) in their health systems.[24] Building on the literature on regulation,[25] three main purposes for institutionalizing HTA can be identified: (i) to make decisions with more consistency, expertise, and information in an area of increasing complexity; (ii) to depoliticize part of the priority-setting activities by shifting the responsibility from politicians to an expert body; and (iii) to enhance the

---

ing Countries are Implementing Universal Health Coverage from the Bottom Up (Washington, DC: World Bank, 2015): 94–95; David A. Watkins et al., "Universal Health Coverage and Essential Packages of Care," in *Disease Control Priorities: Improving Health and Reducing Poverty*, eds. Dean T. Jamison et al. (Washington, DC: The World Bank, 2017), 44; PAHO "Progress Reports on Technical Matters – F. Health Technology Assessment and Incorporation into Health Systems" (September 10, 2015) CD/INF/5; PAHO Res CSP 28.R9 "Health Technology Assessment and Incorporation into Health Systems" (September 19, 2012) CSP28.R9; WHO, "Health Intervention and Technology Assessment in Support of Universal Health Coverage" (March 14, 2014) UN Doc A67/33.

22 Julia Chamova, *Mapping of HTA National Organisations, Programmes and Processes in EU and Norway* (Luxembourg: Publications Office of the European Union, 2017), 26.

23 European Commission, *Inception Impact Assessment on Strengthening of the EU Cooperation on Health Technology Assessment (HTA)* (European Commission, 2016); Banta, "Development of Health Technology Assessment," 131.

24 Y-Ling Chi et al., "What Next After GDP-Based Cost-Effectiveness Thresholds?," *Gates Open Research* 4 (2020); Watkins et al., "Universal Health Coverage," 62; Ursula Giedion, Ana Lucía Muñoz and Adriana Ávila, *Serie de notas técnicas sobre procesos de priorización en salud: Nota 1: Introducción*, Nota técnica 837 (Washington, DC: Inter-American Development Bank, 2015).

25 Mark Thatcher, *Governance Structures and Health Technology Assessment Agencies: A Comparative Approach*, LSE research project 4869 (London: Department of Government, London School of Economics and Political Science, 2010); Claudia Landwehr and Katharina Bohm, "Delegation and Institutional Design in Health-Care Rationing," *Governance: An International Journal of Policy, Administration, and Institutions* 24, no. 4 (October 2011).

legitimacy of priority-setting decisions through a process that allows more transparency, participation, and accountability.

Institutionalization is important because the data involved in HTA is complex to gather, analyse, and interpret. It requires a dedicated and highly trained body of experts with the experience and resources to carry out this task in a rigorous and timely manner. It is not enough to train experts to perform this task as this expertise and knowledge will be lost when these individuals move on from their positions.[26] It is necessary to have institutional arrangements with practices and routines that will allow the continuous accumulation of and improvement in HTA expertise. Moreover, standardized and transparent processes using pre-agreed and publicly available criteria to assess and compare technologies can promote a higher degree of consistency in priority-setting decisions over time.[27] In sum, HTA bodies are in a better position to produce consistent recommendations informed by state-of-the-art evidence and rigorous methods when compared with non-expert bodies or bodies that rely on the individual expertise of some professionals.

Institutionalizing HTA can also be a strategy to depoliticize priority-setting. When part of priority-setting is delegated to institutions with some degree of insularity from ministries, these bodies will attract the blame for rationing decisions that would otherwise be on the shoulders of politicians.[28] This, in principle, would reduce the political costs of decisions that are very unpopular, even when they are reasonable from a policy provision perspective. It is not a coincidence that in many countries institutionalization of HTA started in a context in which the economic pressure on health systems, coupled with public awareness that patients were not receiving optimal care because of scarce resources, resulted in increased political pressure on governments.[29]

The relative insularity of HTA institutions from majoritarian politics may come at the cost of democratic legitimacy, but these institutions rely on different forms of legitimacy. They will aspire to legitimacy through the quality of their procedure (input legitimacy) and the promise of better decisions (output legitimacy).[30] It is expected that HTA bodies will bring output legitimacy to priority-setting if their decisions are believed to be better informed and scientifically rigorous. This is what Keith Syrett called a "technocratic fix" to the legitimacy problem. Moreover, HTA bodies will also seek procedural legitimacy by making their decision-making processes more transparent, inclusive, impartial, and accountable. Many HTA bodies will, for instance, disclose the reasons for their

26 See Justin Parkhurst, *The Politics of Evidence: From Evidence-Based Policy to the Good Governance of Evidence* (Abingdon, OX: Routledge, 2017): 31.
27 Amanda Glassman et al., "Defining a Health Benefits Package: What Are the Necessary Processes?" *Health Systems & Reform* 2, no. 1 (2016): 45.
28 Cotlear et al., *Going Universal*, 79.
29 Lindsay M. Sabik and Reidar K. Lie, "Priority-Setting in Health Care: Lessons from the Experiences of Eight Countries," *International Journal for Equity in Health* 7 (2008): 2.
30 Landwehr and Bohm, "Delegation and Institutional Design."

decisions and create institutional spaces (e.g. public hearings, consultations, and appeals) to channel demand and information from different stakeholders (companies, patients, health systems, experts etc.), and to resolve disagreements between them.[31]

The WHO has affirmed that HTA systems with rigorous research methodology and with transparent and inclusive processes to inform the prioritization of health services play an important role in supporting universal health coverage.[32] The creation and proper functioning of these institutions have also been defended as one way in which states can contribute to the implementation of the right to health.[33]

HTA institutions vary considerably in relation to their role within a health system. They can have advisory functions or regulatory powers, and some have both. HTA institutions exercise advisory functions when they are responsible for producing non-binding recommendations and there is a separation between the body responsible for assessing technologies and those deciding whether these technologies should be funded by a health system. For instance, in Australia, the Pharmaceutical Benefits Advisory Committee's (PBAC) conclusions in the assessment of medicines do not bind the health system, although only those drugs recommended by the PBAC can be considered for listing.[34]

HTA institutions have regulatory powers when their conclusions are mandatory and must be followed by health systems. For instance, the law requires that the technologies recommended following NICE technology appraisals (assessment of clinical and cost-effectiveness of health technologies) must be provided within three months by the NHS Clinical Commissioning Groups (CCGs), the bodies responsible for commissioning healthcare services at the local level.[35] NICE is also an example of a body that has both regulatory powers and advisory functions. Except for technology appraisals, all other NICE guidance (e.g. those related to clinical practice, interventional procedures, and public health) are not binding on the NHS. However, even NICE guidance can impact the provision of treatments as courts have decided that CCGs must provide reasons for not following NICE non-binding recommendations.[36]

31 Ottersen et al., *Making Fair Choices*; Cotlear et al., *Going Universal*, 94–95; Amanda Glassman and Kalipso Chalkidou, *Priority-Setting in Health Building Institutions for Smarter Public Spending* (Washington, DC: Center for Global Development, 2012): 42.

32 WHO, "Health Intervention and Technology Assessment in Support of Universal Health Coverage," (September 13, 2013) SEA/RC66/R4.

33 Benedict Rumbold et al., "Universal Health Coverage, Priority Setting, and the Human Right to Health," *The Lancet* 390, no. 10095 (August 12, 2017).

34 See Lianne Barnieh et al., "A Synthesis of Drug Reimbursement Decision-Making Processes in Organisation for Economic Co-operation and Development Countries," *Value in Health* 17, no. 1 (January-February 2014).

35 The National Institute for Health and Care Excellence (Constitution and Functions) and the Health and Social Care Information Centre (Functions) Regulations 2013.

36 See Chapter 6.

This legal distinction between regulatory/advisory powers will not necessarily be reflected in practice as non-binding recommendations can always, or almost always, be followed by governments. The Canadian *CADTH* Common Drug Review (CDR) produces non-binding recommendations, but publicly funded drug plans follow the CDR's recommendations about 90% of the time.[37] In Australia, the HTA recommendations are also usually followed by the department responsible for resource allocation.[38] In contrast, governments may delay or create obstacles to the implementation of HTA institutions' binding decisions. As discussed previously, there have been concerns about the uneven access to drugs recommended by NICE in England due to insufficient funding.

HTA considerations

Clinical considerations

The application of the scientific method to understand diseases and to test medical interventions is central to modern medicine and HTA makes use of science to inform priority-setting decisions. HTA starts with the following question: is the new technology superior to the existing technology? If it is, then how much better is it? These questions are answered through the review of the scientific literature regarding the safety, efficacy, and effectiveness of the assessed technology. Scientific evidence is central to inform health systems' decisions because it helps to prevent both the overuse (the administration of medical treatments that are more likely to cause harm than good)[39] and the underuse (the failure to deliver services that are likely to improve health)[40] of medical services, which are serious obstacles for adequate care and the efficient allocation of resources.

HTA builds on evidence-based medicine (EBM), which "involves the systematic collection, synthesis and application of all available scientific evidence".[41] The purpose of EBM is to use evidence from scientific research to inform clinical practice in order to improve the quality, safety, and effectiveness of the care provided

37 Canadian Agency for Drugs and Technologies in Health, "*CADTH Presentation on the Common Drug Review to the House of Commons Standing Committee on Health*" (speaking notes for a presentation, Ottawa, ON, House of Commons Standing Committee on Health, April 25, 2007), https://www.cadth.ca/media/media/Standing_Committee_CADTH_Sanders_FINAL_2007Apr25.pdf.

38 Paul Healy and Meir P. Pugatch, *Theory versus Practice: Discussing the Governance of Health Technology Assessment Systems* (London: Stockholm Network, 2009), 21.

39 Shannon Brownlee et al., "Evidence for Overuse of Medical Services Around the World," *The Lancet* 390, no. 10090 (July 2017).

40 Adam G. Elshaug et al., "Levers for Addressing Medical Underuse and Overuse: Achieving High-Value Health Care," *The Lancet* 390, no. 10090 (July 2017).

41 D. Moher et al., "Assessing the Quality of Reports of Randomised Trials: Implications for the Conduct of Meta-Analyses," *Health Technology Assessment* 3, no. 12 (1999): 1.

to patients.[42] As in EBM, HTA will ideally include a systematic literature review of the scientific evidence to gather all the existing research on the assessed treatment. The review should be systematic, using an explicit research strategy and according to recognized methods to prevent biases and to fully capture the state-of-the-art knowledge about a medical treatment.[43]

Safety is measured by the harm (morbidity and mortality) directly related to the use of a technology. Efficacy is the ability of a medical intervention to alter the natural course of a disease for better under the controlled environment of a clinical trial. Effectiveness is the ability of a medical intervention to alter the natural course of a disease for better in real-world conditions of practice and use.[44] The distinction between efficacy and effectiveness is important because clinical trials are normally designed to include patients who meet very specific criteria (which excludes, for instance, participants with comorbidities or those taking other medicines), who will be closely monitored, and use the experimental intervention for a limited period. Therefore, treatments that proved to be safe and efficacious in clinical trials may be shown not to be safe or effective once used by a much larger population over a long period and in non-controlled settings.

Apart from identifying the relevant studies, HTA will also involve assessing the scientific quality of the existing data. One way to assess the quality of the evidence is to classify the existing research on a technology using a hierarchy of levels of evidence. The gold standard at the summit of most hierarchies of this kind are meta-analyses of randomized clinical trials, which pool individual studies and synthesize the evidence to estimate the effects of a particular treatment. Next in the hierarchy come separate randomized clinical trials (RCT), where patients are randomly selected to receive either the experimental treatment or the comparator(s). RCTs are considered to be superior forms of evidence because randomization reduces bias, can control for confounding factors, and adequate sampling minimizes the play of chance.[45] Below RCTs are non-randomized intervention studies, observational studies (the investigator does not apply an intervention, but only observes and compares outcomes for people who use the technology under

42 Banta, "Development of Health Technology Assessment," 124; David L. Sackett et al., "Evidence Based Medicine: What It Is and What It Isn't: It's About Integrating Individual Clinical Expertise and the Best External Evidence," *BMJ* 312, no. 7023 (Jan. 13, 1996).

43 See, for instance, Julian Higgins et al., eds., *Cochrane Handbook for Systematic Reviews of Interventions Version 6.2. (updated February 2021)* (Chichester, UK: Cochrane, 2021). See, also, Finn Børlum Kristensen and Helga Sigmund, eds., *Health Technology Assessment Handbook* (Copenhagen: Danish Centre for Health Technology Assessment, National Board of Health, 2007).

44 See Archie Cochrane, *Effectiveness and Efficiency: Random Reflections on Health Services* (London: The Nuffield Provincial Hospitals Trust, 1971).

45 Michael D. Rawlins, "Evidence, Values, and Decision Making," *International Journal of Technology Assessment in Health Care* 30, no. 2 (April 2014).

study with outcomes for those who do not use the technology),[46] case studies, and expert opinions.[47]

Traditionally, decision-makers would consider that the higher the evidence in this hierarchy the better, and they would rely on other forms of evidence only in the absence of high-hierarchy evidence. However, this approach has been changing as it has been recognized that each form of study has strengths and weaknesses and that high-quality research of lower hierarchy can be more relevant than poor-quality research of a higher hierarchy.[48]

RCTs provide greater confidence in the internal validity of the results (i.e. that the outcome difference between the compared groups in the trial is likely to be related to the tested intervention). However, there are questions about whether resource-intensive RCTs are always necessary, about their external validity or generalizability (i.e. the extent to which the findings in a controlled environment of a trial can be extrapolated to real-world settings), and about their capacity to detect harms caused by the tested intervention given their relatively short duration and the limited number of people involved. Moreover, it is necessary to assess the quality of RCTs taking into account factors such as the size and representativeness of the sample used; whether the chosen method is adequate to answer the research question; if the randomization method allowed all study participants to have the same probability of receiving the tested or the control treatment(s) in the study; whether the comparator used is the standard of care; if the study was double-blinded; and the researchers' possible conflicts of interests that may bias the results.[49]

On the other hand, methods that are placed lower in the hierarchies of evidence level may be sufficient to provide the information needed, they may offer relevant information that is not found in RCTs, or they can even be more reliable than RCTs in answering the relevant questions for a particular HTA. For instance, observational studies occur in non-controlled environments and hence they are more susceptible to confounding variables, which makes it more difficult to prove causality between a health intervention and a given outcome. However, the findings of observational studies tend to be more generalizable because they

46 National Institute for Health and Care Excellence, "Evidence," in *Guide to the Methods of Technology Appraisal 2013* (National Institute for Health and Care Excellence, 2013).

47 See Alison Lesley Weightman et al., eds., *Grading Evidence and Recommendations for Public Health Interventions: Developing and Piloting a Framework* (London: Health Development Agency, 2005).

48 Gordon Guyatt et al., "GRADE Guidelines: 1. Introduction – GRADE Evidence Profiles and Summary of Findings Tables," *Journal of Clinical Epidemiology* 64, no. 4 (April 2011).

49 See, Reinhard Busse et al., "Best Practice in Undertaking and Reporting Health Technology Assessments: Working Group 4 Report," *International Journal of Technology Assessment in Health Care* 18, no. 2 (April 2002): 374; Alejandro R. Jadad et al., "Assessing the Quality of Reports of Randomized Clinical Trials: Is Blinding Necessary?" *Controlled Clinical Trials* 17, no. 1 (February 1996).

capture data from a broader population in a real-world context over a longer period.[50] Therefore, observational studies can play a very significant role in informing HTA recommendations, particularly when they show a very large magnitude of treatment effect (the causal effect of a treatment on an outcome variable of interest) despite the existence of confounders that can potentially decrease the magnitude of this effect.[51]

Therefore, a growing body of literature recommends that all available relevant information across the full spectrum of study designs should be included for a more comprehensive and accurate assessment of new technologies.[52] The *NICE Guide to the Methods of Technology Appraisal*, for instance, recommends that "[w]hatever the sources of evidence available on a particular technology and patient group, they should be integrated into a systematic review."[53]

It is also important to highlight that HTA will normally require evidence beyond what is provided for regulatory approval by regulatory agencies responsible for granting marketing authorization (e.g. the US Food and Drugs Agency or the European Medicines Agency). Marketing authorization is normally granted when the product is shown to be safe and efficacious. This does not suffice for priority-setting decisions which require information about costs, the comparison between the new technology and the existing treatment, and data produced in the real world rather than the controlled environment in clinical trial settings.[54]

For the purposes of HTA, it is important to compare the scientific evidence of a new technology with the existing alternative treatments for the same condition. HTA bodies will be particularly interested in the evidence on how a new technology compares with the standard of care (the currently recommended treatment for a condition).[55] HTA may also take into account evidence about whether there are alternative treatments for the same condition (and how effective they are), the

50 "Understanding Observational Studies," *Drug and Therapeutics Bulletin* 54, no. 9 (September 2016).

51 Gordon Guyatt et al., "An Emerging Consensus on Grading Recommendations?" *BMJ Evidence-Based Medicine* 11, no. 1 (February 2006).

52 Michael Rawlins, "De Testimonio: On the Evidence for Decisions About the Use of Therapeutic Interventions," *The Lancet* 372, no. 9656 (December 2008); Michael F. Drummond et al., "Key Principles for the Improved Conduct of Health Technology Assessments for Resource Allocation Decisions," *International Journal of Technology Assessment in Health Care* 24, no. 3 (July 2008): 252; Rawlins, "Evidence, Values, and Decision Making"; Justin O. Parkhurst and Sudeepa Abeysinghe, "What Constitutes 'Good' Evidence for Public Health and Social Policy-making? From Hierarchies to Appropriateness," *Social Epistemology* 30, no. 5–6 (2016); Angus Deaton and Nancy Cartwright, "Understanding and Misunderstanding Randomized Controlled Trials," *Social Science and Medicine* 210 (August 2018).

53 National Institute for Health and Care Excellence, *Guide to the Methods of Technology Appraisal 2013* (National Institute for Health and Care Excellence, 2013).

54 Michael F. Drummond, "Health Technology Assessment and its Interface with Regulation, Policy and Management," in *Health Technology Assessment and Health Today: A Multifaceted View and their Unstable Crossroads*, eds. Jean E. del Llano-Senaris and Carlos Campillo-Artero (Springer, 2015): 4.

55 Barnieh et al., "Synthesis of Drug Reimbursement," 100.

severity of the condition, and how it affects patients' quality of life and level of impairment (also known as the 'burden of disease').[56] It may also consider data related to the prevalence of the condition in society, although this seems to be less usual.[57]

Lastly, all this material needs to be analysed, synthesized, and discussed to inform a concrete policy recommendation regarding the funding and use of a treatment by the public health system. For instance, interventions that produce statistically significant, but small, differences in a trial may not produce clinically significant results in terms of survival or other clinical benefits. This needs to be weighed against the costs, side effects, and risks to patients. This is why, despite the enormous focus on scientific evidence in HTA, many experts have acknowledged that decisions in this area are never based on evidence alone. Other considerations are (and should be) taken into account in the decision-making. At best, decisions will be *informed* by scientific evidence rather than *based* on it.[58]

Economic considerations

In many HTA systems, the clinical analysis occurs alongside the economic analysis of the technology under assessment.[59] Health economics can help estimate the economic impact of covering a treatment and the relation between its cost and the benefits it can provide to patients. This gives decision-makers information about how to invest the resources to maximize the health benefits gained within a certain amount of resources.

Because resources are scarce, any decision to fund a medical treatment will inevitably displace resources devoted to other interventions. In other words, all expenditure has opportunity costs, which are the foregone gains that could have been obtained if the same resources were invested elsewhere in the health system.[60] Economic analysis is particularly relevant in a context in which a high number of new treatments enter the market, but many offer little or no additional benefits.[61]

A new health technology is normally compared with the existing practice for a particular condition (the "standard care") in terms of costs and health gains.[62]

56 Angelis, Lange, and Kanavos, "Using Health Technology Assessment", 135; Ronald L. Akehurst et al., "Variation in Health Technology Assessment and Reimbursement Processes in Europe," *Value in Health* 20, no. 1 (January 2017): 71.
57 Angelis, Lange, and Kanavos.
58 Kristensen and Sigmund, *Health Technology Assessment Handbook*, 17.
59 Only a small number of countries that have institutionalized HTA do not consider the cost of treatments in their assessments, see Barnieh et al., "Synthesis of Drug Reimbursement."
60 Benedict Rumbold et al., "Public Reasoning and Health-Care Priority Setting: The Case of NICE," *Kennedy Institute of Ethics Journal* 27, no. 1 (March 2017): 121.
61 European Commission, EU cooperation on Health Technology Assessment; Tim Mathes et al., "Methods of International Health Technology Assessment Agencies for Economic Evaluations – A Comparative Analysis," *BMC Health Services Research* 13 (September 30, 2013).
62 Mathes et al.; Kristensen and Sigmund, *Health Technology Assessment Handbook*, 93.

If a new technology is better than the standard of care and will cost the same or less, or if it is equally good and cheaper, then the rational decision, *ceteris paribus*, is to fund the new technology. However, if it is the opposite (i.e. the standard of care is better than the new technology and costs the same or less, or if it is equally good but cheaper), then the standard of care should be kept. The challenging cases are the new technologies that are more expensive and better, or less expensive but worse compared with standard care.[63] The question then is whether it is worth paying the cost of the added health gain brought by the costlier treatment.

Health economics helps to answer this question. There are many kinds of economic analyses in health and it is beyond the scope of this book to explore all of them.[64] It will thus focus primarily on cost-effectiveness analysis (CEA), which is the most common type of economic analysis used in HTA.[65] CEA is used, for instance, by the National Institute for Health and Clinical Excellence (NICE) in England, the Pharmaceutical Benefits Advisory Committee in Australia, the Common Drug Review in Canada, the National Commission for the Incorporation of Health Technologies (CONITEC) in Brazil, and the Health Intervention and Technology Assessment Program in Thailand.[66]

Among HTA bodies that adopt CEA, cost-effectiveness is commonly measured using price per QALY (quality-adjusted life years).[67] QALY is a measure of the health benefits a treatment is expected to provide and it is calculated by estimating the expected years of life gained under the treatment adjusted by the quality of life during these years using a weight that goes from 0 to 1. "Zero" means that the patient is dead and "one" that she is in a state of perfect health, and between these two extremes lie different states of health with varying degrees of sickness and disability.[68] The cost and the number of QALYs offered by the new treatment are then compared with those of the standard of care to calculate the incremental cost-effectiveness ratio (ICER), which is the difference in cost between the new technology and its comparator divided by the difference in QALY gained by using the new technology versus the comparator.

In the example in Table 3.1, the ICER of using treatment A (a new technology) instead of B (the standard of care) is £10k per QALY [(£50k–£10k)/(6QALY–2QALY)], which is another way to say that each QALY gained with

63 Kristensen and Sigmund, 159.

64 For a review of the different types of economic analysis in health see Kristensen and Sigmund, 141.

65 Angelis, Lange, and Kanavos, "Using Health Technology Assessment," 142.

66 Clement et al., "Using Effectiveness and Cost-effectiveness"; Sripen Tantivess et al., "Health Technology Assessment capacity Development in Low- and Middle-Income Countries: Experiences from the International Units of HITAP and NICE," *F1000Research* 6, no. 2119 (December 11, 2017).

67 Barnieh et al., "Synthesis of Drug Reimbursement."

68 On the different methods to estimate quality of life see Mathes et al., "Methods of International Health," 7; Philip Musgrove and Julia Fox-Rushby, "Cost-effectiveness Analysis for Priority Setting," in *Disease Control Priorities in Developing Countries*, eds. Dean T. Jamison and et al., 2nd edition (Washington, DC: World Bank, 2006), 278.

Table 3.1 ICER calculation

Treatment	*Years of life*	*Quality*	*QALY*	*Price (£)*
A	10	0.6	6	50k
B	5	0.4	2	10k
A–B	5	0.2	4	40k

Source: Own creation.

the new treatments costs £10k to the health system. This number is important because there are different ways in which it can be used to inform priority-setting decisions. One is to rank interventions according to ICER in a list, sort the list from the most to the least cost-effective, and adopt those at the top of the list first and continue until resources are exhausted. A more commonly used alternative is to establish an ICER threshold above which treatments will unlikely be funded because they are not considered cost-effective for a particular health system. NICE, for instance, adopts a cutting point of £20k–£30k per QALY gained. That is, as a rule, treatments will not be recommended for funding from the NHS when the cost per QALY gained is above this threshold.

There are different ways to calculate this threshold and experts suggest that health systems should consider economic (e.g. health budget, GDP per capita) and population (e.g. demographics, epidemiology) data in each country to estimate the likely opportunity costs of providing treatments above it.[69]

Many objections have been raised against CEA, particularly when presented in the context of a one-off decision concerning the coverage of a given health technology.[70] This may reinforce the impression that CEA is about putting a price on life. However, CEA should be understood in terms of opportunity costs, focusing on what could be gained with alternative use of the resources. This prevents the provision of non-cost-effective treatments at the expense of other interventions that may offer better value (in terms of health gains) for money.[71]

69 On the different ways to calculate the ICER threshold, see Jessica Ochalek, James Lomas, and Karl Claxton, "Estimating Health Opportunity Costs in Low-Income and Middle-Income Countries: A Novel Approach and Evidence from Cross-Country Data," *BMJ Global Health* 3, no. 6 (November 2018): e000964; Melanie Y. Bertram et al., "Cost–Effectiveness Thresholds: Pros and Cons," *Bulletin of the World Health Organization* 94 (2016); Alyssa Bilinski et al., "When Cost-Effective Interventions are Unaffordable: Integrating Cost-Effectiveness and Budget Impact in Priority Setting for Global Health Programs," *PLoS Med* 14, no. 10 (October); Chi et al., "GDP-Based Cost-Effectiveness Thresholds."

70 S. Bryan and I. Williams, "Adoption of New Technologies, Using Economic Evaluation," in *Encyclopedia of Health Economics*, ed. Anthony J. Culyer, vol. 1 (San Diego: Elsevier, 2014), 29.

71 Nigel Edwards, Helen Crump, and Mark Dayan, *Rationing in the NHS*, Nuffield Trust Policy Briefing 2 (London: Nuffield Trust, 2015), 9.

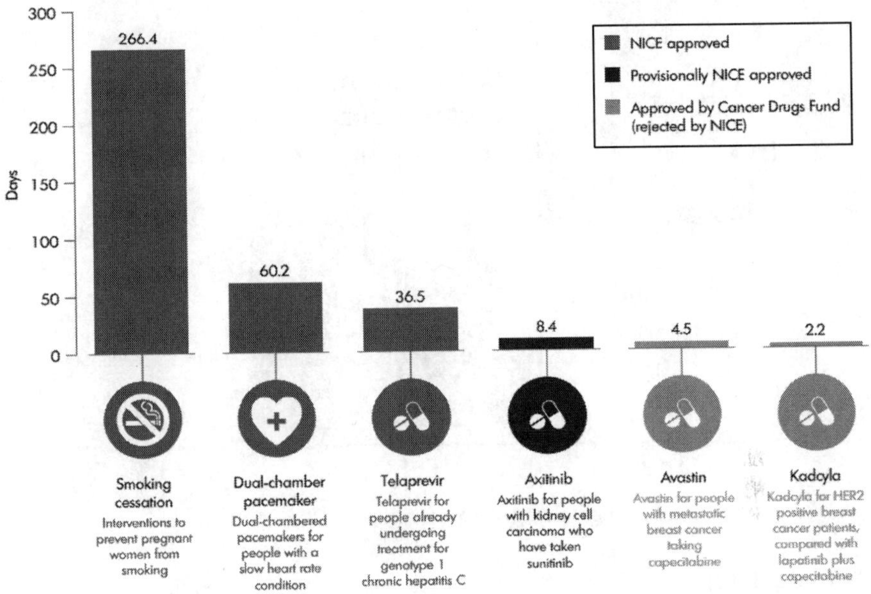

Figure 3.1 Additional days of quality-adjusted life per £1,000 for selected interventions. Source: This image was originally published by the Nuffield Trust. Nigel Edwards, Helen Crump and Mark Dayan, *Rationing in the NHS*, Policy Briefing 2 (London: Nuffield Trust, 2015), 9.

One good example of the risks of ignoring CEA is the Cancer Drugs Fund (CDF) in England. The use of QALY has resulted in many cancer treatments not being recommended for funding by the NHS as, according to NICE, they provided too little benefit despite their high prices. This has always been unpopular and met with fierce opposition from patients and the pharmaceutical industry. The CDF was then created in 2010 to fund cancer treatments not recommended by NICE, to the bewilderment of many who saw no rational reason for creating an exception for cancer treatments and who considered the CDF a politically motivated decision that undermined the work of NICE.[72] Figure 3.1 compares the additional days of quality-adjusted life per £1k spent on different interventions. It helps us visualize that the question is not whether 2.2 quality-adjusted days gained using Kadcyla for HER2 breast cancer are worth £1k, but whether it is worth spending it on Kadcyla instead of smoking-cessation interventions that can offer 266.4 quality-adjusted days for the same amount of money. It is also telling that the CDF proved to be financially unsustainable, and most treatments

72 See Katharina Kieslich et al., "Accounting for Technical, Ethical, and Political Factors in Priority Setting," *Health Systems & Reform* 2, no. 1 (2016): 59.

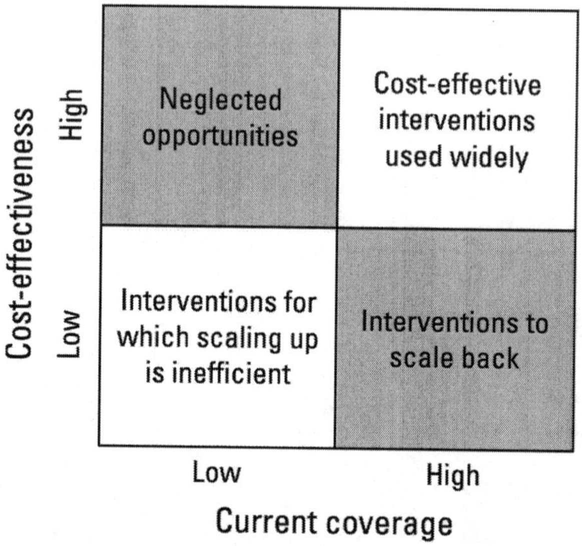

Figure 3.2 Efficiency of interventions. Source: Ramanan Laxminarayan, Jeffrey Chow, and Sonbol A. Shahid-Salles, "Intervention Cost-Effectiveness: Overview of Main Messages", p. 36, in Jamison, Dean T.; Breman, Joel G.; Measham, Anthony R.; Alleyne, George; Claeson, Mariam; Evans, David B.; Jha, Prabhat; Mills, Ann; Musgrove, Philip. 2006. *Disease Control Priorities in Developing Countries, Second Edition*. Washington, DC: World Bank and Oxford University Press. © World Bank. https://openknowledge.worldbank.org/handle/10986/7242 License: CC BY 3.0 IGO.

funded via the CDF did not report a statistically significant improvement in overall survival or clinical benefit.[73]

Cost-effectiveness analysis should not be reduced to merely producing reasons for excluding or scaling back cost-ineffective interventions. It is also useful to indicate interventions that are cost-effective but not yet accessible for the population. This information can be used to challenge unwise policies by showing neglected opportunities for producing greater health impact with a certain amount of resources (see Figure 3.2). CEA can be strategically used to elevate the political pressure on governments for increasing (or not reducing) health budgets to fund them or for reallocating resources to meet those needs, especially where there is public funding for interventions of unknown or limited effectiveness.[74]

73 A. Aggarwal et al., "Do Patient Access Schemes for High-Cost Cancer Drugs Deliver Value to Society? – Lessons from the NHS Cancer Drugs Fund," *Annals of Oncology* 28, no. 8 (August 2017).

74 Glassman and Chalkidou, *Priority-Setting in Health*, 8.

HTA may also include budget impact analysis to assess affordability by quantifying an intervention's short-term net costs for the health system.[75] Even though ICER thresholds may be set considering the budget available, a treatment considered cost-effective may yet be unaffordable because a health system may not have the ability to secure sufficient resources for its provision without severely affecting other services.[76] If issues of cost-effectiveness are separated from matters of affordability (e.g. if the threshold is too high for the existing budget or the budget impact is not considered) there is the risk of undersupply and uneven provision of the assessed treatment, or severe opportunity costs for the health system.[77] This is not a mere hypothetical possibility as there have been concerns about NICE-approved drugs forcing local authorities in England to make tragic disinvestment choices in relevant services because the duty to provide NICE-approved treatments may not come with a corresponding budget increase.[78]

Conversely, a much less cost-effective treatment may have a small budget impact. This is the rationale accepted by some health systems for funding less cost-effective treatments for rare diseases, which the NHS defines as those that affect less than 1 in 50,000 people. Even though the unitary cost of the treatment may be very high, its low prevalence may mean a limited budget impact. The NHS in England, for instance, has a policy for drugs for rare conditions ("highly specialized technologies") that may receive NHS funding even when their ICER is much higher than what would be acceptable for other technologies. However, this was accompanied by the establishment of a budget impact test, according to which the NHS will engage in negotiations with the pharmaceutical company if it spends over £20 million on a particular drug in any of the first three years of funding. The NHS will not have to provide the treatment if no agreement is reached.[79]

Lastly, it is important to acknowledge that one should not assume that the health budget is set in stone. An allocative decision is not always a zero-sum game for the health system from a financial perspective. The total amount available will vary and it is largely a political decision, but this by no means makes the economic analysis less important. Even if additional funding is possible, it will always be limited, and hence decisions about which services or groups should benefit from this additional money should be informed by value-for-money considerations. Likewise, in situations where the total amount of resources for healthcare

75 Bilinski et al., "Cost-Effective Interventions," 2.

76 Cotlear et al., *Going Universal*, 94.

77 Bilinski et al., "Cost-Effective Interventions."

78 Adrian Towse and Martin Buxton, *Three Challenges to Achieving Better Analysis for Better Decisions: Generalisability, Complexity and Thresholds*, Notes on a conference in honour of Bernie O'Brien, OHE Briefing n. 42 (London: Office of Health Economics, October 2006): 13.

79 For a critical analysis of the budget impact test, see Victoria Charlton et al., "Cost Effective but Unaffordable: An Emerging Challenge for Health Systems," *BMJ* 356, no. 8098 (March 25, 2017).

is shrinking, economic analysis will be useful to make decisions about decommissioning and disinvestment to alleviate the impact of a smaller budget on the population's healthcare.

Social values and ethical considerations

The focus on evidence in HTA and the technical complexity of scientific and economic analysis should not distract us from the fact that priority-setting will inevitably involve different social values and conflicting concepts of fairness. Medical science and economic analysis can inform priority-setting decisions, but what makes a decision "correct" is always a matter of value and ethical judgment.[80] Therefore, it is central for HTA bodies to be upfront about the values that inform choices and be mindful about the fairness of their decisions in the eyes of stakeholders, the general public, and other public institutions.

Ethical considerations and social values are not separate from the scientific and economic analysis either. The assessment of scientific evidence is not value-free and there are value judgments in decisions about what counts as harm or benefit of using an intervention, which evidence should be included in the analysis, and how much weight should be given to different sources of evidence. The decision by the Dutch National Health Care Institute to remove a procedure called "bladder instillations" for interstitial cystitis patients from the national basic health insurance package due to insufficient evidence supporting its effectiveness is a telling example. This decision was (unsuccessfully) challenged in court by claimants who argued that the Institute should have given more weight to abundant evidence from physicians' clinical practice and patient experience with the intervention rather than relying exclusively on the results of a few randomized clinical trials with limited quality. Moes et al. argue that this case shows the clash between different epistemic and normative views about what is evidence and how different types of evidence should be weighted.[81]

Even when there is no dispute about the existing evidence, how it is used to inform policy is not value-free either. Choices regarding, for instance, what counts as an acceptable level of risk of harm or as a favourable risk-benefit ratio are value-laden ethical choices that will be central to recommendations about the use and funding of treatments.[82] Value judgments will be particularly important when the evidence is inconclusive or insufficient but a quick decision has to be

80 See Parkhurst, *The Politics of Evidence.*

81 Floortje Moes et al., "Contested Evidence: A Dutch Reimbursement Decision Taken to Court," *Health Economics, Policy and Law* 12, no. 3 (July 2017).

82 See, for instance, Sarah Clark and Albert Weale, "Social Values in Health Priority Setting: A Conceptual Framework," *Journal of Health Organization and Management* 26, no. 3 (2012): 295; Stuart G. Nicholls, Ainsley J. Newson, and Richard E. Ashcroft, "The Need for Ethics As Well As Evidence in Evidence-Based Medicine," *Journal of Clinical Epidemiology* 77 (September 1, 2016); Angelis, Lange, and Kanavos, "Using Health Technology Assessment," 147.

made, such as in cases involving early access to last-chance therapies for patients who are unresponsive to standard care or when the use of experimental treatments is being considered in the context of a pandemic. To avoid waste and to protect patients against unnecessary risks and inconveniences, health systems should limit access to treatments when there is not enough evidence of efficacy, effectiveness or safety (Type I error). But this will increase the risk of a Type II error when they do not allow access to treatment that could have helped the patient. Whether, and under what conditions, an innovative treatment should be covered when the evidence is inconclusive is an ethical and political decision about which type of error is more important to avoid.[83]

Ethical considerations also permeate economic analysis. For instance, which costs will be included in the analysis is a value-laden decision: some, but not all, HTA institutions will include indirect costs and the costs that others (carers, social services, loss of productivity) will have to bear because individuals are sick.[84] The operationalization of CEA will also involve value judgments. The use of QALY is based on the premise that a QALY gained has the same value no matter who benefits from it ("a QALY is a QALY"), which is an ethically debatable assumption. There will be disagreements about whether (and how) QALYs should be adjusted by the age of the patient (so one QALY for a young person will weigh more than one QALY for an older person) or to when the benefits will materialize (so a benefit further in the future will be of less value than a benefit in the present).[85]

Moreover, to the extent that HTA institutions are involved in priority-setting decisions, issues of distributive justice are unavoidable in HTA. Allocative decisions have winners and losers: if funding is denied, people will be left without the care that can potentially improve and extend their lives; if granted, then the opportunity costs for health systems will affect the care of other users. Allocative choices are inherently controversial because people may reasonably disagree about the substantive principle of justice that should guide priority-setting in health care.

CEA aims at the maximization of benefits and its assumption is that, if health is good, then there is a moral imperative to maximize this good in society by prioritizing cost-effective interventions, even if this comes at the cost of excluding low value-for-money treatments. This is controversial and some countries, like Germany, are reluctant to give CEA a central role in priority-setting due to the

83 See Clark and Weale, 304; Kalipso Chalkidou et al., "Evidence-Based Decision Making: When Should We Wait For More Information?" *Health Affairs* 27, no. 6 (November/December 2008).

84 Weyma Lubbe, "Social Value Maximization and the Multiple Goals Assumption: Is Priority Setting a Maximizing Task at All?" in *Prioritization in Medicine: An International Dialogue*, eds. Eckhard Nagel and Michael Lauerer (Heidelberg: Springer, 2015).

85 Dan W. Brock and Daniel Wikler, "Ethical Issues in Resource Allocation, Research, and New Product Development," in *Disease Control Priorities: Improving Health and Reducing Poverty*, eds. Dean T. Jamison et al., 2nd ed. (Washington, DC: The World Bank, 2017), 262.

policymakers' ethical objections and their perception that the public would not accept it.[86] In others, like Colombia, the use of economic analysis for decisions about treatment coverage has been judged a breach of the right to health by the Constitutional Court.[87]

Even those who agree that maximization is a valid ethical imperative for health systems will normally also agree that it is not enough to achieve a fair distribution of resources.[88] Fairness will also include concerns about equity, namely how health gains are distributed among the population. Norheim et al.[89] suggest that equity considerations can be divided into three groups. Group 1 are disease-related criteria, which include giving special consideration to interventions that target severe health conditions, people with a low capacity to benefit (e.g. those who suffer from a less treatable health condition), or those with large past health losses (e.g. chronic disabilities). Group 2 will include criteria related to characteristics that leave some social groups disadvantaged and create health inequalities, including socioeconomic status, area of residence (e.g. rural areas), gender, ethnicity, religion, and sexual orientation. Group 3 criteria relate to the protection against the financial and social effects of ill health offered by some interventions, such as high-cost treatments, the costs of which would be catastrophic if paid out-of-pocket.

Efficiency and equity will often coincide as the most cost-effective treatments are also normally those that will benefit the worst-off the most.[90] However, there are circumstances in which policymakers, after considering the distribution of benefits and the opportunity costs of different policies, will conclude that the most efficient option will not reduce inequality and may even aggravate it. In these cases, health systems have to choose between efficiency and equity. Whether, when, and to what extent equity considerations should outweigh efficiency in a concrete case are ethical choices about which reasonable people may disagree.[91]

NICE, for instance, despite its emphasis on CEA and of having an ICER threshold, may recommend the funding of treatment above this threshold in some circumstances in light of the perceived social values. For instance, treatments above the threshold may be recommended for funding if they extend the

86 Lars Schwettmann, "Let's Talk About Health Economic Evaluation: Relevant Contextual Factors for the German 'Sonderweg'," in *Prioritization in Medicine: an International Dialogue*, eds. Eckhard Nagel and Michael Lauerer (Heidelberg: Springer, 2015).

87 See Chapter 5.

88 See Chapter 2.

89 Ole F. Norheim et al., "Guidance on Priority Setting in Health Care (GPS-Health): The Inclusion of Equity Criteria Not Captured by Cost-Effectiveness Analysis," *Cost Effectiveness and Resource Allocation* 12 (August 2014).

90 Brock and Wikler, "Ethical Issues," 259.

91 Ottersen et al., *Making Fair Choices*; Benedict E. Rumbold and James Wilson, "Reasonable Disagreement and the Generally Unacceptable: A Philosophical Analysis of Making Fair Choices," *Health Economics, Policy and Law* 11, no. 1 (January 2016); Richard Cookson et al., "Using Cost-Effectiveness Analysis to Address Health Equity Concerns," *Value in Health* 20, no. 2 (February 2017).

life of those at the end of life, if they are innovative, or if they can benefit a particular group of patients. The Cancer Drugs Fund mentioned previously was particularly controversial as some considered that these departures from the general NICE standards create unfairness and inefficiency in priority-setting.[92] Another example that raised controversy is the programme for highly specialized technologies, which allows the recommendation of treatments for ultrarare diseases that would not be considered cost-effective according to NICE's usual standards.[93] However, other criteria are explicitly excluded for ethical reasons, such as the individual responsibility of the patient for her health condition.[94]

As seen, the use of clinical evidence and economics in HTA will often involve the conflict of values and ethical judgments. The question of whether a certain allocation of resources is fair cannot be answered by evidence only. Even when exposed to the same evidence and information, fair-minded people may still reasonably disagree on what the outcome should be. Yet, decisions still have to be made despite the substantive disagreements. To solve this problem, there is an increasing emphasis on the fairness of the procedure through which health technologies are assessed.

Procedural considerations

The procedure through which health technologies are assessed matters because it can affect the quality, legitimacy, and legality of HTA. First, a procedure that allows inputs and scrutiny from various experts and stakeholders, and that requires decision-makers to justify their choices, contributes to promoting good standards in the use of evidence to inform policy. Such a procedure contributes to preventing research bias and poor practices such as the cherry-picking of studies that support a certain conclusion, misinterpretation of study results, reliance on poor-quality research, and inaccurate economic models.[95]

Second, as mentioned in the section above, the use of medical science and economics in HTA will involve values and hence the decision-making process should allow these values to be known, discussed, and challenged.[96] The quality of the procedure is also important because it is unlikely that all the stakeholders and the

92 Emma Brockis et al., *A Review of NICE Methods Across Health Technology Assessment Programmes: Differences, Justifications and Implications*, The Office of Health Economics Research Paper 16/03 (London: The Office of Health Economics, April 2016): 13.

93 Victoria Charlton, "Does NICE Apply the Rule of Rescue in Its Approach to Highly Specialised Technologies?" *Journal of Medical Ethics* (March 8, 2021).

94 For a discussion on using social and ethical values to depart from pure cost-effectiveness considerations see Rumbold et al., "Public Reasoning."

95 Parkhurst, *The Politics of Evidence*, 42.

96 Aris Angelis and Panos Kanavos, "Value-Based Assessment of New Medical Technologies: Towards a Robust Methodological Framework for the Application of Multiple Criteria Decision Analysis in the Context of Health Technology Assessment," *PharmacoEconomics* 34, no. 5 (May 2016).

public will reach a consensus on what substantive principles should guide allocative decisions. Therefore, the legitimacy of priority-setting decisions is increasingly dependent on the fairness of the decision-making process by which ethical disagreements are settled.[97] The expectation is that it is possible to come up with procedures we can all accept as fair so that their outputs – including the decisions with which we disagree or that will affect us negatively – will be legitimate.[98]

Lastly, attention to the procedure is necessary to guarantee the legality of HTA. HTA institutions that do not meet the legal requirements of procedural fairness and rationality (which is easier to demonstrate when decision-makers follow an open and informed procedure) may have their decisions reviewed by courts. As seen in Chapter 2, there is an increasing overlap between what courts expect in terms of procedure and what the literature on HTA and UHC has recognized as a fair procedure for priority-setting.

It is beyond the scope of this section to offer a thorough and detailed description of what an HTA procedure should look like. Building on the existing literature, it will just state the premise that transparency, participation, and accountability are the main principles that HTA procedures should endorse in order to promote the quality, legitimacy, and legality of HTA outcomes. These are three broad concepts with several meanings and, for the purposes of this chapter, transparency means that information about the activities and choices of HTA institutions are accurate and accessible. Participation means that HTA bodies allow and facilitate the involvement of stakeholders, experts, and the public in the HTA process. Accountability requires decision-makers to be responsive to external input and scrutiny, to provide justification for their choices. It also requires the possibility of challenging the conclusions of HTA bodies.

Among HTA institutions, the degree of transparency, participation, and accountability will vary a lot in the different stages of HTA. HTA institutions have been criticized for not always being transparent about how they select the technologies for assessment.[99] Some institutions have their agenda set by the government that refers to them the technologies that should be assessed, while others will allow stakeholders (such as pharmaceutical companies) to submit suggestions of technologies for assessment.[100] Agenda-setting is an important issue given that HTA systems have limited resources and whether a technology has been assessed or not can determine funding and access.

97 Daniel Wei Liang Wang and Benedict Rumbold, "Priority Setting and Judicial Accountability: The Case of England," in *Philosophical Foundations of Medical Law*, eds. Andelka M. Philips, Thana C. de Campos, and Jonathan Herring (Oxford: Oxford University Press, 2020).

98 Norman Daniels, *Just Health: Meeting Health Needs Fairly* (Cambridge University Press, 2007); Parkhurst, *The Politics of Evidence.*

99 Sorenson, Drummond and Kanavos, *Ensuring Value*, 5.

100 See, for instance, Healy and Pugatch, *Theory versus Practice*, 25; Sorenson, Drummond and Kanavos, 14; Chamova, *Mapping of HTA.*

During the assessment, there will be different degrees of transparency concerning the conduct of the decision-making process. There may not always be a defined process with clear requirements for starting an assessment process, fixed deadlines for concluding it, and established rules in relation to who will be involved in the assessment, public participation, and appeal. Regarding their decisions/recommendations, some HTA institutions make available and in accessible language the clinical evidence, the economic evaluation, the criteria and the criteria weights in the decision, and the method used to reach their conclusions.[101] They may even provide a detailed justification for why some evidence, criteria, weights, and methods were preferred while others had little or no influence on their decisions. Other HTA institutions, however, are allowed to keep some of the information used in their analyses confidential.[102]

HTA bodies also vary in relation to their openness to the participation of stakeholders, experts, and the public. Some will include consultations with external advisors, public hearings to gather inputs, public consultations to discuss their findings before making a recommendation, and a formal process for appeal against the conclusions, which may be reviewed.[103] NICE, for instance, has an internal appeal process and the data shows that there were appeals against around 30% of the decisions, half of which have been successful.[104] An interesting experience to encourage the participation of lay people in HTA was NICE's Citizens' Council, a deliberative body formed by members of the public to capture the social and ethical values of society to inform NICE recommendations.

There are many reasons for endorsing transparency, participation, and accountability in HTA. They promote fairer and better-informed outputs because the assessment will incorporate more views, expertise, and deliberation. The outputs will also better suit the particular context in which the technologies were assessed, taking into account local values and priorities.[105] It is also expected that those

101 There is a growing literature on "multiple criteria decision analysis" (MCDA) working on decision-making methods that incorporate the multiple criteria and value considerations involved in HTA in a more transparent and consistent manner. MCDA will give each selected criteria a numerical value and a weight that will input into mathematical models to allow the pluri-dimensional comparison between different alternatives. See Praveen Thokala and Alejandra Duenas, "Multiple Criteria Decision Analysis for Health Technology Assessment," *Value in Health* 15, no. 8 (December 2012); Angelis and Kanavos, "Value-Based Assessment." On the importance of transparency in the economic analysis see Thomas Wilkinson et al., "The International Decision Support Initiative Reference Case for Economic Evaluation: An Aid to Thought," *Value in Health* 19, no. 8 (December 2016).

102 Barnieh et al., "Synthesis of Drug Reimbursement"; Chamova, *Mapping of HTA*, 39; Sorenson, Drummond, and Kanavos, *Ensuring value*, 26.

103 Healy and Pugatch, *Theory versus Practice*, 15; Drummond et al., "Key Principles," 248.

104 Drummond et al., 254.

105 Rob Baltussen et al., "Priority Setting for Universal Health Coverage: We Need Evidence-Informed Deliberative Processes, Not Just More Evidence on Cost-Effectiveness," *International Journal of Health Policy and Management* 5, no. 11 (November 2016); Kalipso Chalkidou et al., "Health Technology Assessment: Global Advocacy and Local Realities Comment on 'Priority Setting for Universal Health Coverage: We Need Evidence-Informed

involved in decisions they see as transparent and responsive to their inputs will have more trust in the assessment. A better procedure will also help HTA bodies to build legitimacy and political support among stakeholders and other institutions – Legislatures, ministries, and courts – on which HTA institutions depend for the acceptance, diffusion, and implementation of their recommendations.[106] Lastly, a fair procedure does not have instrumental value only, it is also a requirement of democracy. People should be able to be involved in decisions that affect their lives; and the more important the decision, the more emphasis there should be on participation, transparency, and accountability.[107]

However, it is important to remark that promoting transparency, participation, and accountability can be time- and resource-intensive.[108] The more inclusive and responsive the decision-making process, the more transaction costs it will have and the longer it will take for recommendations to be made, which may delay access to innovative treatments.[109] This is in tension with the demands on HTA bodies for quicker analysis and for the assessment of a wider range of health interventions.[110]

Furthermore, the more power the public and stakeholders have to influence the outcome of the assessment, the higher the risk of the process being captured by powerful, well-funded and organized groups that defend the interests of particular groups of patients and/or pharmaceutical companies.[111] The influence of interest groups with more resources and visibility that bias the agenda and the decisions of HTA bodies has been observed in several countries.[112] Moreover, the more responsive the decision-making process is, and the higher the number of people and considerations it wants to include, the higher the risk of inconsistency across the decisions. Similar treatments may be assessed in different ways, depending on who participates, who takes a position of leadership in the deliberation, which considerations were included, and the weight given to each of them.

Deliberative Processes, Not Just More Evidence on Cost-Effectiveness',” *International Journal of Health Policy and Management* 6, no. 4 (April 2017): 235.

106 John C. O'Donnell et al., “Health Technology Assessment: Lessons Learned from Around the World – An Overview,” *Value Health* 12, no. S2 (June 2009).

107 See Clark and Weale, “Social Values,” 299, 302; Sorenson, Drummond and Kanavos, *Ensuring Value*, 25. See, also, Daniels, *Just Health.*

108 Sorenson, Drummond and Kanavos, 13.

109 Ronald L. Akehurst et al., “Variation in Health Technology Assessment”; Nils Wilking and Bengt Jönsson, *A Pan-European Comparison Regarding Patient Access to Cancer Drugs* (Stockholm: Karolinska Institutet in Collaboration with Stockholm School of Economics, 2005).

110 Towse and Buxton, *Three Challenges*, 8 have also noticed a similar trade-off between the increasing complexity of economic analyses in HTA and the need for quicker assessments and for the assessment of a wide range of interventions.

111 Cotlear et al., *Going Universal*, 79; Kake L. Mandeville et al., “Financial Interests of Patient Organisations Contributing to Technology Assessment at England's National Institute for Health and Care Excellence: Policy Review,” *BMJ* 364 (January 2019).

112 Andres Pichon-Riviere et al., “Stakeholder Involvement in the Health Technology Assessment Process in Latin America,” *International Journal of Technology Assessment in Health Care* 34, no. 3 (2018).

In sum, the expectation that transparency, participation, and accountability will produce better-informed and fairer outcomes has to be weighed against transaction costs and the risks of capture and inconsistency. Where each HTA system will strike the balance in this trade-off is a difficult policy and political choice.

HTA, the rule of rescue, and the courts

The institutionalization of HTA can act as a counterweight to the "rule of rescue" in allocative decisions in healthcare. The rule of rescue can be defined as a human impulse to attempt to do everything possible, at any cost, to help an identifiable person whose health or life is in imminent danger.[113]

In a context of scarcity, where any allocative choice has opportunity costs that will be borne by other users of health services (including future users), the rule of rescue should not be *the* principle (or, arguably, not even *a* principle) used to allocate resources. It is blind to the trade-offs involved in any allocative choice. Helping identified individuals at any cost will end up benefiting a small number of individuals with more voice and visibility at the expense of large populations with fewer resources to be seen and heard. It will also tend to favour the funding of treatments for severely ill patients at the end of life to the detriment of healthcare interventions that do not address urgent needs, but which have an enormous and long-term impact on population health (e.g. preventive and primary care).

HTA allows health systems to make general decisions/recommendations on the funding of treatments through the systematic comparison of different interventions and of groups of patients according to standard methods and preestablished criteria. It is based on these general decisions/recommendations that health systems will then decide on the funding of a treatment to each individual. This promotes a higher degree of objectivity and coherence in allocative decisions. It also enables decisions that are more likely to promote fairness (identified lives are given the same value and consideration as statistical lives) and efficiency (low-benefit and high-cost interventions can be compared against those that offer more benefits at a lower cost).

Yet, it would be naive to believe that HTA will completely exclude the "rule of rescue" in funding decisions. Even health systems that have an explicit framework for cost-effectiveness analysis cannot completely dismiss the rule of rescue when making decisions. At a more general level, the rule of rescue may explain the different criteria put in place to benefit particular groups of patients who are more likely to have funding for life-prolonging treatment denied if the regular rules and procedures are followed. For instance, the Australian PBAC explicitly adopts the

113 National Institute for Clinical Excellence, *Social Value Judgements: Principles for the Development of NICE Guidance* (London: National Institute for Health and Clinical Excellence, 2008).

rule of rescue in very limited circumstances that will mostly apply to orphan drugs for rare diseases. The PBAC, however, makes it clear that "the rule of rescue supplements, rather than substitutes for, the evidence-based consideration of comparative cost-effectiveness."[114] The English NICE, although affirming that it does not apply the rule of rescue,[115] has arguably acted in accordance with it when it allows a higher cost per QALY cutting-point threshold for end-of-life treatments or orphan drugs for ultrarare diseases.[116] Another example is the CDF, in its current form, which allows NICE to recommend the funding of cancer treatments while evidence is being collected to inform HTA. The previous CDF, which funded cancer drugs not recommended by NICE, was an even clearer example of the rule of rescue being applied despite the existence of an HTA system.

The rule of rescue can also motivate decisions concerning specific individuals when, for instance, there is the impulse to provide funding for treatment to a severely ill patient despite a previous decision not to fund it to the cohort to which she belongs. These are the cases in which the rule of rescue may have particular weight because the "victim" is more likely to be identified.[117] Right to healthcare litigation is particularly prone to result in allocative decisions influenced by the rule of rescue. In individual claims for health treatments, judges will be presented with plenty of information about the individual patient litigating for a treatment, including her (often dramatic) personal and family circumstances aggravated by the disease for which treatment is sought. On the other hand, these judges will probably have a very limited understanding of the inequality caused by individual rulings and the opportunity costs and the trade-offs at the populational level of the aggregated impact of hundreds or thousands of such decisions. In other words, those who benefit from right to healthcare litigation will be very well known, but those who bear the opportunity costs of these decisions are obscure to judges or, at best, merely statistical.[118]

114 "Section 5.4 Basis for any claim for the 'rule of rescue'," Submission Structure for Submissions Requiring Evaluation, The Pharmaceutical Benefits Advisory Committee Guidelines, https://pbac.pbs.gov.au/section-5/5-4-basis-for-any-claim-for-the-rule-of-rescue.html. For a critical analysis of the concept of the rule of rescue and its justification by the PBAC, see Richard Cookson, C. McCabe and A. Tsuchiya, "Public healthcare resource allocation and the Rule of Rescue," *Journal of Medical Ethics* 34, no. 7 (2008).

115 "The Principles That Guide the Development of NICE Guidance and Standards," *Our Principles, National Institute for Health and Care Excellence*, https://www.nice.org.uk/about/who-we-are/our-principles.

116 See Shepley Orr and Jonathan Wolff, "Reconciling Cost-Effectiveness with the Rule of Rescue: The Institutional Division of Moral Labour," *Theory and Decision* 78 (2015): 535.

117 Cookson, McCabe, and Tsuchiya, "Public Healthcare Resource Allocation", argue that these are the cases that fit the definition of "rule of rescue" because there is an "identified victim". Accordingly, policies such as those applied by NICE and the PBAC are merely giving severity of illness more weight in the decision-making but are not referring to specific individuals with urgent needs.

118 Daniel Wei Liang Wang, "Courts and Health Care Rationing: The Case of the Brazilian Federal Supreme Court," *Health Economics, Policy and Law* 8, no. 1 (January 2013).

Therefore, how courts judge the right to healthcare cases and how they interact with HTA bodies are key factors to determine the weight the rule of rescue will have in the distribution of healthcare resources within a health system.

Conclusion

Chapter 2 argued that UHC requires fair priority-setting. It allows the expansion of coverage and the reduction of health inequalities and promotes financial protection. Moreover, where resources are scarce, priorities should be set in a way that provides legitimate justifications for the non-fulfilment of health needs despite the recognition of legal entitlements to receive healthcare. If this is correct, then health systems should give a central role in priority-setting to HTA that is informed by scientific evidence, economic analysis, ethical considerations, and social values, and that is made through transparent, inclusive, and accountable processes.

The aim of the present chapter is not to offer a comprehensive description of HTA and HTA institutions. The purpose here is rather modest: to explain what HTA is, the rationale for the creation of HTA institutions, and the multiple considerations and dilemmatic choices involved in HTA.

It is important to highlight that HTA bodies – despite their relative independence and their focus on evidence, methods, ethical reasoning, and procedural fairness – do not change the fact that priority-setting is inexorably political. Allocative choices are political decisions that will not always follow HTA recommendations, although priority-setting that ignores HTA or contradicts its recommendations (e.g. the non-provision of cost-effective treatments or the funding of treatments with limited evidence of efficacy) must satisfy a much higher burden of justification. Moreover, the decision to create an HTA institution; the amount of power and autonomy it has; how transparent, inclusive, and accountable the decision-making process is; the considerations it will take into account in the assessment; if their outputs are binding or mere recommendations; and whether their decisions/recommendations actually determine the rights of users and the duties of health systems, are all policy choices that result from the confluence of many variables.[119] The rest of this book will try to show that the law and the courts are two of these variables.

119 See Ole F. Norheim, "Disease Control Priorities Third Edition Is Published: A Theory of Change is Needed for Translating Evidence to Health Policy," *International Journal of Health Policy and Managment* 7, no. 9 (2018): 774–775. See, also, Thatcher, *Governance Structures.*

4 Brazil

Right to healthcare litigation: the problem and the institutional responses

Imagine a healthcare policy with the following features: scientific evidence plays almost no role in it because stringent analysis of the effectiveness or safety of treatments is not an essential requirement; the cost-effectiveness of treatments will not be assessed either and hence efficiency in public spending is ignored; the allocative choices are not made according to any reasonable principle of distributive justice, but rather to an individual's capacity to litigate; and this policy will have to be implemented no matter if there are other needs more urgent, there is the possibility of alternative use of the resources, or there are different preferences among elected representatives, public authorities, or other stakeholders. From any perspective, this would be a bad healthcare policy and would never fulfil the requirements of fair priority-setting. However, this is how the Brazilian courts are allocating a significant amount of public resources when enforcing the right to healthcare as an individual trump card against rationing decisions.

The Brazilian Federal Constitution declares that the right to health is a fundamental right of all and a duty of the State. It also established a public health system based on the principles of universality, equality of access, and comprehensive and integrated coverage (Articles 196–8). Brazilian judges were also given the power to consider any case in which a right is threatened or violated (Article 5, XXXV), and a claim against the State can be issued via ordinary actions, class actions (*ação civil pública*), a protection writ against public authorities (*mandado de segurança*), and special procedures in small-claim courts (*juízados especiais*), where legal representation is not necessary. These constitutional and jurisdictional provisions have entitled citizens who were denied a health treatment by the public health system to sue the State claiming that they have the right to receive the treatment they need funded by the public health system.

This chapter will build on the existing literature and on emerging data about this phenomenon in Brazil to answer three questions: what is demanded by claimants; what the economic impact of the decisions on the public health budget is; and how courts judge these cases. The answers to these questions reveal that litigation in Brazil has reached an impressive scale and has made the courts a major player in the allocation of healthcare resources, but in a way that makes the public health system less fair and efficient.

DOI: 10.4324/9781315149165-4

The second part of this chapter compares three responses aimed at reducing the negative impact of litigation on the Brazilian public health system: (i) the case law of the Supreme Federal Court (STF) and the tests it has tried to establish over the last decade to define the judicially enforceable duties created by the constitutional right to health; (ii) the recommendations by the National Council of Justice (CNJ) – the body responsible for improving the Judiciary's strategic planning and administration – aimed at building courts' institutional capacity to judge the right to healthcare cases; and (iii) the Federal Law 12.401/11, which created a new health technology assessment (HTA) system in Brazil.

The case of Brazil offers important lessons for the legal and policy debates on how courts can impact access to healthcare and priority-setting. First, it shows how and why adjudicating health rights via individual complaints can create an undesirable collective outcome by making a health system less fair and efficient. Second, the comparison between the different institutional responses to right to healthcare litigation challenges the expediency of the idea proposed by part of the social rights literature that courts should build their institutional capacity to adjudicate on social policy issues. Third, it argues that where a functioning HTA system is in place, there are good reasons for courts to avoid making allocative decisions but rather focus on controlling authorities' decision-making processes. Yet the case of Brazil shows that courts' deference to rationing decisions, even when they are informed by HTA, cannot be taken for granted.

Right to healthcare litigation: unfairness and inefficiency

This section analyses healthcare litigation in Brazil based on empirical evidence on what is demanded by claimants, how courts judge the cases, and the economic impact of the decisions on the public budget.

It is virtually impossible to have a comprehensive view of the phenomenon in the whole country. Brazil is organized in a Federal system and the Federal government, 26 states, the Federal District, and over 5,500 municipalities can become defendants in claims for health treatments.[1] To date, there is no unified database to access information from court cases against all these entities.

1 In Brazil there is a national public health system, the Sistema Único de Saúde (SUS), and the duty to provide health services is shared by every entity of the Federation, although each entity has different responsibilities. The Brazilian courts, however, have constantly decided that patients can file judicial claims for any health treatment against any entity (see Daniel Wei Liang Wang et al., "The Impact of Health Care Judicialization in the City of São Paulo: Public Expenditure and Federal Organization," *Revista de Administração Pública* 48, no. 5 (September/October, 2014)). This position has been recently confirmed by the Supreme Federal Court (STF) in the case RE 855178/2019.

There have been national surveys[2] and research using artificial intelligence to collect and analyse the right to healthcare cases nationally.[3] They have produced interesting results that will be cited in this chapter, but their data has limitations that do not allow a nuanced and detailed understanding of the phenomenon. Therefore, for more fine-grained analysis, this chapter will focus mainly on the data available on healthcare litigation cases filed against a few selected defendants: the Federal government and the states of Santa Catarina, Rio de Janeiro, Minas Gerais, Sao Paulo, Paraná, and Rio Grande do Sul. Although these jurisdictions are not representative of the whole country, they are where most of the right to healthcare litigation in the country is concentrated.[4]

What is demanded?

Healthcare litigation is mainly driven by individual claims for drugs.[5] Drugs that have not been "incorporated" in the national public health system (SUS) (i.e. have not been included in the official lists of drugs or clinical guidelines and protocols) account for most of what is spent by health systems to comply with judicial decisions ordering the provision of treatment.

Wang et al., aggregating data from 6,604 court cases filed in State and Federal courts in the capital cities of São Paulo, Santa Catarina, and Rio Grande do Sul from 2010 to 2015 found that 66% of the claims for health treatments were demanding the provision of drugs; 71% of these claims were for drugs not incorporated in SUS and 5% did not even have marketing authorization at the time the claim was filed.[6]

These findings vindicate previous research showing that the percentage of cases involving judicial claims for drugs not incorporated in SUS was 80.6% in the state of Rio de Janeiro[7] and 92.5% in the city of Rio de Janeiro (the capital city of the

2 National Council of Justice, *Justiça em Números* (Brasília: National Council of Justice, 2017, 2018, 2019, 2020).

3 Institution of Education and Research – Insper, *Judicialização da Saúde no Brasil: perfil da demanda, causas e propostas de solução*, Justiça Pesquisa – Relatório Analítico Propositivo (Brasília: National Council of Justice, 2019).

4 Relatório de Auditoria 009.253/2015-7, TCU; Octávio Luiz Motta Ferraz, *Health as a Human Right: The Politics and Judicialization of Health in Brazil* (Cambridge: Cambridge University Press, 2020), 112; National Council of Justice, *Relatórios de cumprimento da Resolução CNJ n. 107* (Brasília: National Council of Justice, 2015).

5 Fabíola Sulpino Vieira, *Direito à Saúde no Brasil: seus contornos, judicialização e a necessidade da macrojustiça*, Texto para Discussão 2547 (Brasília: Instituto de Pesquisa Econômica Aplicada, 2020), 28.

6 Daniel Wei Liang Wang et al., "Health Technology Assessment and Judicial Deference to Priority-Setting Decisions in Healthcare: Quasi-Experimental Analysis of Right-to-Health Litigation in Brazil," *Social Science & Medicine* 265 (November 2020).

7 Vera Lúcia Edais Pepe et al., "Characterization of Lawsuits for the Supply of 'essential' Medicines in the State of Rio de Janeiro, Brazil," *Cadernos de Saúde Pública* 26, no. 3 (March 2010).

State of Rio de Janeiro).[8] Other academic articles and reports, instead of analysing the percentage of lawsuits in which a non-incorporated drug was demanded, have assessed the percentage of non-incorporated drugs among all drugs judicially claimed – 68% in the state of Santa Catarina[9] and the city of Florianopolis (the capital city of the State of Santa Catarina);[10] 71% in the state of Sao Paulo;[11] 45% in the city of Sao Paulo (the capital city of the State of Sao Paulo);[12] 50% in the State of Minas Gerais;[13] and 58% in the State of Rio Grande do Sul.[14]

It is important to highlight the difference between these two methods for calculating the data. The second method – which counts the number of non-included drugs among all those judicially claimed – underestimates the importance of claims for non-incorporated drugs as the main driver of right to healthcare litigation. In many cases, patients demand more than one drug. For example, in the state of Rio de Janeiro, it was found that among the drugs judicially claimed, 52% were not incorporated in the pharmaceutical policy.[15] However, when analysing the number of cases in which at least one of these drugs is claimed, the number rises to 80.6%. In the state of Sao Paulo, it was found that in 87% of the cases in which patients were litigating for drugs already provided by the public health system, they were also claiming access to non-incorporated treatments.[16]

8 Tatiana Aragão Figueiredo, "Analysis of Drugs Dispensed by Court Order in the County of Rio de Janeiro: The Application of Scientific Evidence in Decision-Making Process" (Master's diss., Sergio Arouca National School of Public Health, 2010).

9 Auditoria Operacional RLA 18/00189572, Relatório de Instrução – Apreciação Definitiva, TCESC, 02/10/2019, 34; Silvana Nair Leite et al., "Legal Actions and Administrative Demands Related to the Guarantee of the Right to Drugs Access in the city of Florianópolis-SC," *Revista de Direito Sanitário* 10, no. 2 (2009). See, also, Januária Ramos Pereira et al., "Situation of Lawsuits Concerning the Access to Medical Products by the Health Department of Santa Catarina State, Brazil, during the Years 2003 and 2004," *Ciência & Saúde Coletiva* 15, no. S3 (November 2010).

10 Leite et al., "Legal Actions and Administrative Demands."

11 Ana Luiza Chieffi, Rita de Cassia Barradas Barata and Moisés Golbaum, "Legal Access to Medications: A Threat to Brazil's Public Health System?" *BMC Health Services Research* 17 (July 19, 2017).

12 Wang et al., "Impact of Health Care Judicialization."

13 Luciana de Melo Nunes Lopes et al., "Comprehensiveness and Universality of the Pharmaceutical Assistance in Times of Judicialization of Health Care," *Saúde e Sociedade* 28, no. 2 (2019).

14 Bruno Naundorf, Patrícia de Carli and Bárbara Goulart, "O Estado do Rio Grande do Sul e os Impactos da Judicialização da Saúde na Gestão Pública," in *Dilemas do Fenômeno da Judicialização da Saúde,* Coletânea Direito e Saúde, eds. Alethele de Oliveira Santos and Luciana Tolêdo Lopes, vol. 2 (Brasília: CONASS, 2018), 214.

15 Pepe et al., "Supply of 'Essential' Medicines." See also João Maurício Brambati Sant'Anna, "Essentiality and pharmaceutical care: an exploratory study of individual legal demands for access to medicines in the State of Rio de Janeiro" (Master's diss., Sergio Arouca National School of Public Health, 2009).

16 Daniel Wei Liang Wang, Fernanda Terrazas, and Ana Luiza Chieffi, "Incorporating Drugs through Litigation: The Case of the State of Sao Paulo" (Annual Meeting of the Law and Society Association, 2012).

One plausible hypothesis to explain this difference is that when people litigate for a non-incorporated medicine, they make the most of their effort and include in the lawsuit all the medicines in the same medical prescription. In other words, drugs included in the pharmaceutical policy are "free riders" claimed together with drugs not provided by the health system. Litigants put forward such a claim because if they have a judicial decision in their favour, they will receive the drugs under more convenient conditions. The Federal Government, for instance, when complying with a judicial decision, delivers the drug by mail to the patient's house.[17] Moreover, patients make sure that their supply will not be interrupted, as may happen to other patients, since health authorities are less likely to stop providing the drugs to these patients because contempt of court is a criminal offence.

It has also been noticed that in many cases patients went to court claiming drugs that belong to the pharmaceutical policy because they were prescribed for off-label or off-protocol use.[18] The former means the prescription of a drug for unapproved clinical indications or to unapproved subpopulations; the latter is the prescription of drugs that are incorporated in the SUS to patients who do not meet the clinical criteria established by clinical protocols and guidelines. For instance, Macedo et al. and Chieffi et al. analysed judicial claims for high-cost drugs incorporated in the SUS and found that in 81.3% of them the clinical guidelines and protocols did not recommend their use for the claimant's condition.[19]

Similar results were found in the State of Paraná, where only 8 out of the 42 most frequently claimed drugs were incorporated at SUS and most of the claims for incorporated treatments were for off-protocol use. Among those that were not incorporated, some had never been assessed by CONITEC (the Brazilian HTA body) whereas others have been assessed but public funding was not recommended. For instance, the drugs claimed via courts with the largest and the third-largest impact on Paraná's health budget – Omalizumab and Ustequinumab – were not recommended by CONITEC, and the second-largest – Betagalsidase – had not been assessed.[20]

17 The Federal Attorney General's Office, *Intervenção Judicial na Saúde Pública: Panorama no âmbito da Justiça Federal e Apontamentos na seara das Justiças Estaduais* (Brasília: The Federal Attorney General's Office, 2012).

18 Relatório de Auditoria 009.253/2015-7, TCU; Marina Amaral de Ávila Machado et al., "Judicialization of access to medicines in Minas Gerais state, South eastern Brazil," *Revista de Saúde Pública* 45, no. 3 (June 2011); Wang, Terrazas, and Chieffi, "Incorporating Drugs through Litigation"; Figueiredo, "Drugs dispensed by court order"; Ana Márcia Messeder, Claudia Garcia Serpa Osorio-de-Castro, and Vera Lucia Luiza, "Can Court Injunctions Guarantee Access to Medicines in the Public Sector? The Experience in the State of Rio de Janeiro, Brazil," *Cadernos de Saúde Pública* 21, no. 2 (April 2005).

19 Eloisa Israel de Macedo, Luciane Cruz Lopes, and Silvio Barberato-Filho, "A Technical Analysis of Medicines Request-Related Decision-Making in Brazilian Courts," *Revista de Saúde Pública* 45, no. 4 (August 2011); Chieffi, Barradas, and Golbaum, "Legal Access to Medications," 8.

20 Deise Pontarolli, Paula Rossignoli, and Cláudia Moretoni, "Panorama da Judicialização de Medicamentos na Secretaria Estadual de Saúde do Paraná," in *Dilemas do Fenômeno da Judi-*

There is also a small percentage (5–10%) of claims for treatments without marketing authorization, which were not registered with the Brazilian National Health Surveillance Agency (ANVISA), the agency responsible for the regulation of drugs in Brazil.[21] In cases where courts order the provision of unregistered drugs or for off-label use, they are forcing public expenditure on treatments the safety and effectiveness of which have not been evaluated or confirmed by the agency.

In these cases, besides the risk to patients, the cost of providing these treatments can be very high. For example, in the state of Sao Paulo, R$40 million (around US$19 million)[22] was spent to comply with judicial decisions ordering drugs for cancer from 2005 to 2006. However, 17% of this amount was spent on drugs without scientific evidence that they could bring any benefit to patients who were claiming them, either because the drug was not registered with the ANVISA or because the existing clinical guidelines and protocols did not recommend it for the patient due to her diagnosis or clinical condition (off-protocol use).[23] Similar data were found by Vieira and Zucchi: three out of ten cancer drugs provided by the city of São Paulo to comply with judicial orders were not registered with the ANVISA and most of the rest lacked evidence of their effectiveness under the claimants' circumstances. At that time, in the city of São Paulo, just 7.2% of the drugs funded as a result of judicial orders were drugs for cancer, although they represented 75% of the total spent to buy judicially ordered medicines.[24]

One reason why non-registered treatments are so expensive is that registration is followed by price regulation, which sets a cap on the maximum price for a drug in Brazil. Moreover, unregistered drugs cannot be incorporated at SUS, so there is no opportunity for the health system to negotiate the price. In the case of Eculizumab, the judicial claims for this treatment started in 2009 but the patent-holder company did not apply for market authorization until 2015. It was eventually registered in 2017 and a 50% drop in its price followed. Up to the moment

cialização da Saúde, Coletânea Direito e Saúde, eds. Alethele de Oliveira Santos and Luciana Tolêdo Lopes, vol. 2 (Brasília: CONASS, 2018), 181–185.

21 See Wang et al., "Health Technology Assessment"; Izamara Damasceno Catanheide, Erick Soares Lisboa and Luis Eugenio Portela Fernandes de Souza, "Characteristics of the Judicialization of Access to Medicines in Brazil: a systematic review," *Physis Revista de Saúde Coletiva* 26, no. 4 (October 2016); Machado et al., "Judicialization of Access to Medicines"; Pereira et al., "Lawsuits Concerning the Access to Medical Products"; Pepe et al., "Supply of 'Essential' Medicines"; Figueiredo, "Drugs Dispensed by Court Order"; Ana Luiza Chieffi and Rita de Cássia Barradas Barata, " 'Judicialization' of Public Health Policy for Distribution of Medicines," *Cadernos de Saúde Pública* 25, no. 8 (August 2009); Fabiola Sulpino Vieira and Paola Zucchi, "Distortions to national drug policy caused by lawsuits in Brazil," *Revista de Saúde Pública* 41, no. 2 (April 2007).

22 Unless otherwise specified, the values in US dollars in this chapter were calculated using the average exchange rate in the last month of the respective year.

23 Luciane Cruz Lopes et al., "Rational Use of Anticancer Drugs and Patient Lawsuits in the State of São Paulo, Southeastern Brazil," *Revista de Saúde Pública* 44, no. 4 (August 2010).

24 Vieira and Zucchi, "Distortions to National Drug Policy."

when the writing of this book was completed, it had not been made available by SUS due to the reluctance of the drug company to reduce the price further, possibly because the potential users are already receiving it through litigation.[25]

More recent data shows that the financial impact of a few high-cost drugs provided following a judicial order is even more accentuated. At the Federal level, out of the R$1.3 billion (US$372.5 million) spent to comply with judicial decisions in 2016, 61% was spent on unregistered treatments, 91% was spent on the ten most expensive drugs (none of them was then incorporated in SUS), and almost half of the total amount went to buy one single treatment (Eculizumab).[26]

Apart from drugs, courts have also ordered the provision of other treatments without robust evidence of safety and effectiveness. In the case *STA 223* (2008), the Supreme Federal Court (STF) decided that the health system should pay for experimental surgery performed by an American surgeon, who had to be brought to Brazil with all expenses (flights, hotel, and a US$150,000 treatment) paid for by the State. In *RE 368546* (2011) the STF decided that six people had the right to receive treatment for pigment rethinosis in Cuba, with all expenses covered by the State, despite the medical consensus that this treatment does not work.[27] In another case, the Ministry of Health was ordered to pay for an experimental US$870,000 surgery in the United States plus the expenses related to the patient and her parents' transportation and living costs abroad.[28]

The safety and effectiveness of treatments should be the first things to be considered when designing healthcare policies. However, there is another element that cannot be neglected: cost-effectiveness. Even if it is proved that a new treatment is safe and effective, it is important to assess whether it is more effective than the existing treatments and, if it is, whether the gains it produces justify its cost. Ideally, patients would receive optimal care, but the scarcity of resources is a ubiquitous reality and thus cost-effectiveness should be considered by health systems when deciding what can be provided to patients.

Machado et al. found that there were alternative treatments available in the SUS for 73% of the drugs not then incorporated in SUS that were provided via

25 Ana Carolina Morozowski and Daniel Wei Liang Wang, "Soliris: A esperança na corda bamba de sombrinha," *Direito em Comprimidos*, September 20, 2020, https://direitoemcomprimidos.com.br/soliris/.

26 Advocacia Geral da União, "Judicialização da Saúde no Âmbito da União em Números: Recursos Extraordinários 566471 e 657718" (PowerPoint presentation, Brasília, May 2017); Christabelle-Ann Xavier, "Judicialização da Saúde: Perspectiva Crítica sobre os Gastos da União para o Cumprimento das Ordens Judiciais," in *Dilemas do Fenômeno da Judicialização da Saúde*, Coletânea Direito e Saúde, eds. Alethele de Oliveira Santos and Luciana Tolêdo Lopes, vol. 2 (Brasília: CONASS, 2018), 55–56.

27 The Brazilian Ophthalmology Association, the institution that represents ophthalmologists in the country, participated in the judicial proceeding and confirmed before the STF that the treatment is ineffective.

28 Octavio Luiz Motta Ferraz and Daniel Wei Liang Wang, "As Duas Portas do SUS", *Folha de São Paulo*, June 19, 2014, A3, https://www1.folha.uol.com.br/opiniao/2014/06/1472761-octavio-ferraz-e-daniel-wang-as-duas-portas-do-sus.shtml.

judicial order.[29] In Vieira and Zucchi's sample, this rate was 80%.[30] In these cases, patients successfully demanded modern (and more expensive) treatments that are allegedly better than the drugs available in the SUS.

The case of analogous insulin, the most litigated treatment in several cities and States, offers a vivid example.[31] The SUS provides human insulin to patients, but litigants want access to the allegedly superior analogous insulin. In 2014, CONITEC, the body responsible for HTA in Brazil, assessed two types of analogous insulin and did not recommend their incorporation in SUS due to the lack of evidence of their superiority and to their much higher cost.[32] In 2018, there was another assessment and CONITEC found again that there was no robust evidence that they are safer or more effective than their human versions. It also estimated that the budget impact for the health system of providing this analogous insulin instead of human insulin for types I and II diabetes could be up to R$ 90 billion (US$ 24 billion) over five years.[33] Yet, for most judges, if the patient has a prescription for the analogous insulin, then her right to health will trump priority-setting considerations.[34]

Lastly, Norheim and Gloppen developed a methodology using Quality Adjusted Life Years (QALY) and the country GDP per capita to establish thresholds to grade health treatments according to levels of priority for the population. Applying this methodology to a sample of litigated drugs in Brazil, the authors concluded that most of them should be classified as having a low priority since

29 Machado et al., "Judicialization of Access to Medicines."

30 Vieira and Zucchi, "Distortions to National Drug Policy."

31 See Wang et al., "Health Technology Assessment"; Virgílio Afonso da Silva and Fernanda Vargas Terrazas, "Claiming the Right to Health in Brazilian Courts: The Exclusion of the Already Excluded," *Law and Social Inquiry* 36, no. 4 (Fall 2011); Daniel Wei Liang Wang et al., "Judiciário e fornecimento de insulinas análogas pelo sistema público de saúde: direitos, ciência e políticas públicas," Casoteca Direito GV, Produção de Casos 2011, http://direitosp.fgv.br/casoteca/judiciario-fornecimento-de-insulinas-analogas-pelo-sistema-publico-de-saude-direitos-cienci; Figueiredo, "Drugs Dispensed by Court Order"; Daniel Wei Liang Wang, and Octavio Luiza Motta Ferraz, "Reaching Out to the Needy? Access to Justice and Public Attorneys' Role in Right to Health Litigation in the City of Sao Paulo" *SUR International Journal on Human Rights* 10, no. 18 (June 2013).

32 Ministério da Saúde, *Insulinas Análogas de Longa Duração – Diabetes Mellitus tipo II*, Relatório de Recomendação da Comissão Nacional de Incorporação de Tecnologias no SUS – CONITEC – 103 (Brasília: Ministério da Saúde, 2014).

33 Comissão Nacional de Incorporação de Tecnologias no SUS, *Insulinas análogas de ação prolongada para o tratamento de diabetes mellitus tipo I*, Relatório de Recomendação 440 (Brasília: Comissão Nacional de Incorporação de Tecnologias no SUS, 2018); Comissão Nacional de Incorporação de Tecnologias no SUS, *Insulinas análogas de ação prolongada para o tratamento de diabetes mellitus tipo II*, Relatório de Recomendação 434 (Brasília: Comissão Nacional de Incorporação de Tecnologias no SUS, 2018).

34 Wang et al., "Health Technology Assessment"; Wang et al., "Judiciário e fornecimento de insulinas."

they provide small or marginal health benefits at a high opportunity cost for the healthcare system.[35]

How the courts judge

Patients' rate of success in judicial claims for health treatments is very high. According to Wang et al., it goes from 92% in lower courts to 98% in appeal courts. That means it is almost certain that the Judiciary will eventually order SUS to provide the claimed drugs. At the appeal level, the research did not find any statistically significant difference in the success rate of claims for treatments that have not been incorporated in SUS or that did not have marketing authorization. That means courts ignore the health system's regulatory and policy decisions. Judgements are mostly made based solely on the information provided by the patients' physicians.[36]

These findings confirm a pattern that has been identified in literature reviews of the right to healthcare litigation phenomenon in Brazil, which concluded that patients' rate of success is very high (nearly 100% in some courts) and that most cases are decided based on the information available in the patients' medical prescription.[37]

Some examples can make these numbers more concrete. Duran et al. analysed 144 cases demanding HIV drugs that were not then incorporated in SUS's policy for HIV and found that the State of São Paulo Court of Appeal judged 85% of them in favour of the patient.[38] Moreover, in the lower courts, the rate of success is absolute: all cases were judged in favour of the patient. The court's predominant view is that the right to health is an individual right and only in a small number of cases did it consider that economic and policy reasons can justify the non-provision of a drug to a patient.

Marques and Dallari analysed cases judged by lower courts in the state of Sao Paulo and found that patients won in more than 90% of the cases.[39] Additionally, in more than 80% of the decisions, the judge affirmed that the patient's right to healthcare cannot be restricted by budgetary or policy considerations. Grinover et al. found that, from 2010 to 2012, the State of São Paulo Court of Appeal,

35 Ole F. Norheim and Siri Gloppen, "Litigating for Medicines: How Can We Assess Impact on Health Outcomes," in *Litigating Health Rights: Can Courts Bring More Justice to Health?* eds. Alicia Yamin and Siri Gloppen (Harvard University Press, 2011), 313.

36 Wang et al., "Health Technology Assessment."

37 Catanheide, Lisboa and de Souza, "Judicialization of Access to Medicines"; Vanessa Santana Gomes and Tânia Alves Amador, "Studies Published in Indexed Journals on Lawsuits for Medicines in Brazil: A Systematic Review," *Cadernos de Saúde Pública* 31, no. 3 (March 2015).

38 Camila Duran Ferreira et al., "O Judiciário e as políticas públicas de saúde no Brasil: o caso AIDS," in *Prêmio Ipea 40 Anos: Monografias Premiadas* (Brasília: Ipea, 2004).

39 Silvia Badim Marques and Sueli Gandolfi Dallari, "Safeguarding of the Social Right to Pharmaceutical Assistance in the State of São Paulo, Brazil," *Revista de Saúde Pública* 41, no. 1 (February 2007).

the State of Minas Gerais Court of Appeal, and the 3rd Circuit Federal Court of Appeal have judged over 90% of the cases in favour of the litigant patient.[40]

Pepe et al.[41] and Sant'Ana[42] found that patients won 100% of the cases in the lower courts in the state of Rio de Janeiro. Sant'Ana also found that patients won all the cases in the Court of Appeal.[43] In the sample analysed by Ventura et al., all the claimants in the city of Rio de Janeiro had their preliminary injunction claims decided in their favour.[44] In the state of Rio Grande do Sul, in 93% of the cases the claimant had a preliminary injunction granted by the court, in 96% of them the final ruling in the lower courts was completely or partially in favour of patients, and 89% of the cases that reached the State of Rio Grande do Sul Court of Appeal were decided in favour of patients.[45]

Wang et al. analysed 502 cases from 12 courts (the Supreme Federal Court, the Superior Court of Justice, five State Courts of Appeal, and five Federal Courts of Appeal) in which analogous insulin was claimed.[46] They found that patients won in 88% of them. Furthermore, in five courts the rate of success was 100% and in two of them, it was more than 95%. The case of analogous insulin is especially interesting because, as already discussed, there is a scientific dispute about its superiority over regular insulin. This was an argument used by the defendant health authorities in courts to justify the non-provision of the analogous insulin. Yet, most often courts considered that it was for the patient's doctor, rather than the health authorities, to decide which treatment should be provided to them.

Similar findings regarding the source of evidence used by courts were found by Ventura et al.: in 97% of the cases the judicial decision was based solely on the medical information provided by the claimants' doctors and no further evidence regarding the quality of the treatment claimed, the actual need of the patient, or the alternative treatments available for her was required.[47]

The problem with this deferential attitude towards a doctor's opinion is that physicians do not always base their prescription on the best scientific evidence available.[48] This may happen because of the difficulty for practitioners to keep

40 Ada Pellegrini Grinover et al., *Avaliação da prestação jurisdicional coletiva e individual a partir da judicialização da saúde* (CEBEPEJ/DIREITOGV, 2014).

41 Pepe et al., "Supply of 'Essential' Medicines."

42 Sant'Ana, "Essentiality and Pharmaceutical Care."

43 Sant'Ana.

44 Miriam Ventura et al., "Judicialization of the Right to Health, Access to Justice and the Effectiveness of the Right to Health," *Revista de Saúde Coletiva* 20, no. 1 (2010).

45 João Biehl, Mariana P. Socal, and Joseph J. Amon, "The Judicialization of Health and the Quest for State Accountability: Evidence from 1,262 Lawsuits for Access to Medicines in Southern Brazil," *Health and Human Rights Journal* 18, no. 1 (June 2016). See, also, Denise Vieira Travassos et al., "The Judicialization of Health Care: A Case Study of Three State Courts in Brazil," *Ciência & saúde coletiva* 18, n. 11 (November 2013).

46 Wang et al., "Judiciário e fornecimento de insulinas."

47 Ventura et al., "Judicialization of the Right to Health."

48 James C. Moon et al., "Getting Better Value from the NHS Drug Budget," *BMJ* 341 (December 17, 2010).

up to date with all the new scientific information; the biases in the dissemination of scientific research; the marketing strategies of pharmaceutical companies; and conflicts of interest.[49] This form of judicial reasoning is hence an obstacle for the use of evidence-based medicine to inform priority-setting decisions in Brazil. Moreover, what is best for an individual patient may not be cost-effective or affordable for the health system.

In sum, applicants' high rate of success can be explained by the prevalent interpretation of the right to health as an individual trump card against priority-setting decisions, coupled with the lack of stringent scientific evidence requirements for the funding of treatment via courts. Brazilian courts' predominant approach when judging claims for health treatments is in line with the case law of the Supreme Federal Court (STF), the highest Court of Appeal and the Constitutional Court in Brazil.

In the first case related to the funding of health treatment decided by the STF,[50] the claimant sought a judicial order for SUS to fund an experimental treatment only available in the United States (the costs included transportation, the treatment costs, and foreign living expenses). In this decision, the STF made a statement that has been constantly quoted by lower courts and by the STF itself:

> [In choosing] between protecting the inviolability of the right to life, an inalienable Constitutional fundamental right, and a financial and secondary interest of the State, I believe — once this dilemma is established — ethical and legal reasons leave the judge with only one possible option: unwavering respect for life.

The STF departed from this view in a few cases and recognized that the public health system cannot focus exclusively on the specific needs of the applicant patient and should consider the allocative impact of its decisions.[51] However, the reasoning in the 1996 case has been dominant in the STF. It is worth mentioning and quoting again the case *RE 368546*,[52] in which the government was obliged to fund treatment for pigment rethinosis in Cuba despite scientific evidence that it is ineffective. One of the Justices (Marco Aurelio) downplayed the extensive evidence against the effectiveness of the treatment and the objections against its high costs for the public health budget by affirming:

> I cannot accept that the lack of economic resources can be articulated to deny health care to a citizen … from what I read in the media, the successful treatment for this disease is indeed in Cuba.

49 See, for instance, Ben Goldacre, *Bad Pharma: How Drug Companies Mislead Doctors and Harm Patients* (New York: Farrar, Straus, and Giroux, 2012).

50 Pet 1246 MC, STF, 31/01/1997.

51 See Daniel Wei Liang Wang, "Courts and Health Care Rationing: The Case of the Brazilian Federal Supreme Court," *Health Economics, Policy and Law* 8, no. 1 (January 2013).

52 RE 368546, STF, 13/04/2011.

Similarly, another Justice (Luiz Fux) reasoned:

> I am very determined when it comes to hope. I never believed in the version that the pigment rethinosis could not be cured in Cuba. Quite the opposite, I think that they [Cubans] are specialists in this area and there should be hope concerning the cure.

In a subsequent case,[53] the STF decided that the public health system should provide a high-cost treatment (US$409,500 per year) although the treatment had never been incorporated in the SUS nor had it been registered with the ANVISA.

As will be discussed further in this chapter, a recent STF judgment may set a precedent that will change the case law in this field to limit the circumstances in which courts can order the provision of medical treatment. Whether this will actually change the interpretation of the right to health as entitling patients to receive any treatment they are prescribed despite the "financial and secondary interests of the State" is yet to be seen.

Collective claims

Right to healthcare litigation in Brazil is mainly driven by individual lawsuits,[54] but there are also collective claims, normally demanding access to drugs not regularly provided by the SUS to a group of identified patients or to all patients in a given jurisdiction (which can be a city, a State, the Federal District, or the whole country).[55] The former is very similar to individual lawsuits and the only difference is that there is more than one claimant. Courts decide these cases in the same way that they decide individual claims. The latter lawsuits, on the other hand, raise different issues because they are more structural in the sense that they aim at producing far-reaching reforms that affect a multiplicity of parties.[56]

Interestingly, the same courts that show almost no restraint in reviewing rationing decisions in individual cases are more reluctant to decide in favour of claimants when the claim is collective and structural.[57] As already shown, in individual cases, courts tend to ignore the impact of their decisions on the public

53 STA 761, STF, 27/11/2014.

54 According to the research carried out by Grinover et al., *Avaliação da prestação jurisdicional*, collective claims represent less than 1% of right to healthcare litigation cases in Brazil.

55 There are also lawsuits requiring the improvement of health facilities, see Wang and Ferraz, "Reaching Out to the Needy?".

56 Owen M. Fiss, "The Social and Political Foundations of Adjudication," *Law and Human Behavior* 6, no. 2 (1983): 123.

57 See Wang et al., "Judiciário e fornecimento de insulinas"; Wang and Ferraz, "Reaching out to the Needy?"; Florian F. Hoffman and Fernando R. N. M. Bentes, "Accountability and Social and Economic Rights in Brazil," in *Courting Social Justice: Judicial Enforcement of Social and Economic Rights in the Developing World*, eds. Varun Gauri and Daniel M. Brinks (New York: Cambridge University Press, 2010), 224–225.

health budget and the other users of the SUS, the need to set priorities in healthcare, and the limited capacity and legitimacy of courts to assess scientific evidence and to make allocative decisions. Conversely, in collective claims with potential structural effects, all these elements are considered by courts to justify their deference to rationing decisions made by health authorities.[58]

As shown by Wang et al.,[59] the same courts that grant access to analogous insulin to practically any patient who goes individually to claim it turns down collective claims for the incorporation of this insulin for the regular provision by the SUS. In collective cases, courts tend to reason that resources are scarce and judges are not in the best position to second-guess the decisions made by health authorities.

Two decisions by the STF make clear the preference for adjudicating the right to health individually rather than collectively: *SL 256* (2010) and *STA 424* (2010). The latter involved a request for universal provision of three drugs (not incorporated in the SUS) for treating microcephalia. The former was a complaint to oblige the health system to pay for transportation, food, and accommodation costs of any patient in the city of Araguaína who needed to receive treatment in another city. The STF rejected both claims, arguing that the Judiciary should not require health authorities to fulfil duties that are overly "general" because this may unduly affect the public budget and would "impair the regular functioning and management of the health system, reduce efficiency in patient care and reduce the resources available [for the health system]".

Nonetheless, both decisions emphasized that the drugs in one case, and the transportation, food, and accommodation in the other, must be provided if the need is proved on an individual basis. In the case *SL 256* (2010), apart from the general demand for the SUS to pay for the transportation, food, and accommodation to all citizens of Araguaína, there was also a request for the provision of these services to a group of identified individuals, which was granted by the court.

The fact that individual and collective cases tend to be decided differently can be explained by the fact that in individual lawsuits there is the impression that the court decision has no potential to cause much impact, whereas a collective claim can have large-scale policy implications.[60] This impression is false because the aggregate effect of individual lawsuits can be enormous, as will be shown in the next section.

In the recent STF judgment RE 566471 (2020) there are several *obiter dicta* in which some Justices expressed the opinion that the right to health should be preferably adjudicated via collective, rather than individual, claims. According to these *dicta*, collective claims would allow the court a more thorough understanding

58 Wang et al., "Judiciário e fornecimento de insulinas"; Hoffman and Bentes, "Accountability and Social and Economic Rights in Brazil," 224–225.

59 Wang et al.

60 See David Landau, "The Reality of Social Rights Enforcement," *Harvard International Law Journal* 53, no. 1 (Winter 2012).

of the problem (including budgetary and distributive issues), a more inclusive dialogue between the court and stakeholders, and judicial interventions that can promote policy changes of a structural nature.[61] The *dicta*, however, have not engaged with concerns that this form of adjudication would involve courts in complex meso- or macro-level resource allocation that, in general, courts are poorly suited to make.[62] In any case, it is uncertain whether these *dicta* will have any impact on future decisions of the STF or lower courts.

Budget impact

Brazilian courts' interpretation of the right to health, coupled with relatively easy access to courts, and the increasing demand for new health technologies, have all created the conditions for the increasing involvement of courts in decisions about the allocation of healthcare resources. It is estimated that between 200,000 and 300,000 claims for health treatments are being filed in Brazilian courts every year.[63]

As expected, this has had a significant impact on the public health budget. Graph 4.1 shows the amount spent by the Federal Government and five States to buy drugs the funding of which was ordered by courts. It is worth noting that, although the expenditure at the Federal level stands out, the impact at the State level should not be underestimated as five States together have outspent the Federal Government.

These numbers, however, are just a fraction of the total cost of the healthcare litigation for the public purse. First, they include drugs only. Although most claims are for drugs, there is litigation for other treatments the cost of which is not systematically calculated by the government or for which there is not necessarily a requirement for an extra monetary outlay despite having opportunity costs. This includes, for instance, court rulings ordering the immediate hospitalization of a patient in an intensive care unit despite the existence of waiting lists for accessing this service. Second, although these are the jurisdictions with the highest number of court claims for health treatments, the data in Graph 4.1 does not cover the amount spent by the other 21 States, the Federal District, and over 5,000 municipalities. Third, it does not account for the legal and administrative costs related to the legal dispute and to the provision of treatments following court decisions, which are far from negligible.[64]

61 See the opinions of Justice Gilmar Mendes and Edson Fachin. A similar approach by the Brazilian Judiciary in healthcare-related claims was suggested by Pedro Felipe de Oliveira Santos, "Beyond Minimalism and Usurpation: Designing Judicial Review to Control the Mis-Enforcement of Socio-economic Rights," *Washington University Global Studies Law Review* 18, no. 3 (2019).

62 See Chapter 2.

63 Ferraz, *Health as a Human Right*, 107.

64 Natalia Pires de Vasconcelos, "Writ of Mandamus or Ministry of Health? Managers, Prosecutors and Institutional Responses to Judicialization" (PhD thesis, University of São Paulo, 2018).

Yearly expenditure on drugs provided in compliance with judicial decisions adjusted by inflation in million of US$

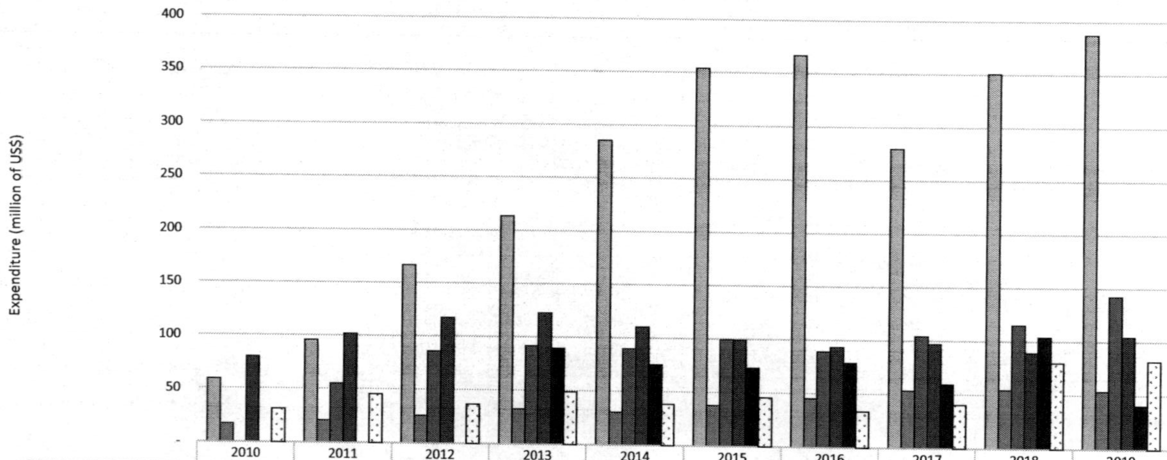

	2010	2011	2012	2013	2014	2015	2016	2017	2018	2019
Federal government	5,90,53,079	9,58,38,916	16,65,72,775	21,39,44,707	28,54,41,180	35,37,40,718	36,64,09,021	27,98,85,935	35,08,26,045	38,73,51,003
Parana State	1,71,94,197	2,05,53,530	2,58,81,603	3,27,78,006	3,07,74,780	3,79,28,042	4,54,98,314	5,34,52,084	5,49,82,447	5,37,77,154
Rio Grande do Sul State	-	5,51,72,333	8,61,75,316	9,18,44,621	9,02,51,717	9,96,90,497	8,93,99,505	10,44,15,594	11,52,76,504	14,25,97,403
São Paulo State	7,99,71,071	10,18,25,071	11,74,88,259	12,25,82,668	11,05,52,185	9,94,74,527	9,34,93,596	9,72,78,136	8,92,43,252	10,47,20,332
Minas Gerais State	-	-	-	9,00,12,395	7,52,45,781	7,30,95,864	7,89,66,961	5,97,59,528	10,42,27,348	4,06,51,473
Santa Catarina State	3,13,01,255	4,53,74,540	3,65,24,081	4,90,14,323	3,83,54,053	4,59,18,739	3,37,28,601	4,06,01,845	8,01,37,951	8,20,59,788

Graph 4.1 Yearly expenditure on drugs provided in compliance with judicial decisions adjusted by inflation in millions of US$. Source: Ministry of Health, State of Parana Department of Health, State of Rio Grande do Sul Department of Health, State of São Paulo Department of Health, State of Minas Gerais Department of Health, State of Santa Catarina Department of Health. Data were obtained through a direct request by the author to the respective bodies. Values in R$ were adjusted to 2019 price levels using the implicit price deflator for the Government expenditure component of the Health Satellite Account (IBGE) between 2010 and 2017, and the Consumer Price Index (IPCA) in 2018 and 2019. Values converted to US$ using the average exchange rate for 2019 (3.94 BRL/USD).

The absolute numbers are impressive, and so is the growth from 2010 onwards. These numbers are even more significant considering that the overall public expenditure in healthcare and drugs has either stagnated or decreased (when controlled by inflation) in recent years due to a serious economic crisis and conservative governments with a fiscal austerity agenda.[65]

It is also important to understand how these values compare with the health budget and with other health policies. For example, in 2016 the Federal Government spent more on court-ordered drugs than on its world-renowned HIV antiretroviral distribution policy. Since 2015, the Federal Government expenditure on the provision of drugs to comply with judicial decisions has represented, on average, 7% of what it spent on drugs and about 20% of the budget for highly specialized treatments (which includes high-cost drugs for rare diseases) in each respective year.[66] At the Federal level, the disproportionate impact of a few very expensive drugs is also noteworthy. As mentioned, in 2016, 90% of the amount spent on medicines ordered by courts went to buy ten high-cost drugs and about 50% was on one single medicine (Soliris).[67] None of them was then incorporated in SUS and some did not even have regulatory approval (which accounted for 61% of the amount spent on court-ordered drugs).[68]

At the sub-Federal level – particularly States – the scale of the impact of right to health litigation is also noteworthy and seems to replicate some of the patterns found at the Federal level: most of the expenditure was for drugs that were not incorporated in SUS, a small number of drugs is responsible for most of the expenditure, and a significant part of the health budget is being allocated by courts.[69]

Table 4.1 shows the percentage of what is spent by some State governments to buy drugs following a court order in relation to the total health budget. In Santa Catarina and Rio Grande do Sul the numbers are very impressive. However, even in places where the percentage is low, it is important to remember that expenditure determined by courts is being compared with the budget available for state governments to cover all the healthcare services under their responsibility (which includes drugs, and ambulatory and inpatient hospital care).

65 Fabiola Sulpino Vieira, Sergio Francisco Piola and Rodrigo Pucci de Sá e Benevides, *Vinculação Orçamentária do Gasto em Saúde no Brasil: resultados e argumentos a seu favor*, Texto para Discussâo 2516 (Brasília: Instituto de Pesquisa Econômica Aplicada, 2019).

66 Vieira, *Direito à Saúde no Brasil;* Luiza Pinheiro Alves da Silva, *Orçamento Temático De Acesso A Medicamentos: Análise De 10 Anos De Recursos Federais Destinados À Assistência Farmacêutica* – Avaliação das execuções financeiras do Ministério da Saúde com medicamentos de 2008 a 2018 (Brasília: Inesc, 2019), 19.

67 Vieira, Piola and Benevides, *Vinculação Orçamentária do Gasto em Saúde.*

68 Xavier, "Judicialização da saúde."

69 Data provided by the Minas Gerais Department of Health through direct contact by the author; Machado et al., "Judicialization of Access to Medicines"; Relatório de Auditoria 009.253/2015-7, TCU; Diana Sakae, "Otimização de recursos: judicial versus política pública" (PowerPoint presentation, State of Santa Catarina Department of Health, 2020).

Table 4.1 State expenditure on drugs provided in compliance with judicial decisions in relation to the state government health expenditure

	2010	*2011*	*2012*	*2013*	*2014*	*2015*	*2016*	*2017*	*2018*	*2019*
Paraná State	2.56%	2.85%	3.34%	3.60%	3.17%	4.00%	4.97%	5.34%	5.48%	5.37%
Rio Grande do Sul State	–	8.04%	10.17%	8.34%	8.41%	10.14%	9.14%	10.07%	10.66%	13.26%
São Paulo State	1.66%	1.98%	2.33%	2.42%	2.42%	2.31%	2.28%	2.15%	2.01%	2.31%
Minas Gerais State	–	–	–	5.41%	4.78%	4.96%	5.33%	3.81%	7.70%	2.39%
Santa Catarina State	5.63%	7.38%	5.81%	7.78%	5.99%	7.32%	5.59%	6.16%	10.65%	11.28%

Source: State expenditure on drugs provided in compliance with judicial decisions: State of Parana Department of Health, State of Rio Grande do Sul Department of Health, State of São Paulo Department of Health, State of Minas Gerais Department of Health, State of Santa Catarina Department of Health. Data were obtained through a direct request by the author to the respective bodies. State government health expenditure extracted from Sistema de Informações sobre Orçamentos Públicos em Saúde Indicadores Estaduais (SIOPS). Health expenditure excludes Federal transfers, which are used for specific purposes and cannot be used by State governments to comply with judicial orders.

For instance, in São Paulo, although the impact of court orders on the overall health budget seems relatively modest if compared to other states, the comparison with other healthcare policies funded by the government of Sao Paulo shows the magnitude of this phenomenon there. In 2016–2017, it represented 35% of the State's budget for drugs during the same period.[70] Naffah Filho et al. estimated that in 2010 the state of São Paulo spent 4.5 times more to comply with judicial decisions than on hospitalization for organ transplantation. This amount was also equivalent to 90% of what was spent on the 123 million clinical diagnoses made by the public health system in that State; 28% more than what was spent on dialysis; and 29% more than what was spent on chemotherapy and radiotherapy.[71] In the State of Paraná, the amount spent from 2013 to 2017 on drugs which provision was ordered by courts was about 49% of the State budget for drugs during this period.[72]

At the municipal level, the increase in litigation and its costs has also been noticed. In the city of São Paulo – the richest and most populated city in Brazil – the amount spent on complying with healthcare litigation decisions in 2018 was around R$13.5 million (US$ 3.7 million). This represented over 5% of the city's budget for drugs in that year.[73] In cities with smaller budgets, the impact of healthcare litigation can be even more dramatic. For example, in Buritana, a small city of 15,000 inhabitants, more than 50% of the budget for drugs was spent on providing treatment ordered by courts and one single patient won in court the right to receive a treatment that cost the municipality 16% of its entire budget for drugs.[74] A 2016 survey covering over 4,000 municipalities found that half of them have responded to judicial claims for health treatments. Most of the claims were for drugs and hospital beds (including in intensive care units). The municipalities declared that their main concern in relation to judicial claims is their lack of financial and human resources to comply with court orders. [75]

In conclusion, the amount spent by the public health system to comply with judicial decisions is consuming a significant share of the public health budget. Given that the public health budgets cannot keep up with the growth in litigation, courts are having a major impact in reallocating public healthcare resources in Brazil. Courts show almost complete disregard for scientific evidence and policy considerations such as cost-effectiveness, distributive fairness, budget capacity,

70 Sérgio Swain Muller, "Judicialização da saúde" (PowerPoint presentation, Seminário sobre Gestão e Saúde, Insper/CONASS), https://slideplayer.com.br/slide/17057062/.

71 Michel Naffah Filho, Ana Luiza Chieffi, and Maria Cecília M. M. A. Correa, "S-Codes: A New System of Information on Lawsuits of the State Department of Health of São Paulo," *Boletim Epidemiológico Paulista* 7, no. 84 (2010): 28.

72 Pontarolli, Rossignoli, and Moretoni, "Panorama da Judicialização de Medicamentos," 179.

73 Gabriela Pinheiro Lima Chabbouh, "O impacto da judicialização da saúde sobre o município de São Paulo: orçamento e organização administrativa" (master's diss., Universidade Federal do ABC, 2019).

74 Cristiane Segatto, "O paciente de R$800 mil," *Época*, March 26, 2012.

75 Carla Estefânia Albert, "Análise sobre a judicialização da saúde nos municípios," *Revista Técnica CNM* (2016).

and the health needs of the population. Moreover, given that litigation is mainly driven by individual claims, courts bias public spending towards goods that can be individually consumed (e.g. drugs) rather than on public services that benefit whole populations (e.g. preventative health programmes).

Litigation also creates a two-tier public health system – the upper-tier for those who litigate and have access to any treatment irrespective of cost, and the other for the rest of the population who have access to more limited care. Healthcare resources are distributed according to a morally arbitrary principle, namely the capacity to litigate, which is certainly not evenly distributed in society.[76] It can be expected that the right to healthcare litigation will progressively become more accessible as people are better informed, there is more public investment in legal aid, and pharmaceutical companies have incentives to encourage and sponsor litigation.[77] This can make right to health litigation apparently less unfair, but the fact that more people litigate and thus go up to the courts created upper-tier means that litigation will affect more severely the rest of the population in the tier below.

The institutional responses

The impact of courts on healthcare policies has become too big to be ignored. This section will discuss the three most overarching responses to control its negative consequences on the public health system. Two come from the judicial branch itself and the third is the Federal Law 12.401/11. All these proposals

76 There is data indicating that right to health litigation creates an anti-poor bias because claimants from higher socio-economic groups and from more affluent areas tend to be over-represented in these cases: see Ferraz, *Health as a Human Right*; Virgílio da Silva and Terrazas, "Claiming the Right to Health"; Octavio Luiz Motta Ferraz, "Harming the Poor Through Social Rights Litigation: Lessons from Brazil," *Texas Law Review* 89, no. 7 (June 2011); Wang and Ferraz, "Reaching out to the needy?". See, however, João Biehl et al., "Between the Court and the Clinic: Lawsuits for Medicines and the Right to Health in Brazil," *Health and Human Rights Journal* 14, no. 1 (June 15, 2012); Marcelo Medeiros, Debora Diniz and Ida Vanessa Doederlein Schwartz, "The Thesis of Judicialization of Health Care by the Elites: Medication for Mucopolysaccharidosis," *Ciência & Saúde Coletiva* 18, no. 4 (April 2013).

77 The evidence on pharmaceutical companies encouraging and funding right to health litigation by connecting patients, doctors, and lawyers is abundant: see Ana Luiza Chieffi and Rita de Cássia Barradas Barata, "Legal Suits: Pharmaceutical Industry Strategies to Introduce New Drugs in the Brazilian Public Healthcare System," *Revista de Saúde Pública* 44, no. 3 (June 2010); Naffah Filho, Chieffi and Correa et al, "S-Codes"; Medeiros, Diniz and Schwartz, "Judicialization by the Elites"; Daniel Wei Liang Wang and Octavio Luiz Motta Ferraz, "Pharmaceutical Companies vs. the State: Who Is Responsible for Post-Trial Provision of Drugs in Brazil?," *The Journal of Law, Medicine & Ethics* 40, no. 2 (Summer 2012); Orozimbo Henrique Campos Neto, Luiz Alberto de Oliveira Gonçalves and Eli Iola Gurgel Andrade, "Estratégias do poder econômico interferindo no fenômeno da judicialização da saúde," in *Coletânea Direito e Saúde*, vol. 2, *Dilemas do Fenômeno da Judicialização da Saúde,* eds. Alethele de Oliveira Santos and Luciana Tolêdo Lopes (Brasília: CONASS, 2018).

have in common the fact that they try to establish a sphere of judicial restraint in which courts should defer to the decisions made by health authorities. Thus, they try to oppose the Brazilian courts' prevailing interpretation that there is an absolute individual right to receive any prescribed health treatment, which cannot be limited by health authorities' priority-setting decisions or by the lack of robust scientific evidence. However, they disagree on what courts should do when there are claims for drugs not incorporated in the SUS. This is a central issue since, as discussed earlier in this chapter, these claims are one of the main drivers of health-care litigation in Brazil.

Self-restraint and institutional capacity: responses from the judicial branch

Courts' lack of institutional capacity and the limits of the adjudicative process are some of the most common critiques against courts deciding on the provision of welfare benefits via social rights adjudication. Judges, according to this argument, are trained in law and legal processes and lack the knowledge, expertise, and resources to decide on multifaceted issues of policy, especially those involving the allocation of scarce resources. Moreover, the adversarial model of adjudication tends to reduce polycentric problems which "involve many affected parties and a somewhat fluid state of affairs" to bilateral disputes and is poorly prepared to gather and analyse complex social data.[78] Courts will know a lot about a case, but little about its milieu and thus will not be able to see the trade-offs and follow-throughs in the allocation of scarce resources.[79]

On the other hand, those who advocate for a more active role of judges in social rights adjudication affirm that courts, when protecting civil and political rights, also deal with complex issues that are similar to those raised by social rights adjudication. Thus, the judicial protection of social rights creates challenges for courts that are not so different from those they commonly face. Furthermore, judges can be provided with relevant information by the parties, their lawyers, witnesses, and court-appointed experts. Judges can also specialize in social policy issues through experience and legal education, in the same way that they can specialize in other fields of law. Finally, the judicial process can be made more participatory – open to *amici curiae* and public hearing – to enable courts to deal with the complex issues brought before them in social rights cases.[80]

78 Lon L. Fuller, "The Forms and Limits of Adjudication," *Harvard Law Review* 92, no. 2 (December 1978): 394.

79 Donald L. Horowitz, "The Judiciary: Umpire or Empire?" *Law and Human Behaviour* 6, no. 2 (1982).

80 See, for instance, Aoife Nolan, Bruce Porter, and Malcolm Langford, *The Justiciability of Social and Economic Rights: An Updated Appraisal*, CHRGJ Working Paper 15 (Center for Human Rights and Global Justice, 2007): 14–15; Virginia Mantouvalou, "In Support of Legislation," in *Debating Social Rights*, eds. Conor Gearty and Virginia Mantouvalou (Oxford: Hart, 2011); Roberto Gargarella, "Dialogic Justice in the Enforcement of Social

The responses to the right to healthcare litigation phenomenon advanced by the Supreme Federal Court (STF) and the National Council of Justice (CNJ) can be contextualized in this debate about the capacity and legitimacy of courts to decide on the provision of welfare policies. The STF is the last Court of Appeal in the Brazilian Judiciary and the constitutional court. The CNJ is part of the judicial branch but has no judicial power and cannot review judicial decisions. Its main role is to issue resolutions and recommendations aimed at improving courts' strategic planning and administration.

Both institutions recognize that courts have institutional limitations and therefore can only be secondary decision-makers on the issue of healthcare provision. However, at the same time, they try to overcome these limitations to allow courts a prominent role in making and reviewing rationing decisions.

The response advanced by the STF and the CNJ can be better understood as complementary parts of the same policy by the Judiciary to address the problems created by the right to healthcare litigation. This is not surprising since there is a strong connection between both institutions. The CNJ is formally an autonomous institution, but it is expected that the STF, and especially the STF Chief Justice, will have a significant influence on the CNJ. The presidency of the CNJ, which sets the institution's agenda, is chaired by the Chief Justice of the STF. Moreover, the STF has the prerogative to appoint two other members of the CNJ. The affinity between the recommendations of the CNJ and the decisions of the STF will become clear in the following subsections.

The Supreme Federal Court: public hearings and tests for judicial restraint

The STF held a public hearing in 2009 with over 50 experts (including health professionals, public authorities, scholars, and civil society representatives), heard over six days, to supply the STF with "technical, scientific, administrative, political and economic" information related to the healthcare litigation phenomenon in Brazil.[81]

The public hearing was motivated by the acknowledgement that litigation has had a significant impact on the public health system and that the court needed support from different specialists and stakeholders to make better decisions.[82] Chief Justice Gilmar Mendes (as he then was) held the public hearing and declared in his opening speech that "either the idea that courts should have no

Rights: Some Initial Arguments," in *Litigating Health Rights: Can Courts Bring More Justice to Health?*, eds. Alicia Yamin and Siri Gloppen (Cambridge, MA: Harvard University Press, 2011).

81 Gilmar Mendes, "Opening of the Public Hearing n. 4 at the Supreme Federal Court", *Supreme Federal Court*, March 5, 2009. www.stf.jus.br/arquivo/cms/processoAudienciaPublicaSaude/anexo/Abertura_da_Audiencia_Publica__MGM.pdf.

82 Mendes.

role in healthcare issues or that there is a right to any health treatment is untenable" and that a balanced view should be found, taking into consideration "the judicial decisions' implications without compromising … the right to health".[83] Lastly, he affirmed that he expected the public hearing would result in technical information able to inform the court's analysis of the cases and also support a broader and pluralist debate for the improvement of health policies.[84]

Initiatives like public hearings can be seen as an institutional mechanism to protect more activist courts against criticisms concerning their lack of institutional capacity and legitimacy. It has also been presented as a tool for courts to promote deliberative democracy by enabling open and inclusive participation and discussion. This public hearing held by the STF was praised by analysts as a good example of how courts should proceed in right to healthcare cases.[85]

A general analysis of the quality of the participation and deliberation in public hearings held by courts is beyond the scope of this chapter. Nonetheless, it is important to mention that the potential benefits of deliberation promoted via public hearings have to be weighed against the possibility that judges "may cherry-pick from available studies to support a foregone conclusion", especially when there is a large amount of conflicting data and the interpretation of complex facts is required.[86] Furthermore, the outcome of the dispute (the judicial decision) may not reflect the deliberation about it given that judges cannot be punished for not grounding their reasons on the deliberation.[87] The 2009 public hearing in the STF seems to vindicate these concerns raised by the literature.

Following this public hearing, the STF established a test to identify the cases in which the SUS's refusal to fund a health treatment breaches the right to health and should thus be judicially redressed. This test was mentioned in several cases judged by the STF a few months after the public hearing was held and, according to Chief Justice Gilmar Mendes, it was based on the conclusions drawn from this event.[88]

According to this test, the government is legally obliged to offer universal access to treatments already incorporated in the SUS (i.e. on the official lists and clinical protocols and guidelines). On the other hand, courts should not order the SUS to provide unregistered treatments (treatments that did not receive marketing authorization from ANVISA, the Brazilian drugs agency). Lastly, if a treatment is registered but not incorporated in the SUS, then courts can order their

83 Mendes, 9.
84 Mendes, 10.
85 See Gargarella, "Dialogic Justice," 237; Aoife Nolan, *Children's Socio-Economic Rights, Democracy and the Courts* (Oxford: Hart, 2011), 78.
86 Jeff King, *Judging Social Rights* (Cambridge: Cambridge University Press, 2012), 242.
87 Mark Tushnet, *Weak Courts, Strong Rights: Judicial Review and Social Welfare Rights in Comparative Constitutional Law* (Princeton, NJ: Princeton University Press, 2008): 94.
88 See Wang, "Courts and Health Care Rationing," 81.

to provide a non-incorporated treatment in exceptional circumstances and for patient claimants who cannot afford it themselves, which creates unprecedented means-tested access to care within the SUS.

The STF, however, is divided on what counts as an exception that allows the courts to order the provision of a non-incorporated treatment. For some Justices, courts should order the SUS to fund them whenever there is a medical opinion confirming that the patient needs it and that there is no suitable therapeutic alternative available at SUS. If this opinion prevails, then there will probably be no substantial change in the courts' approach when judging these cases. STF will only reaffirm the pervasive interpretation of health as entitling patients to receive any treatment that a physician considers optimal even if the health system has not assessed it or has decided against funding it. This, in practice, rules out explicit priority-setting.

Other Justices, however, insist that the need of the patient to receive the claimed treatment and the suitability of the alternative treatments available at SUS should be assessed through the lens of evidence-based medicine. Some Justices have also suggested that courts should not order the provision of treatments that have been assessed by SUS and there was an explicit decision not to incorporate it. This condition, if accepted, would narrow the scope of judicial intervention and give SUS the final word in priority-setting. An STF decision on the wording of the *ratio decidendi* to settle these disagreements within the court is pending.

Nevertheless, in both scenarios, although in different degrees, the STF will probably be overestimating courts' institutional capacity to adjudicate on complex issues of science and policy. The availability of a therapeutic alternative at SUS to the non-incorporated treatment claimed by patients will be key to determine the outcome of cases. However, it is not clear what counts as a therapeutic alternative and how courts will compare different treatment options. This is particularly challenging when new technologies with disputed evidence are being considered and claimants (together with their lawyers and doctors) and health authorities disagree. There are also issues of cost and budget when comparing alternatives. A treatment may be marginally better than the one offered by the SUS but at a much higher cost.[91]

This all brings us back to the problem of courts' institutional capacity to make priority-setting decisions and may help explain the purpose of the CNJ recommendations aiming at building courts' institutional capacity, as will be discussed in the subsection that follows.

The National Council of Justice: building courts' institutional capacity

Following the 2009 public hearing held by the STF, the CNJ issued Recommendation 31/2010 proposing policies that reinforce and complement

91 See Chapter 3.

what had been put forward by the STF. For the reasons previously presented, the affinity between the CNJ and the STF was to be expected. Justice Gilmar Mendes, the then President of the CNJ, was also the Chief Justice of the STF who organized and chaired the 2009 public hearing and who wrote the leading opinion of the judgment in which the test previously discussed was established.

Recommendation 31/2010 "recommends to courts the implementation of measures aiming at supporting judges [...] to assure better solution for the judicial claims related to healthcare". It affirmed that the main problems caused by healthcare litigation in Brazil were due to the lack of medical/scientific information available to judges in the claims for health treatments. It also stated that the health authority's managerial capacity, the existing public policies, the organization of the SUS, and the need to guarantee the sustainability and manageability of the SUS should all be taken into consideration by courts when judging the cases.

The CNJ recommended courts to, among other things:

a) Make available technical support from doctors and pharmacists to assist judges in assessing the clinical evidence presented by litigants;
b) Advise judges to analyse the cases based on complete and comprehensive information; to avoid the provision of drugs that are experimental or not registered with the ANVISA and; to consult, whenever it is possible, health authorities before issuing a preliminary injunction;
c) Include health law legislation as a subject to be examined in the public entrance exams for judges.

Building on Recommendation 31/2010, CNJ Resolution 238/2016 determined that every court in Brazil should have a Technical Support Team (*NAT-Jus*) staffed with health professionals to provide judges with scientific information about the treatments that are claimed by patients. The opinions of the Technical Support Teams are saved in an electronic database (*e-NatJus*), which can be accessed by other judges and their clerks. Resolution 238/2016 also requires courts to create health law divisions, so healthcare-related cases are decided by specialist judges. In sum, the CNJ recommends courts exercise some degree of self-restraint while trying to build courts' institutional capacity to make allocative decisions themselves.

Better-trained, informed, and assisted judges can impact the right to healthcare litigation in different ways. First, judges with more information will be able to filter out claims that are based on poor evidence. Moreover, the more courts know about healthcare policies, the warier they will probably be in reviewing the health authorities' rationing decisions because they will be given a broader perspective on the challenges for delivering quality and timely healthcare to a population. They will understand, for instance, that the SUS has to make "tragic choices", that there are opportunity costs, and that priority-setting is necessary and complex.

On the other hand, by building courts' institutional capacity, the CNJ also tries to create better conditions for judges to make allocative decisions in healthcare. This is in line with the STF case law, which has been attempting to create a sphere of judicial self-restraint while leaving space for courts to order the funding of treatment based on the individual needs of a patient and their assessment of the evidence. Providing courts with more knowledge, information, and support from health professionals could, in principle, allow them to better perform this task.

However, it is questionable whether better-trained judges assisted by health professionals will be able to gather and evaluate factual information to make sound policy decisions. Even if we reduce these decisions to a mere medical/scientific issue, it would be unrealistic to expect that a group of doctors and pharmacists will have the necessary diversification of expertise to make a comprehensive scientific assessment of all the treatments that are being litigated for. This task is even more daunting considering that the main driver of litigation is a wide array of new technologies for which the scientific evidence may be inconclusive or disputed. In countries where HTA is taken seriously, this task is carried out by highly specialized and resourced bodies that can gather and assess large amounts of data applying stringent scientific methods and that are open to inputs from stakeholders and experts.

Nonetheless, let us assume, for the sake of the argument, that courts supported by health professionals can create a system that is able to comprehensively assess treatments using high-quality evidence and methods. That will still not solve all the problems caused by healthcare litigation because whether a health system should fund a treatment is not merely a medical problem that science can solve. It is a matter of public policy. Doctors and pharmacists will not be able to consider cost-effectiveness, affordability, opportunity costs, public health priorities, and the preferences of stakeholders before recommending the provision of a given treatment.

Even if we add specialists from other fields to the group of medical experts, it would still be naive to expect that they can give the right answer to whether or not a treatment should be provided. Priority-setting involves problems of social fact (e.g. how a certain disease affects the population's health), polycentricity (e.g. the socio-economic effects of providing a given treatment on the public health system), politics (e.g. the priorities of a community with regards to healthcare spending), and social values (e.g. the trade-off between maximizing benefits and reducing inequality when allocating scarce resources) that cannot be reduced to a technical decision that can be objectively made by a body of experts attached to courts. Moreover, public policies are inescapably speculative, and their impact is hard to predict, which requires the managerial capacity to make and review decisions according to the consequences and to respond promptly to changing circumstances.[92]

This all underscores the importance of procedural legitimacy in priority-setting. Since there is no unequivocal right decision, it is essential that it be made according to a fair procedure.[93] From this perspective, the expectation that courts can second-guess administrative and political allocative decisions with better-trained

92 Jeffrey King, "Flexibility," chap. 9 in *Judging Social Rights* (Cambridge: Cambridge University Press, 2012).

93 See Norman Daniels, *Just Health: Meeting Health Needs Fairly* (Cambridge University Press, 2007).

judges and expert assistance, but without the virtues of the public administration (for example, expertise and flexibility) and a politically accountable process, seems untenable. Moreover, those advantages of the political and administrative processes may be undermined by decisions of reviewing courts which reverse choices from the political and administrative sphere based on a different opinion or source of evidence.[94]

To overcome some of these obstacles, one could imagine the CNJ recommending the creation of a very sophisticated "bureaucracy under judicial auspices" to carry out health technology assessments and decide on whether a treatment should be provided in each case.[95] Even if we assume that courts have the resources and capacity to do so, it can be questioned whether this would be more sensible than relying on, and controlling, the procedure used at the administrative level by health authorities who have the structure and expertise to perform this task. The section that follows will discuss this argument further.

Federal Law 12.401/11: health technology assessment

Federal Law 12.401/2011 was based on two draft bills: the 338/2007, proposed by Senator Flávio Arns ("Arns' Bill"); and the 219/2007, by Senator Tião Vianna ("Vianna's Bill"). Both draft bills state that the right to healthcare litigation is the main justification for their enactment. Nevertheless, they see the problem from different perspectives and put forward different solutions for it.

In the official justification for his draft bill, Senator Arns affirms that access to healthcare cannot be restricted by clinical protocols and guidelines or by official lists of treatments. According to him, the SUS's official lists of treatments are not frequently updated, restricting patients' access to new technologies. He also mentioned that there is no formal administrative process to assess and incorporate health technologies in the SUS, which means that there is no deadline for the assessments to be concluded, no right to an administrative appeal, and no participation from the civil society. He proposed the creation of a public body – composed of government and civil society representatives – for assessing health technologies and deciding on their incorporation in the SUS through a formal administrative process. However, the government would still have to provide treatments not incorporated in the SUS if there is no effective substitute therapy

94 See Daniel Wei Liang Wang, "Social Rights and the Nirvana Fallacy," *Public Law* (July 1, 2018).

95 The idea of a 'bureaucracy under judicial auspices' to assist courts in cases involving legislative facts was suggested by Kenneth Culp Davis, *Discretionary Justice: A Preliminary Inquiry* (Urbana: University of Illinois Press, 1971), 118; Adrian Vermeule, *Law and the Limits of Reason* (New York: Oxford University Press, 2008), and has been recently advanced by Paul Yowell, "Empirical Research in Rights-Based Judicial Review of Legislation," in *Current Problems in the Protection of Human Rights–Perspectives from Germany and the UK*, eds. Katja S. Ziegler and Peter M. Huber (Oxford: Hart, 2012).

available and there is a medical prescription declaring that the claimed treatment is necessary to avoid death or serious harm to the patient.

Vianna's Bill had a different approach. In his draft's justification, Senator Vianna affirmed that the provision of drugs ordered by courts is forcing the public purchase of high-cost treatments the effectiveness of which is not always proven. According to him, this is harmful to the SUS because it gives pharmaceutical companies the power to lobby patients and doctors to convince them that the treatments they sell are the best and that patients can access them free of cost through courts. He affirms that because resources are scarce, priorities have to be set by the SUS in order to benefit the largest number of people. Vianna's Bill also proposed that the SUS should only provide treatments that are registered with the ANVISA and included in the official lists of treatments. Thus, Vianna's Bill would give health authorities the final decision on the provision of healthcare and would rule out claims for drugs not incorporated in the SUS.

In spite of the different proposals and opposing perspectives, both draft bills were analysed conjointly by the National Congress because they legislate about the same issue. Vianna's Bill was formally rejected and Arns' Bill was approved to become Federal Law 12.401/2011. However, the proposals put forward by Vianna's Bill were introduced as amendments to Arns' Bill. Thus, Federal Law 12.401/2011 is an amalgam of both draft bills: it established that the government should only provide treatments that are incorporated in the SUS (as proposed in Vianna's Bill) and created an institution responsible for assessing health technologies through a formal administrative process (as proposed in Arns' Bill).

Federal Law 12.401/11 establishes that the provision of treatment in the SUS can only be made according to its official lists and clinical protocols and guidelines. It also banned the provision of, or reimbursement for, experimental treatments and drugs not registered with the ANVISA or not authorized by it. These rules are, in principle, similar to those established by the STF after the public hearing and by the CNJ's recommendation. The main difference is the rule proposed for treatments not incorporated in the SUS or claimed for off-protocol use, which are the main drivers of litigation. The CNJ and the STF accept that courts have the power to order the funding of treatments in these cases. Federal Law 12.401/11 does not allow this exception.

Federal Law 12.401/11 created a body responsible for HTA – the National Council for Incorporation of Technologies in the National Health System (CONITEC). CONITEC makes recommendations to inform the SUS's funding decisions and creates and amends clinical protocols and guidelines. CONITEC assesses health technologies based on the scientific evidence regarding their effectiveness, accuracy, and safety, as well as health economic evaluation by comparing a new technology with those already incorporated in terms of cost-effectiveness and budget impact.

This legislation also established that the incorporation, exclusion, or alteration in the use of treatments has to be made through an administrative process that is open to public participation through public hearings and consultation. The appraisal is made by independent experts in research institutions and the assessment must be concluded within 180 days, and extended by a further 90 days, if necessary. Interested parties also have the right to administrative appeal against CONITEC′s recommendations.

Presidential Decree 7646/2011, which regulates Federal Law 12.401/11, established that CONITEC is composed of representatives from health-related public bodies, civil society, and the Ministry of Health. This Decree also added that the CONITEC's reports will be forwarded to the Ministry of Health Secretary for Science and Technology (SCTIE) for the final decision on the incorporation of a technology. If the SCTIE decides to incorporate the assessed technology, then it must be made available in the SUS within 180 days.[96]

Before the final version of Federal Law 12.401/11 was approved, the then President of the Republic, Dilma Roussef, vetoed the article which stated that, if the deadline for the conclusion of a technology's assessment was reached and no recommendation had been issued, then the technology should be made available in the SUS until the decision is finally made. She also vetoed an article stating that the economic impact of a technology is not a reason to deny its incorporation in the SUS. The justifications given for both vetoes are very similar. The President asserted the importance of scientific and economic assessment of a health technology before any decision on its provision is made. She affirmed that providing non-assessed treatments brings risk to patients' health and is an inadequate way of allocating public resources. Moreover, according to her, the SUS has to consider the economic impact of a treatment in order to optimize and rationalize the allocation of public funds. Differently from the proposals of the CNJ and the position of the STF so far, which give courts the last word on the provision of non-incorporated drugs, Federal Law 12.401/2011 makes it clear that the final decision on the provision of healthcare should be in the hands of health authorities.

According to CONITEC's first body of directors, the pressure for the incorporation of new health technologies comes from many groups in society – including patients and pharmaceutical industries – but they were especially concerned about judicial decisions that compel the provision of drugs based on "the right to health as an individual rather than a collective right".[97] According to them, there is a common opinion among judges and the general public that if a drug is not provided, it is because the SUS is poorly managed. A more robust HTA system was thus seen as necessary to challenge and change this perception. This would be achieved through a system that can increase the number of clinical protocols and guidelines, update them more frequently, and make the procedure

96 For a thorough description of the HTA system in Brazil, see Denizar Vianna Araújo, Marcella de Souza Cruz Distrutti and Flávia Tavares Silva Elias, "Health Technologies Prioritization: The Brazilian Case," *Jornal Brasileiro de Economia da Saúde* 9, no. S1 (2017).

97 Helaine Carneiro Capucho et al., "Incorporation of Technologies in Health in Brazil: A New Model for the Brazilian Public Health System (Sistema Único de Saúde – SUS)," *Boletim do Instituto de Saúde* 13, no. 3 (July 2012).

for incorporation of new technologies more informed, transparent, inclusive, and accountable.[98]

Following the enactment of Federal Law 12.401/11 the Federal Attorney General's Office (AGU), the body responsible for the legal representation of the Federal Government, issued several legal opinions (*pareceres*) putting forward a new strategy for government lawyers to respond to claims for health treatments. The legal opinions affirm that, in response to the increasing number of lawsuits claiming treatments against the SUS based on weak scientific evidence, it is important for the government's lawyers to make reference to CONITEC and the administrative process created by Federal Law 12.401/11. The strategy is to convince courts that the SUS's pharmaceutical policy is based on methodologically stringent scientific analysis to guarantee that the treatments provided are safe, effective, and, at the same time, rationalize and optimize the allocation of financial resources.[99]

The legislative history of Federal Law 12.401/2011, the analysis of its first body of directors, and the legal opinions issued by the AGU have all made clear the government's strategy to use the new HTA system to convince courts not to review healthcare rationing decisions. The government was working on the assumption that a better administrative procedure for HTA – more transparent, participative, accountable, timely, and scientifically sophisticated – would be conducive to promoting a more deferential attitude from courts and, consequently, reduce the negative impact of healthcare litigation on the SUS.

This does not mean that courts have no role in controlling the decisions made by health authorities. The AGU's legal opinion 804/2012 suggests that, instead of reviewing rationing decisions based on their own sources of evidence and policy preferences, courts could order the assessment of the claimed drug and control the legality and reasonableness of the process within CONITEC.

Although litigation was one of the drivers for the creation of CONITEC, there is no evidence that judicialization impacts CONITEC's recommendations. Even though this is a frequently discussed topic within the institution, it does not seem to be a determinant for the outcomes of HTA.[100] However, litigation may be relevant for the agenda-setting at CONITEC as the Ministry of Health itself mentioned court orders and the "pressure" from litigation as reasons for submitting technologies for CONITEC assessment.[101]

On the other hand, there is evidence that CONITEC has had no impact on court decisions. Wang et al. analysed a large sample of cases in which individuals

98 Capucho et al.

99 See Federal Attorney General's Legal Opinions 803/2012; 804/2012; 805/2012; 810/2012.

100 Kleize Araújo de Oliveira Souza, Luis Eugênio Portela Fernandes de Souza and Erick Soares Lisboa, "Legal Actions and Incorporation of Medicines into SUS: The Performance of Conitec," *Saúde debate* 42, no. 119 (October/December 2018).

101 Ministério da Saúde, *Avaliação de tecnologias em saúde: seleção de estudos apoiados pelo Decit* (Brasília: Ministério da Saúde, 2011), 14.

claimed the provision of drugs that have been assessed by CONITEC. Their hypothesis was that a CONITEC assessment report not recommending the incorporation of a medicine would decrease the probability of a judicial order for SUS to fund it. However, through logistic regression and interrupted time-series analysis, they found no evidence to suggest that a CONITEC report (either recommending or not a treatment) has affected the probability of courts ordering the provision of a treatment. It is even more telling that CONITEC reports are very rarely mentioned by judges even when their existence is brought to their attention by the litigants.

The example of analogous insulins makes these findings very concrete. In September 2014, CONITEC published two reports that did not recommend their incorporation because, despite being much more expensive, there was no robust evidence that they were more effective and safer than the analogous insulin available at SUS. These reports, however, had no effect on judicial decisions. In claims for analogous insulin, courts decided in favour of claimants in 94.6% of 932 judicial decisions prior to the CONITEC report in September 2014 and 95.7% of 418 judicial decisions afterwards.[102]

The creation of CONITEC can be seen as a positive indirect effect of the right to healthcare litigation as it institutionalized HTA and, at least on paper, gave it centrality in decisions about the incorporation of treatments in SUS. It is an interesting paradox that courts, by creating unfairness and inefficiency, may have forced the SUS to create a fairer and more efficient system for priority-setting. CONITEC could have also changed the role of courts in healthcare: from trumping rationing decisions to overseeing the legality and reasonableness of priority-setting decisions informed by CONITEC. However, CONITEC reports have been mostly ignored by courts. Therefore, rather than promoting fair priority-setting, courts are actually used to bypass priority-setting institutions and allow litigants privileged access to healthcare resources based on individual needs and rights.

Conclusion

Right to healthcare litigation in Brazil has limited the capacity of the health system to set priorities fairly. It makes the public health system less efficient because an enormous amount of resources is spent based on limited evidence and in a way that does not maximize the potential benefits. It also creates inequality by creating a two-tier public health system and distributing resources according to patients' capacity to litigate.

It would certainly be possible to cherry-pick decisions in which many would agree that the court made the right ruling in an individual case, that is, granting healthcare for a patient who was denied a treatment that was safe, effective, cost-effective, affordable, and needed. However, this is not a good argument to

102 Wang et al., "Health Technology Assessment."

justify courts applying the right to health like most of them do in Brazil. If courts order the provision of almost any treatment that patients claim, then both right and wrong decisions will be delivered without any criteria to distinguish between them. What is needed is a procedure that allows a more efficient and fair allocation of resources.

The CNJ and the STF, although trying to establish a sphere of self-restraint and deference, still assume that courts can appropriately make allocative decisions in healthcare if they go beyond the limits imposed by the traditional adjudicative model and incorporate attributes that are normally present in the administrative arena. As Horowitz observed: "[I]nstitutions in competition with each other tend to resemble each other. Each assumes the characteristics of the other to minimize competitive disadvantages".[103] This is perceived as a way to make sure that health authorities do a good job and, if they do not, to substitute judicial rulings for their decisions.

However, the question is whether, and under what circumstances, courts can do a better job than the primary decision-makers.[104] Why should they try to build their institutional capacity and legitimacy to make substantive allocative decisions in healthcare when there is an administrative body created and equipped specifically to make them? If the administrative process is adequate (based on robust evidence and fair principles and procedures) and properly followed in concrete cases, then why replicate it under the auspices of courts? It is probably naive to expect courts to create a better procedure to decide on the provision of healthcare than the one that already exists at the administrative level. This would also be unnecessarily costly.

If health authorities' processes are defective, then it would be better if courts controlled the procedure, occasionally ordering a decision to be remade, rather than ignoring what was decided by health authorities and trying to decide it from scratch. If compared with health authorities, courts are ill-suited to engage with scientific issues (e.g. whether treatment A is more effective than B) or economic and policy considerations (e.g. to balance the needs of a claimant against those of others and the State's budget capacity).

Courts, however, are in a good position to oversee and scrutinize the process through which these decisions are made to guarantee the conditions for fair priority-setting. Such an approach was expected from Brazilian courts following the enactment of Federal Law 12.401/11. Judicial control of procedure is now facilitated by a more inclusive, transparent, accountable, and evidence-informed health technology assessment system. It was expected that such a process would make clear to courts that priority-setting is as necessary as it is complex. It was also hoped that this new system would be perceived by courts as being more

103 Horowitz, "The Judiciary: Umpire or Empire?" 141.
104 Horowitz, 207.

legitimate and hence attract greater judicial deference.[105] However, these expectations have not materialized. Courts are still interpreting the right to health to allow individual needs to trump rationing decisions, no matter the fairness of the process through which they are made.

The STF will have the opportunity to reverse this situation if the position that gives health authorities the final word on the funding (or not) of health treatments eventually prevails in the *ratio decidendi* of the judgment in case RE 566471. This, coupled with the judicial control of the administrative process through which priorities are set, would imply a significant change in the way the right to health is interpreted by courts. Instead of judging the right to health as an individual trump card against rationing decisions, it would be applied as the right to access a healthcare system in which resources are distributed through fair priority-setting processes.[106]

105 The hypothesis that courts are more deferential to rationing decisions when health authorities' reasons and procedures are explicit was suggested by Daniels, *Just Health*, 123; and Flood and Essajee, "Setting Limits on Health Care: Challenges in and out of the Courtroom in Canada and Down-under" in *Rationing Health Care: Hard Choices and Unavoidable Trade-offs*, eds. André den Exter and Martin Buijsen (Antwerp: Maklu, 2012), 184.

106 See Chapter 2.

5 Colombia

Demanding but undermining fair priority-setting via courts

Colombia stands out among the countries where courts have been involved in decisions about resource allocation in healthcare. This is due to the impressive number of individual claims for treatments there and to the breadth of the structural changes in the health system that resulted, at least in part, from court decisions.

Among the countries for which statistics have been produced, Colombia has by far the highest absolute and per capita number of judicial claims for health treatments. The scale of right to healthcare litigation in Colombia can be better understood through the results of a study that estimated that the number of such judicial claims per million people in Colombia was 16 times larger than in Brazil, the second-highest in the list.[1] Apart from the impressive number of individual claims for health treatments, the Judiciary has also contributed to promoting broad changes in the Colombian health system through structural remedies and the constitutionality control of key healthcare legislation.

With such an expansive role, it is unsurprising that the Judiciary has contributed to setting the pace and direction for important changes in the Colombian health system. There is already extensive scholarship on right to healthcare litigation in Colombia and vast data on this phenomenon is available. The existing literature focuses mainly on the socio-economic profile of litigants, what has been claimed through courts, how judges decide, the financial impact of decisions on the health budget, and the authorities' compliance with structural decisions. However, as mentioned earlier in this book, this sort of approach to studying health litigation, which focuses on court cases and their immediate impact, leaves a blind spot: much is known about the benefits and beneficiaries of litigation, whereas the opportunity costs are less visible. This is likely to result in the

1 Ottar Mœstad, Lise Rakner, and Octavio L. Motta Ferraz, "Assessing the Impact of Health Rights Litigation: A Comparative Analysis of Argentina, Brazil, Colombia, Costa Rica, India, and South Africa," in *Litigating Health Rights: Can Courts Bring More Justice to Health?* eds. Alicia Yamin and Siri Gloppen (Harvard University Press, 2011).

DOI: 10.4324/9781315149165-5

overestimation of the positive impact of courts as those who were left worse-off because of judicial intervention tend to be overlooked.[2]

In order to shed light on this spot and offer a different perspective on right to healthcare litigation in Colombian, this chapter will focus on the impact of courts on how priorities are set in the Colombian healthcare system. The central question is whether courts have promoted or impaired fair priority-setting of healthcare resources in Colombia. In other words, have judicial rulings created incentives or obstacles for the Colombian health system to allocate scarce resources informed by robust scientific and economic evidence, guided by fair principles of justice, and through a transparent, inclusive, and accountable process?[3]

To answer this question, it will review the existing (both academic and grey) literature on the right to healthcare litigation in Colombia. It will then analyse how litigation and judicialization fit in the broader context of important administrative and legislative reforms in the Colombian health system over the last 30 years. Judicialization is the product of a context that courts themselves have helped to create. Understanding the effects of health system reforms and the impact of judicial decisions on the health system allows this chapter to draw conclusions about whether courts have contributed or hindered fair priority-setting in Colombia.

The argument in this chapter is that while courts have required and prompted important reforms towards fairer priority-setting, they have also created obstacles for fairer priority-setting by constantly judging explicit healthcare rationing unlawful. As shown by the judgments in hundreds of thousands of individual claims for health treatments, Colombian courts tend to not accept that the rationing of potentially beneficial health treatment can be the result of legitimate priority-setting choices and insist on finding that this is always a breach of constitutional rights. Moreover, the 2015 Colombian Constitutional Court decision in *C-313* declared that it is unconstitutional to take into account economic considerations (e.g. cost-effectiveness analysis and budget impact analysis) when deciding on the funding of health treatment needed by a patient. If I am right that courts have been an obstacle for fair priority-setting, then it is likely that they have contributed to aggravating many of the problems in the Colombian health system that some expected litigation could have helped to address.

The case of Colombia offers the unique opportunity, which will be seized by this chapter, to discuss some important questions for understanding the impact of courts on priority-setting more generally. How can an unlimited (and judicially enforceable) duty to fund expensive health technologies be reconciled with the universal and fair provision of quality health services for a large population and with the health system's financial sustainability? What role, if any, can health technology assessment play in a health system working under legal constraints for using economic analyses in priority-setting?

2 See Chapter 1.
3 See Chapter 2.

Law 100/1993: universality in search of equality

In 1993, a major health reform was introduced through Law 100. This legislation was intended to change a scenario in which most of the poor in Colombia could not access needed care or had to pay for it out-of-pocket because they lacked effective healthcare coverage. This reality resulted from a very fragmented health system composed of a social security system funded by payroll taxes that covered just one quarter of the population, a private system for the upper and upper-middle classes who could afford it, and an underfunded public health system that was actually more frequently used by the better-off.[4]

Law 100 unified the social security, the public and the private systems under the General System of Social Security in Health (SGSSS). In this unified system, all covered individuals are affiliated to an insurance company (EPS) regulated by the State. Individuals can choose the EPS to which they will be affiliated and EPSs compete against each other to attract users (and the funding that follows them). EPSs, however, are not directly paid by their affiliates.

Under SGSSS, there are two schemes: the contributory scheme for those able to pay, and a subsidized scheme for the poor. The contributory scheme is funded via a mandatory payroll tax for those in the formal labour market and earning above a certain income level. Payroll taxes are pooled into an equalization fund (initially FOSYGA and, since 2015, ADRES), which would then pay each EPS a risk-adjusted premium per person affiliated. The subsidized scheme is funded by revenues from the public budget and subsidized by a small fraction of the resources from the contributory system. Until very recently, the pool of resources per capita was significantly higher for the contributory scheme, resulting in a significantly lower premium paid to EPS and hence a reduced benefits package for those in the subsidized scheme.

Law 100 also established a prioritization plan for progressively including all the poor in the subsidized system, within available resources, and giving priority to the worst-off according to socio-economic criteria such as income and social vulnerability. The 1993 reform also organized service provision around the definition of explicit lists for the covered population: the compulsory health plan (POS). POS were positive lists defining what would be covered by the health system and they co-existed with negative lists defining what would not be covered. When new interventions were included in POS, the premium paid by FOSYGA to EPS for each patient would be adjusted following a financial impact analysis.[5]

4 Amanda L. Glassman et al., eds., *From Few to Many: Ten Years of Health Insurance Expansion in Colombia* (Inter-American Development Bank/Brookings Institution, 2009), 3–4.

5 Aurelio Mejía and Ana Lucía Muñoz, *Serie de notas técnicas sobre procesos de priorización en salud: nota 5: Institutos de evaluación de tecnologías sanitarias: recomendaciones para su estrucutración a partir del caso Colombia*, Nota técnica IDB-TN-1253 (Interamerican Development Bank, 2017).

This was one of the first attempts in Latin America to move from implicit to explicit healthcare rationing.[6]

However, while every insured person had access to a defined basket of health services covered by POS, the basket in each scheme was different. Due to the difference in the value of insurance premiums paid by FOSYGA to EPSs, those in the contributory scheme had access to a more generous and comprehensive set of services if compared to those in the subsidized scheme.[7] Although both schemes offered access to primary care and selected high-cost treatments, the main difference was in the secondary and tertiary care. Each scheme would also give access to different providers (e.g. hospitals and doctors). Law 100 stated that the packages for both schemes should be fully unified by 2001 (Article 162) but, as will be seen later in this chapter, this did not happen until 2012.

Law 100 aimed at creating a system that could increase coverage, promote fairness, and make explicit the duties and rights in healthcare. The results were, overall, positive. It allowed Colombia to extend coverage to practically the whole population: from 25% of the population covered in 1993 to almost 100% 20 years later.[8] Moreover, it resulted in increasing public health spending and improvements in health services access and utilization, as well as in financial protection and health outcomes, particularly for the poor.[9]

These results were achieved despite several challenges that the Colombian health system has faced over the years. Contrary to what had initially been planned, coverage expansion was in large part due to the growth of the subsidized scheme, which is almost fully dependent on an already overstretched national budget.[10] This was the result of a policy choice to expand coverage to include lower-middle classes unable to join the contributory scheme. It was also the consequence of economic and social problems that have limited the expansion of the contribu-

6 Ursula Giedion, Giota Panopoulou and Sandra Gómez-Fraga, *Diseño y ajuste de los planes explícitos de beneficios: el caso de Colombia y México* (Santiago, Chile: United Nations Economic Commission for Latin America and the Caribbean/Swedish International Development Cooperation Agency, 2009), 10.

7 Glassman et al., *From Few to Many*, 5; Giedion, Panopoulou and Gómez-Fraga, *Diseño y ajuste*, 48.

8 Claudia Patricia Vaca González, "El plan de beneficios de colombia ¿qué lecciones nos deja?" (presentation, International Development Bank/Criteria, April 2015).

9 Tania Dmytraczenko and Gisele Almeida, eds., *Toward Universal Health Coverage and Equity in Latin America and the Caribbean: Evidence from Selected Countries*, Directions in Development – Human Development (Washington, DC: World Bank Publications, 2015), 69; Glassman et al., *From Few to Many*, 49, 71–72; Catalina Gutiérrez Sourdís, Olga Lucía Acosta Navarro, and Eduardo Andrés Alfonso Sierra, "Financiación de la Seguridad Social en Salud: Fuentes de recursos y su administración" in *La salud en Colombia: Logros, retos y recomendaciones*, edited by Óscar Bernal and Catalina Gutiérrez (Bogotá: Universidad de Los Andes, 2012), 122–127; Ursula Giedion and Manuela Villar Uribe, "Colombia's Universal Health Insurance System," *Health Affairs* 28, no. 3 (May/June 2009).

10 Sourdís, Navarro and Sierra, Financiación de la Seguridad Social en Salud, 119; Everaldo Lamprea, and Johnattan García, "Closing the Gap Between Formal and Material Healthcare Coverage in Colombia," *Health and Human Rights Journal* 18, no. 2 (December 2016).

tory scheme, in particular, the economic instabilities that caused large unemployment and increased the informal labour market, and the displacement of large populations due to the long civil war. This meant that the gap between patients' expectations and the health system's capacity to meet them remained large, and so was the inequality in the access to care between those in the contributory and in the subsidized schemes.

The health system created by Law 100 has been heavily criticized precisely for the inequality created by a two-tier system that offered different packages depending on the scheme (contributory or subsidized) and the lack of frequent and comprehensive updates in the POS benefits basket, especially for those in the subsidized scheme. These were considered serious policy failures and political mistakes in the management of the Colombian health system.

Nevertheless, and without glossing over the government's wrongs and omissions, the tardiness in unifying the packages and the infrequent updates can also be understood as policy choices made under less-than-ideal conditions. As illustrated in the WHO Universal Health Coverage (UHC) cube (see Figure 5.1), the path of any health system towards UHC is made of difficult trade-offs, including the choice between extending coverage to include more people or increasing the list of services for those already covered.

The main direction that was chosen for the Colombian health system in Law 100 was clear. Despite the unsteady performance of the economy, there has been a significant increase in healthcare spending (see Graph 5.1) and in coverage

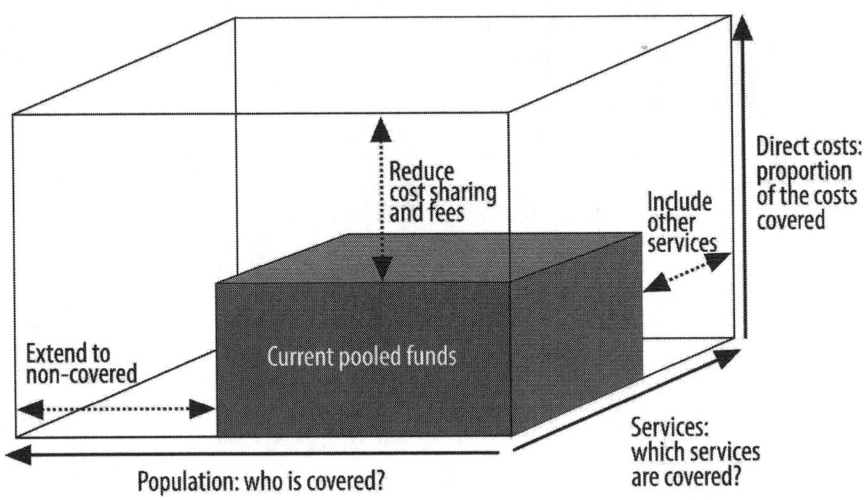

Figure 5.1 Three dimensions to consider when moving towards universal coverage. Reproduced from The world health report: health systems financing: the path to universal coverage, World Health Organization, Executive Summary – removing financial risks and barriers to access, Page xv, Copyright 2014.

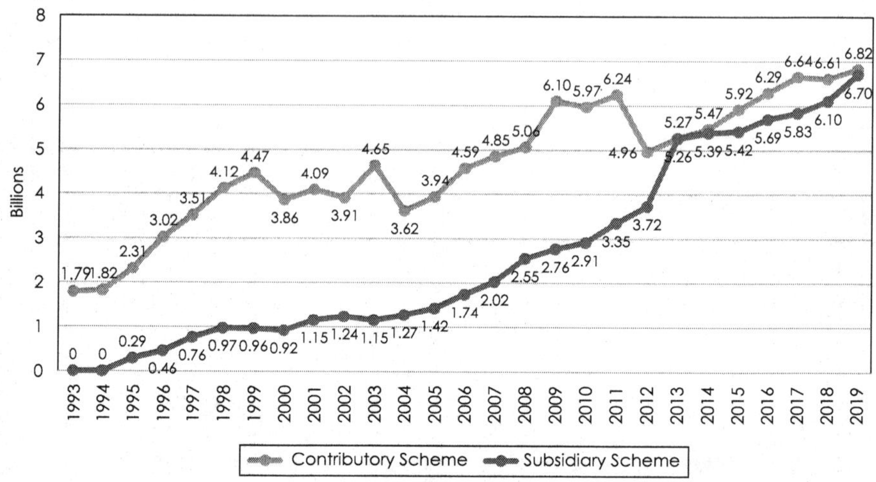

Graph 5.1 Healthcare expenditure by scheme (billions of constant 2019 USD$). Annotations: 1) Data from 1993–2003 was converted from 2000 constant COP$ to 2019 constant COP$; 2) Data from 2012–2016 was converted from 2016 constant COP$ to 2019 constant COP$; 3) The exchange rate for December 31, 2019 was $ 3,277.14. Sources: 1993–2003: Gilberto Barón-Leguizamón, *Cuentas de salud de Colombia 1993-2003*, El gasto nacional en salud y su financiamento (Bogotá D.C: Ministerio de la Protección Social/Departamento Nacional de Planeación, 2007), 102; 2004–2011: Ministerio de Salud y Protección Social, *Cifras financieras del Sector Salud, Gasto en salud de Colombia 2004-2011*, Boletín bimestral no. 2 (January–February, 2014), 19; 2012–2016: Ministerio de Salud y Protección Social, *Cifras Financieras del Sector Salud, Fuentes y usos de los recursos del Sistema General de Seguridad Social en Salud (SGSSS)*, Actualización 2016, Boletín bimestral No. 13 (2016), 9; 2017 (Subsidiary Scheme): Ministerio de Salud y Protección Social. Matriz de Continuidad (Bogotá: Ministerio de Salud y Protección Social 2020); 2017 (EPS Contributory Scheme): Ministerio de Salud y Protección Social, Informe al Congreso de la República, Cuatrienio 2014–2018, 2017–2018. (Bogotá: Ministerio de Salud y Protección Social 2018), 127; 2018–2019: Administradora de los Recursos del Sistema General de Seguridad Social en Salud - ADRES, Ejecución presupuestal URA (2020).

extension through the expansion of the subsidized scheme to progressively achieve universal coverage (see Graph 5.2).[11] In a context of limited resources, fast coverage expansion to include and protect more people within the health

11 Fernando Montenegro Torres and Oscar Bernal Acevedo, *Colombia Case Study: The Subsidized Regime of Colombia's National Health Insurance System*, UNICO Studies Series 15 (Washington, DC: The World Bank, 2013), 10.

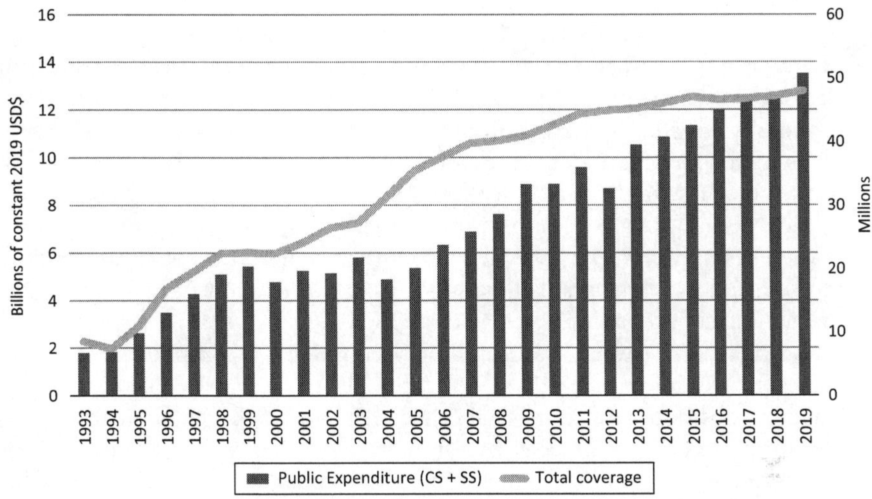

Graph 5.2 Public expenditure and healthcare coverage in Colombia. Annotations: CS – contributory scheme, SS – subsidized scheme. Source: 1993: Author's calculations based on Population Estimates of DANE and the percentage of the population in the Subsidiary Scheme which was retrieved from here: https://www.minsalud.gov.co/sites/rid/Lists/BibliotecaDigital/RIDE/VP/DOA/boletin-aseguramiento-i-trimestre-2017.pdf; 1994: Author's calculations based on Population Estimates of DANE and the percentage of the population in the Subsidiary Scheme which was retrieved from here: https://slideplayer.es/slide/1724547/ and https://www.minsalud.gov.co/sites/rid/Lists/BibliotecaDigital/RIDE/VP/DOA/boletin-aseguramiento-i-trimestre-2017.pdf; 1995-2018: Ministerio de Salud y Protección Social, Comportamiento del aseguramiento (Bogotá: Ministerio de Salud y Protección Social, 2020); 2019: Ministerio de Salud y Protección Social. Cifras de aseguramiento en salud (Bogotá: Ministerio de Salud y Protección Social, 2020).

system limits the fiscal space for including new technologies in the benefits baskets for the covered population.

The lack of frequent updates in the benefits baskets (POS) and the differences between the POS in each scheme are also frequently mentioned as one of the main causes of the enormous number of judicial claims for the funding of health treatments in Colombia. However, as will be discussed in the next section, this is likely an oversimplification of the relationship between litigation and the extension of POS packages. Right to healthcare litigation has also added to the financial pressure on the Colombian health system, which was a key obstacle for the Colombian health system to expand and unify POS while expanding coverage to the entire population. Litigation is a consequence but also probably a cause of the shortcomings in POS packages that left many health needs unmet.

Individual claims: *tutelas*

Colombia is second to none in the number of judicial claims for the funding of health treatments. The first court cases regarding access to health treatment started soon after the promulgation of the 1991 Constitution. In this constitution, there is no explicit right to health – except for minors (Article 44) – but health is a public service under the responsibility of the State and it is part of social security, which is a "right of all" (see Articles 48 and 49). Despite the absence of an explicit general right to health in the Constitution, since the earliest right to healthcare cases, courts have considered that they could order the health system to provide health treatments if there was a threat to the constitutional right to life, which includes the right to live with dignity.[12]

The connection between health and the right to life was consolidated through several cases – for instance T-491/1992, SU-111/1997, and T-1204/2000 – in which the Constitutional Court established that one of the requirements for a successful judicial claim for health treatment is the demonstration that a person's vital minimum, which includes a life with dignity and physical integrity, is threatened without access to the claimed treatment. This opened the door for the use of *tutelas* (an expedite writ created by the 1991 Constitution that allows individuals free of cost access to justice, and without the need of a lawyer, in cases of alleged breaches of fundamental rights) to litigate for basically any form of healthcare intervention.

Another crucial Constitutional Court decision was SU-480/1997. It confirmed the right of patients to access non-POS treatments (i.e. treatments that had not been included in the list of treatments to be covered by EPSs) when there is a threat to life and bodily integrity. Moreover, it established that if courts grant access to non-POS treatments against an EPS (the insurance company), then the EPS should be reimbursed by FOSYGA (the equalization fund). This meant that the financial burden of complying with the judicial decisions was transferred from EPSs to the public budget that would have to cover FOSYGA's deficit.

This rule created incentives for EPSs to encourage and assist patients to use *tutelas* to access non-POS treatments via courts so the companies could transfer to the public budget the costs of providing treatment.[13] It also reinforced the incentives for health professionals and providers to prescribe non-POS treatments instead of on-list treatments. Health providers saw reimbursement for non-POS

12 Everaldo Lamprea, *Derechos en la práctica: jueces, litigantes y operadores de salud en Colombia (1991–2014)* (Bogotá: Universidad de los Andes, 2015), 5; Corey Prachniak-Rincón and Jimena Villar de Onís, "HIV and the Right to Health in Colombia," *Health and Human Rights Journal* 18, no. 2 (December 2016): 161.

13 César Rodríguez-Garavito, "La judicialización de la salud: síntomas, diagnóstico y prescripciones," in *La salud en Colombia: Logros, retos y recomendaciones*, eds. Óscar Bernal, Catalina Gutiérrez (Bogotá: Universidad de Los Andes, 2012), 538.

treatments as an extra source of income.[14] The medical profession supported the possibility of patient access to non-POS treatments arguing that it protects their professional autonomy to choose the best treatment for their patients.

The pharmaceutical companies also saw in the *tutelas* the opportunity to sell their products without having to go through the regulatory requirements for POS inclusion, which included price regulation.[15] There is evidence of questionable practices such as agreements between EPSs and pharmaceutical companies to encourage judicial claims for drugs to be reimbursed by FOSYGA at overpriced rates, and the dissemination of dubious information about the inferiority of generics in comparison to patented drugs.[16] Pharmaceutical companies have also supported patient groups and charities that, through legal support and information campaigns, help patients to file tutela claims for treatments. This practice has raised concerns about conflicts of interest, particularly when patient groups promote access to brand-name drugs even when generic versions are available in POS.[17]

Colombian courts have decided in favour of patient claimants in the large majority of cases. About 80% of the *tutelas* for health treatment are decided in favour of patient claimants, a rate that has increased in recent years.[18] Judges tend to rely almost exclusively on the information provided by the patient's prescribing doctor, even if the prescription is based on limited scientific evidence or goes against the recommendation of scientific bodies.[19] If the decisions that are partially in favour of the patient are included, then the rate of success goes up

14 Ministerio de Salud y Protección Social, *Estructura del Gasto en Salud Pública en Colombia*, Papeles en Salud 17 (Bogotá: Ministerio de Salud y Protección Social, 2018), 31–32.

15 See Ursula Giedion, Ricardo Bitrán and Ignez Tristao, eds., *Health Benefit Plans in Latin America: A Regional Comparison* (Washington, DC: Inter-American Development Bank – Social Protection and Health Division, 2014), 101; Úrsula Giedion et al., *La priorización en salud paso a paso: cómo articulan sus procesos México, Brasil y Colombia* (Washington, DC: Inter-American Development Bank, 2018), 187; Ministerio de Salud, *Estructura del Gasto*, 32.

16 Rodríguez-Garavito, "La judicialización de la salud," 538; César Rodríguez-Garavito, "Constructing and Contesting the Global Intellectual Property Legal Field: The Struggle over Patent Rights and Access to Medicines in Colombia," in *Balancing Wealth and Health*, eds. Rochelle Dreyfuss and César Rodríguez-Garavito (Oxford: Oxford University Press, 2014).

17 Lamprea, *Derechos en la práctica*, 20–21.

18 Everaldo Lamprea, "The Judicialization of Healthcare: A Global South Perspective," *Annual Review of Law and Social Science* 13 (October 2017): 440; Defensoría del Pueblo de Colombia, *La tutela y los derechos a la salud y a la seguridad social 2018* (Bogotá: Defensoría del Pueblo de Colombia, 2019), 60.

19 Everaldo Lamprea, "Colombia's Right to Health Litigation in a Context of Healthcare Reform," in *The Right to Health at a Public/Private Divide: A Global Comparative Study*, eds. Colleen M. Flood and Aeyal Gross (New York: Cambridge University Press, 2014); Benjamin Hawkins and Arturo Alvarez-Rosete, "Judicialization and Health Policy in Colombia: The Implications for Evidence-Informed Policymaking," *Policy Studies Journal* 47, no. 4 (November 2019); Rodrigo Uprimny and Juanita Durán, *Equidad y protección judicial del derecho a la salud en Colombia*, Serie Políticas Sociales 197 (Bogotá: ECLAC/GIZ, 2014), 46.

to about 95%.[20] Moreover, the claims that did not result in a ruling ordering the funding of claimed treatment are mostly because the patient started receiving the treatment before the court decision was made.[21]

The judicial interpretation of the Constitution to include a judicially enforceable individual right to healthcare, the accessibility of courts via *tutelas*, the courts' inclination to decide in favour of patients, and the incentives created by EPSs' right to reimbursement, have all contributed to the drastic increase in the volume of litigation for health treatment since 1999. The number of *tutelas* has increased exponentially and steadily (except for a short period in 2009–2010) and went from around 21,000 in 1999 to over 207,000 in 2018 when it reached its peak (see Table 5.1).

Historically, most healthcare-related *tutelas* claimed access to drugs, although this has changed recently.[22] There have been claims for the funding of treatments that were not then included in the patients' respective POS (either in the contributory or the subsidized scheme) but also for treatments that were already included in POS. A report by the *Defensoría del Pueblo* (the institution responsible for the protection of fundamental rights in Colombia) shows that most *tutelas* have claimed access to treatments that are included in POS. Moreover, the proportion of litigation for POS-included treatments has been growing significantly in the last few years. It went from 56% in 2003 to 86% in 2019.[23] The most obvious hypothesis to explain why there are legal claims for treatments included in POS – which should be regularly available to patients – is that EPSs have been failing to offer the treatments in the compulsory package and that the administrative procedures for complaining against these failures do not work properly.[24]

However, when the analysis is restricted to drugs only, then the proportion of non-POS treatments increases.[25] This is relevant information because, as will be seen later in this chapter, drugs represent a very large share of what the health system spends on reimbursement for non-POS treatments. Moreover, the data from *Defensoría del Pueblo* has to be taken with a pinch of salt as there are treatments in the grey area, namely those about which there may be disagreement whether

20 Rodríguez-Garavito, "La judicialización de la salud," 526.

21 Defensoría del Pueblo de Colombia, *Informes "La tutela y el derecho a la salud"*, período 1999–2010 (Bogotá: Defensoría del Pueblo de Colombia); Defensoría del Pueblo de Colombia, *La tutela y los derechos 2018*, 86; Rodríguez-Garavito, 526.

22 Uprimny and Durán, *Equidad y protección judicial*, 25; Defensoría del Pueblo de Colombia, *La tutela y los derechos a la salud y a la seguridad social 2019* (Bogotá: Defensoría del Pueblo de Colombia, 2020), 181.

23 Defensoría del Pueblo de Colombia, *La tutela y los derechos 2019*, 177.

24 Rodríguez-Garavito, "La judicialización de la salud," 531.

25 Defensoría del Pueblo, *Informes "La tutela y el derecho a la salud"*, período 1999-2010; Defensoría del Pueblo de Colombia, *La tutela y los derechos 2018*, 136; Tatiana Andía, *El "efecto portafolio" de la regulación de precios de medicamentos: la respuesta de la industria farmacéutica a la regulación de precios de medicamentos en Colombia*, Nota Técnica IDB-TN-1507 (Washington, DC: Interamerican Development Bank, 2018), 9; Defensoría del Pueblo de Colombia, *La tutela y los derechos* 2019, 181.

Table 5.1 Number of health-related *tutelas* per year

Year	*Health-related* tutelas	*Annual growth %*
1999	21,301	–
2000	24,843	16.63
2001	34,319	38.14
2002	42,734	24.52
2003	51,944	21.55
2004	72,033	38.67
2005	81,017	12.47
2006	96,226	18.77
2007	107,238	11.44
2008	142,957	33.31
2009	100,490	-29.71
2010	94,502	-5.96
2011	105,947	12.11
2012	114,313	7.90
2013	115,147	0.73
2014	118,281	2.72
2015	151,213	27.84
2016	163,977	8.44
2017	197,655	20.54
2018	207,734	5.10
2019	207,368	-0,18
Total	**2,251,239**	

Sources: Defensoría del Pueblo de Colombia, *La tutela y los derechos a la salud y a la seguridad social 2018* (Bogotá: Defensoría del Pueblo de Colombia, 2019), 84; Defensoría del Pueblo de Colombia, *La tutela y los derechos a la salud y a la seguridad social 2019* (Bogotá: Defensoría del Pueblo de Colombia, 2020), 67.

they are included or not in POS. Studies using different criteria have found an almost equal proportion between POS-included and non-POS treatments and an even higher proportion of claims for the latter.[26]

The enormous number of *tutelas* for health treatment and the financial burden of complying with judicial decisions prompted several reforms aimed at reducing litigation. Law 1122/2007 established a rule that gave to EPSs' "scientific technical committees" – CTCs – the role of evaluating individual requests for the funding of non-POS treatments. The idea was that claims for the funding of non-POS treatments should be resolved at the administrative level, rather than by courts. CTCs (formed by EPSs' physicians and managers) decisions, however, were made under the shadow of *tutelas.* According to Law 1122/2007, if the

26 Uprimny and Durán, *Equidad y protección judicial*, 23.

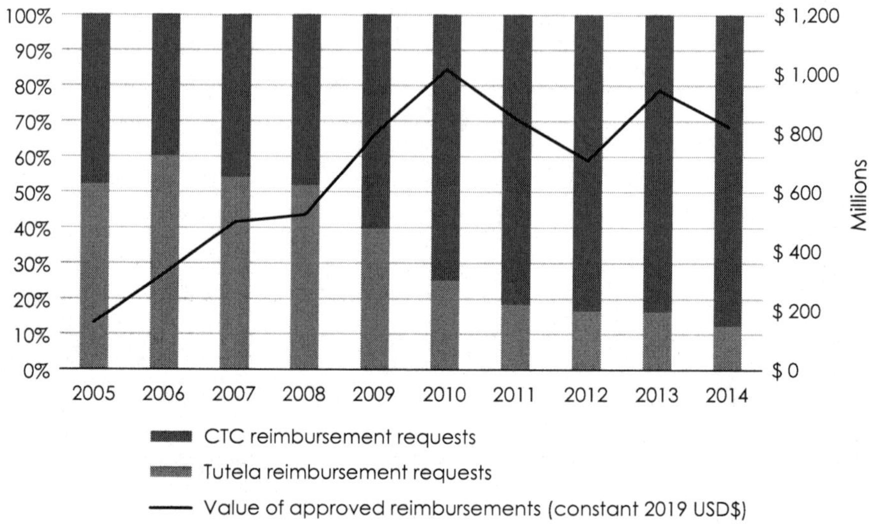

Graph 5.3 Evolution of approved reimbursements ($) and the composition of reimbursement requests. Source (evolution of expenditure): 2009–2014: Ministerio de Salud y Protección Social, *Cifras Financieras del Sector Salud*, Boletín bimestral no. 11 (July–August, 2015), 11; 2015: Ministerio de Salud y Protección Social, *Seguimiento A Recobros No Pos Régimen Contributivo – Resultados 2014 y 2015* (Bogotá: Ministerio de Salud y Proteccíon Social, 2016); 2017: La República, "Valor de los Recobros no PBS en 2017," La República, 2018. Original data source is from ADRES. Source (composition of expenditure): Jaime Ramírez Moreno, "The healthcare social emergency: from regulatory contingencies to citizen disappointment," Revista Gerencia y Politicas de Salud S9, no. 18 (February–June, 2010): 124–143; (2009–2014): Ministerio de Salud y Protección Social, *Cifras Financieras del Sector Salud*, Boletín bimestral no. 11 (July–August, 2015).

EPS, following a CTC evaluation, denied the funding of a non-POS treatment sought by the patient, but a court subsequently orders its funding, then the EPS would have to pay 50% of its cost (the other half would be paid by FOSYGA, the equalization fund). On the other hand, an EPS was entitled to full reimbursement by FOSYGA if a non-POS treatment was authorized by its CTC. In a context in which patients have easy access to justice and will almost certainly win in court, this system created incentives for EPSs to authorize the exceptional funding of non-POS treatments and then claim full reimbursement from FOSYGA.[27]

As a result, while the number of *tutelas* has decreased momentarily in the immediate years following this legislation, the number of reimbursements from CTC authorization has increased over time and surpassed those from *tutela*

27 Lamprea, "Colombia's Right to Health Litigation," 147.

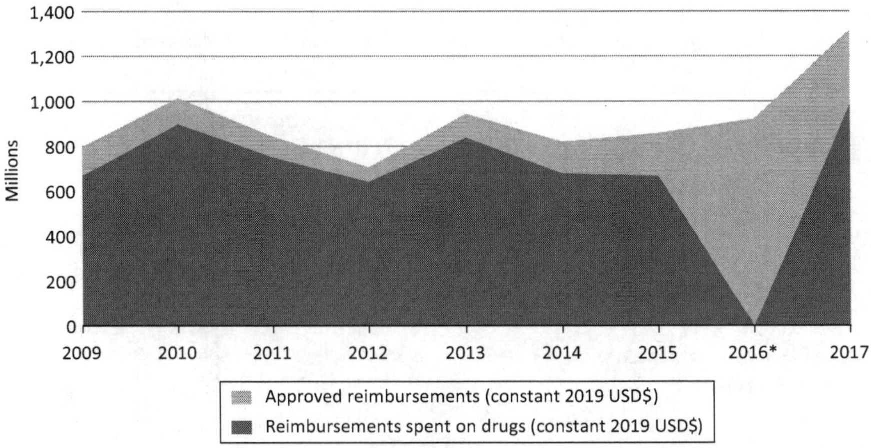

Graph 5.4 Total reimbursements and portion spent on drugs in Colombia. *Data on drug expenditure was not available for 2016. Source: 2009–2014: Ministerio de Salud y Protección Social, *Cifras Financieras del Sector Salud*, Boletín bimestral no. 11 (July–August, 2015), 11; 2015: Ministerio de Salud y Protección Social, *Seguimiento A Recobros No Pos Régimen Contributivo – Resultados 2014 y 2015* (Bogotá: Ministerio de Salud y Proteccíon Social, 2016); 2017: La República, "Valor de los Recobros no PBS en 2017," La República, 2018. Original data source is from ADRES.

orders. This was all concomitant to the increase in the amount spent by the health system on reimbursements for non-POS treatments (see Graph 5.3).

Moreover, most of the costs of reimbursement for non-POS treatments are due to the funding of drugs (see Graph 5.4), and a very large share of it is spent on a small number of high-cost drugs.[28] In 2011, for instance, 38 drugs accounted for almost 90% of reimbursements for non-POS interventions.[29] As in Brazil, it is a very small number of drugs that are responsible for most of the costs generated by claims for treatments that have not been included in the health systems' benefits baskets.

As already mentioned, the rules related to the reimbursement of non-POS treatments created incentives for the prescription and CTC authorizations of branded treatments despite the availability of cheaper generic versions in POS.[30] Moreover, the treatments reimbursed were very often of questionable efficacy and not cost-effective.[31] According to Sourdís and Rippol, 40% of the reimbursed

28 Giedion, Bitrán and Tristao, *Health Benefit Plans*, 88; Lamprea, *Derechos en la práctica*, xvi; Ministerio de Salud y Protección Social, *Seguimiento A Recobros No Pos Régimen Contributivo – Resultados 2014 y 2015* (Bogotá: Ministerio de Salud y Proteccíon Social, 2016), 23.

29 Sergio I. Prada et al., "Higher Pharmaceutical Public Expenditure after Direct Price Control: Improved Access or Induced Demand? The Colombian case," *Cost Effectiveness and Resource Allocation* 16 (2018): 2.

30 Giedion et al., *La priorización en salud*, 184.

31 Giedion, Bitrán, and Tristao, *Health Benefit Plans*, 87.

Table 5.2 Expenditure on pharmaceuticals and the proportion of expenditure on "non-pos" (reimbursement) drugs in relation to POS drugs and total drugs expenditure in Colombia

	Expenditure on pharmaceuticals in Colombia (in billions of constant 2018 US$)						
	2012	*2013*	*2014*	*2015*	*2016*	*2017**	*2018**
POS	0,79	0,93	1,01	1,19	1,29	1,37	1,45
Non-POS (reimbursement + out-of-pocket)	2,33	2,67	2,72	2,66	2,74	2,86	3,08
NO POS (reimbursement)	0,75	1,01	0,90	0,87	0,93	1,08	
Non-POS (out-of-pocket)	1,58	1,66	1,83	1,78	1,82	1,78	
Total	3,12	3,60	3,73	3,85	4,03	4,23	4,52
	The proportion of expenditure on "non-pos" (reimbursement) drugs in relation to POS drugs and total drugs expenditure (in %)						
Non-POS (reimbursement)/ POS	95	108	89	74	72	79	
Non-POS (reimbursement)/ total	24	28	24	23	23	26	

Own creation.
Source: Oscar Andía, "La regulación de precios de medicamentos: insuficiente y neutralizada. ¿Tiene alguna salida el sistema de salud colombiano?," *El pulso*, http://www.periodicoelpulso.com/2019_agosto/monitoreo-1.html
*Since 2017, the POS was replaced by PBS.

treatments were for non-approved use in Colombia and 30% were not approved by the FDA.[32]

The enormous impact of reimbursement for non-POS drugs on health expenditure can be better understood through the data on the market for pharmaceuticals in Colombia. Although the number of drug sales in Colombia changed little from 2012 to 2018, the amount spent on pharmaceuticals increased steadily during this period. More telling is the fact that reimbursements for non-POS drugs represent about 25% of the entire drug market in Colombia and has a size comparable to the expenditure on POS-included drugs (see Table 5.2).

In practice, easy access to treatments via courts or CTC created a situation in which the official benefits packages (POS) have not corresponded to

32 Catalina Gutiérrez Sourdís and Julián Urrutia Ripoll, "Hacia un sistema de priorización en salud para Colombia," in *La salud en Colombia: Logros, retos y recomendaciones*, eds. Óscar Bernal and Catalina Gutiérrez (Bogotá: Universidad de Los Andes, 2012), 403.

patients' healthcare entitlements, nor to the effective duties of the health system in Colombia. A very significant amount of healthcare spending decisions in Colombia has been made by courts or under their shadow. This has certainly promoted and facilitated access to some treatments, such as drugs that were able to bypass the regulatory and technology assessment mechanisms in the health system. However, it has also strained public resources and affected the financial sustainability of the health system, which has very likely affected the provision of other services.

As discussed in the previous section, the Colombian health system has consistently expanded coverage to almost achieve universal coverage in a relatively short period. This section shows that reimbursements via *tutelas*, and CTC working under the threat of *tutelas*, have forced public expenditure on non-POS treatments, mostly on high-cost drugs. The financial efforts to expand coverage and to fund non-POS treatments are comparable: the amount spent annually on non-POS drugs is equivalent to the cost of including almost 9 million people in the subsidized regime.[33]

The opportunity costs of reimbursements should not be overlooked. Frequent POS updates to allow the universal and regular provision of more services were competing for resources (and losing) against coverage expansion to include more people and against the reimbursements for non-POS treatments following judicial order or CTC decisions. It could be argued that the expansion of POS would have reduced reimbursements but, as will be seen in subsequent subsections, there does not seem to be evidence that expanding POS has led to less litigation or less reimbursement for treatments. Moreover, the financial strain caused by reimbursement has most likely resulted in more implicit rationing of treatments already covered by POS, which affects care at the point of use and may explain why there is still so much litigation for POS-included treatments.

There have been attempts to address the massive volume and impact of *tutelas*. This section mentioned the legislative reform to reduce litigation by giving more power to CTCs. Other initiatives from the government and from the Judiciary itself will be discussed in the sections that follow.

T-760/2008: the structural enforcement of the right to health

Apart from the thousands of individual *tutelas* (and also because of them), the Colombian Judiciary has also made judgments that included remedies of a structural nature intended to promote macro changes in the Colombian health system. The most well known is probably the Constitutional Court of Colombia (hereafter, the Court) decision in case T-760/2008.

33 Andía, *El "efecto portafolio" de la regulación de precios de medicamentos*. For comparative purposes, in 2017, 22.7 million people were affiliated in the subsidized scheme (https://www.minsalud.gov.co/proteccionsocial/Paginas/cifras-aseguramiento-salud.aspx).

In this case, the Court unequivocally recognized health as a self-standing fundamental constitutional right in Colombia. Thus, it does not have to be connected to a right explicitly listed in the constitution (e.g. the right to life) to be protected by courts. This was of symbolic importance, although this recognition had virtually no impact in practice as courts had never hesitated to find the connection between health and other rights when adjudicating concrete cases.

It is important to notice that the right to health was not recognized by the Constitutional Court as an absolute right. Building on the General Comment n.14 of the UN Committee on Economic, Social and Cultural Rights (GC14), the Court declared that health is a right of progressive realization within available resources, which implies (as the Court itself acknowledged) that not all individual claims connected to it can be judicially fulfilled. Nonetheless, according to the Court, and in line with GC14, the right to health creates an immediately enforceable minimum core and a duty to have at least a plan to progressively realize it.

The Court, however, departed from GC14 when it, in practice, recognized a judicially enforceable right to receive any potentially beneficial treatment for any serious health condition. The Court accepted that the health system may not be obliged to fund treatment in some limited circumstances (e.g. treatments for a purely cosmetic purpose) but it recognized a judicially enforceable right to any treatment that a physician considers necessary to prevent a threat to the patient's health, life, personal integrity, or dignity. Moreover, according to the Court, the fact that a treatment is not included in POS cannot be an obstacle for patients to access it funded by the health system. T-760 also stated that whenever a needed treatment is not in POS, this means a regulatory failure that breaches human rights and should be redressed by courts. Again, the Court is not innovating on this point as T-760 merely vindicated the interpretation of the Constitution that was already widely applied by Colombian courts in right to healthcare cases.

The most innovative aspect of T-760, however, is the attempt to reduce the high number of individual claims by addressing the "regulatory failures" in the health system that were perceived by the Court as the structural causes of litigation. The Court issued several structural remedies determining a series of obligations for multiple authorities. Some of these measures, although ambitious in scope, are examples of an "experimentalist" intervention by the Judiciary. That is, the judgment set policy outcomes but made provisional and flexible orders instead of specific and definitive commands; it emphasized transparency and inclusion of stakeholders in the implementation of the judicial rulings and; it gave the Court the power and the tools to monitor the authorities' compliance with the decision and to adjust its orders in light of the circumstances.[34]

34 Charles F. Sabel and William H. Simon, "Destabilization Rights: How Public Law Litigation Succeeds," *Harvard Law Review* 117, no. 4 (2004). See, also, César Rodríguez-Garavito, "Beyond the Courtroom: the Impact of Judicial Activism on Socioeconomic Rights in Latin America," *Texas Law Review* 89 (2011).

Some of these structural remedies are worth highlighting. First, the Constitutional Court ordered that the EPSs' scientific-technical committees (CTC) should have increased authority to decide on the access to all non-POS treatments, which was previously restricted to drugs only. The decision in T-760 also confirmed the rule that EPSs were entitled to receive full reimbursement from FOSYGA for treatments authorized through CTCs, and a 50% reimbursement if the treatment is denied by its CTC but later ordered via *tutelas*. It also ordered measures to facilitate timely and appropriate FOSYGA reimbursements to EPS for costs associated with non-POS treatments. The guarantee of EPS's "constitutional right" to reimbursement from FOSYGA for the cost of non-POS treatments was judged as fundamental for protecting the right to health.

The Court expected that an effective administrative procedure for accessing non-POS treatments would reduce the number of *tutelas*. Nonetheless, the decision in T-760 itself reduced the authority of CTCs when it established that a previous administrative claim to a CTC was not a necessary condition for filing a *tutela*. Moreover, if a CTC and the patient's treating physician disagree on whether the claimed treatment is necessary, the opinion of the latter shall prevail.

The Constitutional Court also called for the regular and comprehensive update of the benefits in the POS packages. It reiterated that the content of POS should be determined by the Executive branch considering the demographic and epidemiological profile of the population, the technologies available in the country, and the financial condition of the health system. The Court also established procedural requirements that should be respected when updating POS, such as transparency, the inclusion of stakeholders, and the use of evidence. Moreover, it ordered the government to bring more clarity to the POS content to address the problem of treatments in the grey area (i.e. when there is uncertainty about whether an intervention is included in POS or not). The Court also established that treatments in the grey area should be considered in POS if needed by the patient and connected to a POS-included intervention.

Furthermore, T760/2008 ordered the progressive unification of the POS packages for the contributory and subsidized schemes. The judgment considered that the indefinite separation between the POS packages in each scheme, despite the provision in Law 100/1993 that they should have been unified by 2001, was a breach of the right to health.

"State of emergency" in health and C-252/2010

In response to (and also in defiance of) T760/2008, the then president Álvaro Uribe (2002–2010) declared a "state of emergency" in the health system in December 2009 to allow himself extraordinary executive powers to implement reforms in the health system through executive decrees. The justification for this declaration was the more than US$1 billion deficit that the Colombian health system was running under at that time. The uncontrolled growth in reimbursements for non-POS treatments was mentioned as one of the main reasons for this huge deficit that, according to the government, threatened the sustainability of the health system and created inequality.

Rather than tackling the structural problems identified by the Court in T-760, the emergency measures focused on adding new funds to healthcare through sin taxes and also on limiting reimbursements for non-POS treatments. Although there was no explicit mention of restricting the use of *tutelas* to access healthcare, many at the time feared that this could be one of the consequences of the "state of emergency". Uribe had already unsuccessfully attempted to rule out the use of *tutelas* for socio-economic rights in 2002, soon after his presidential inauguration.[35]

This declaration of emergency proved to be very controversial and faced strong and vocal opposition from civil society, including activists, patient groups, social movements and the medical profession. Large demonstrations were organized in defence of the right to health and *tutelas*. The declaration of emergency decree (except for what related to sin taxes for funding the health system) was eventually declared unexecutable (*inexequible*) by the Constitutional Court in its judgment in C-252/2010 (April 2010). The Court considered that the need for emergency measures had not been demonstrated since the "crisis" in the health system was caused by persistent and well-known structural problems for which the government itself was responsible. The decision also reaffirmed patients' constitutional right to claim health treatments through *tutelas*.

Has T-760 achieved its aims?

The unification of the packages following the Court judgment in T-760 started in 2009, but the judges charged with monitoring the implementation of the decision were under the impression that the government of the then president Uribe was not genuinely interested in complying with it.[36]

Law 1438/2011 eventually completed the unification for all the covered population in 2012 and determined the biannual comprehensive update of POS packages. This legislation was passed under a new government that came to power in the previous year promising a deep reform in the health system, which included a unified and regularly updated POS.[37] Currently, the number of resources per capita in the subsidized and in the contributory schemes are very similar. This is certainly challenging from a public finance perspective given that more than half of the people are insured in the subsidized scheme and thus rely mostly on public funds.[38]

35 Lamprea, *Derechos en la práctica*, 87.

36 David Landau, "The Reality of Social Rights Enforcement," *Harvard International Law Journal* 53, no. 1 (Winter 2012): 226.

37 Arturo Alvarez-Rosete and Benjamin Hawkins, "Advocacy Coalitions, Contestation, and Policy Stasis: The 20 Year Reform Process of the Colombian Health System," *Latin American Policy* 9, no. 1 (June 2018): 42.

38 Alejandro Gaviria, *Strengthening Governments' Capacity to Discern Value: The Need to Address Technological Pressure on Health Expenditure*, Breve 13 (Washington, DC: Inter-

T-760/2008 is frequently praised in the literature as a good example of how courts should judge social rights because it addressed structural (rather than individual) problems and promoted institutional dialogue and openness. It is beyond the scope of this chapter to offer a full assessment of the impact of T-760, but it has certainly failed to achieve one of its central aims, namely, to reduce the number of *tutelas* for healthcare.

The reduction in the number of *tutelas* in the years immediately following T760/2008 was seen by some analysts as evidence that the structural remedies were effective in achieving the intended aim.[39] However, as seen, the number of *tutelas* started to rise again a few years later and quickly surpassed the numbers from before T760/2008 (see Table 5.1). This was accompanied by the increase in reimbursements during the same period. From 2010 to 2018, the amount spent on reimbursements increased 31% and currently represents almost 10% of the total spent on both the contributory and the subsidized schemes.[40]

Moreover, the financial situation of the health system, one of the concerns in T-760, has worsened. The deficit in the Colombian health system keeps growing, including the debts of ADRES (previously FOSYGA) with EPSs (around US$1.8 billion in 2019), and of EPSs with healthcare providers (over US$3 billion in 2019), which most likely result in implicit rationing and affect the quality of care at the point of use.[41] In 2020, the Colombian government has promised to zero out these debts using public funds.[42]

These results frustrate the expectation that the structural rulings in T-760 could have the enduring effect of reducing litigation and alleviating the health system's financial crisis.[43] Although frustrating, this is unsurprising. The Court expected that a more transparent, accountable, and fair system would reduce the need for *tutelas* to access health treatment. This would be achieved through regular, inclusive, comprehensive, and evidence-informed POS updates; stronger administrative mechanisms for resolving claims for treatments; and the unification of packages to reduce inequality. However, the Court failed to acknowledge that no health system, no matter how well-managed or organized, can afford every potentially beneficial health treatment for all, especially when the develop-

American Development Bank, 2016), 4; Jairo Humberto Restrepo-Zea, Lina Patricia Casas-Bustamante, and Juan José Espinal-Piedrahita, "Universal Coverage and Effective Access to Healthcare: What Has Happened in Colombia Ten Years after Sentence T-760?," *Revista de Salud Pública* 20, no. 6 (2018): 674.

39 See, for instance, Rodríguez-Garavito, "La judicialización de la salud," 519.

40 Restrepo-Zea, Casas-Bustamante and Espinal-Piedrahita, "Universal coverage and effective access," 675.

41 La República, "El déficit de la salud se financiará con deuda pública: Juan Pablo Uribe," *La República*, February 13, 2019, https://www.larepublica.co/economia/el-deficit-de-la-salud-se-financiara-con-deuda-publica-juan-pablo-uribe-2827267.

42 Defensoría del Pueblo de Colombia, *La Tutela y los Derechos* 2019, 18.

43 See, for instance, Audrey R. Chapman, Lisa Forman, and Everaldo Lamprea, "Evaluating Essential Health Packages from a Human Rights Perspective," *Journal of Human Rights* 16, no. 2 (2017).

ment of new technologies keeps widening the gap between patients' expectations and health systems' capacity to meet them.[44]

The reforms put forward in T-760 had the potential to improve fairness in priority-setting in Colombia. Yet, a serious discussion about priority-setting was foreclosed when the Court insisted that rationing decisions breach the Constitution and should be reversed by courts, leaving health authorities no real discretion to set priorities explicitly. This creates incentives for patients with unfulfilled health needs, which will continue to exist despite all reforms, to keep filing *tutelas* that will then be decided by courts based on limited evidence, ignoring the opportunity costs for the health system and without considering issues of distributive justice and procedural fairness for the allocation of scarce resources. In sum, the Constitutional Court tried to address the problem of the large number of *tutelas* by promoting structural changes in the system while ignoring that its interpretation and application of the right to health is one of the main causes of litigation. The Court would make the same mistake again years later.

Law 1751/2015 and C-313/2014

Law 1751/2015, which came into force in 2017, is also known as the *Statutory Health Law*. In Colombia, "statutory laws" regulate constitutional rights and are above ordinary legislation. The importance of Law 1751/2015 cannot be underestimated. First, and vindicating the Constitutional Court decision in T-760, it finally recognized in legislation the right to health as a fundamental right.

One of the main goals of this legislation, which also builds on T-760, was to establish the precise content of the right to health.[45] In its original draft, it established that (i) treatments should not be provided if there is no evidence of effectiveness, safety, and efficacy and (ii) that statutory legislation should be enacted to create institutional mechanisms to decide on the provision of treatments to be covered by the health system. In other words, there would be a negative list (what should not be funded by the health system for reasons of safety, efficacy, and effectiveness) and a positive list (what should be funded based on criteria and processes that were yet to be defined).

However, the Constitutional Court, when controlling the constitutionality of the draft bill that would later become Law 1751/2015, ruled in C-313/2014 that a positive list is unconstitutional and that the health system can only deny the provision of treatments that are in the negative list. This implies a duty to cover any health treatment unless it is explicitly excluded.[46] This decision implicitly

44 See Chapters 2 and 3.

45 Alvarez-Rosete and Hawkins, "Advocacy Coalitions," 45.

46 A negative list has existed in Colombia since Law 1450/2011 that was defined by a regulatory body (CRES) to determine the interventions that would not be reimbursed by FOSYGA. This list included interventions for cosmetic purposes, that had to be performed abroad, were experimental, or were not healthcare-related.

ruled out the adoption of any criteria other than effectiveness, safety, and efficacy for making funding decisions. In practice, this excludes the possibility of considering cost-effectiveness, budget impact, and distributive justice in priority-setting. The Court also declared that needed care should be immediately provided and cannot be interrupted due to economic reasons. Furthermore, the Court declared that the fiscal sustainability of the health system cannot justify the denial of efficient and timely provision of needed health services.

In sum, the Constitutional Court not only denied the health system the final word on the funding of health treatments, but it also limited the use of economic analysis for limiting or excluding treatment coverage. This decision frustrated the attempt in the original draft bill to make priority-setting more explicit and thus bring clarity regarding the rights of patients and the duties of the health system, as required by the Constitutional Court itself in T-760. It also rendered illegal a system like the one put forward in Law 100/1993 that attempted to move in the direction of explicit rationing by organizing treatment provision around positive lists.

As a result of this judgment, Law 1751/2015 established that the health system can only deny funding for treatments that are purely for cosmetic purposes, have no evidence of safety and efficacy or effectiveness, do not have marketing authorization, are experimental, or are only available abroad. Yet, the possibility of services under these categories being funded following a court order still exists.[47]

The Court, by modifying fundamental elements of the health reform, actually reinforced the status quo in the Colombian health system in a way that was very coherent with its precedents. That is, the funding of health treatment was not limited by POS packages and explicit rationing informed by economic, policy, and distributive considerations was practically never accepted by the Judiciary.

In 2016, POS was eventually replaced by the Basic Health Plan (PBS).[48] The PBS, instead of listing the treatments to which the covered population would be formally entitled, only determines the treatments the coverage of which will be funded through the insurance premiums paid by ADRES (previously, FOSYGA) to EPSs.[49] PBS is thus a benchmark to calculate the premium EPSs are entitled to receive per patient and does not work as a positive list that determines and limits the duties of the health system in terms of service coverage. As in the previous system, patients are still entitled to access treatments outside the PBS via judicial or administrative claims.

CTCs were also replaced by an electronic system (MIPRES) in which those who were prescribed a non-PBS treatment can apply online directly to the

47 Sentencia T-061/19, CCC, 14/02/2019.

48 See Resolution 5592/2015.

49 Law 1753/2015 extinguished the FOSYGA and its functions were transferred to the newly created the Administradora de los Recursos del Sistema General de Seguridad Social en Salud – ADRES.

Ministry of Health, which will then analyse the claim and make a funding decision based on the information provided by the patient's treating physician. The Ministry of Health, as expected, decide under the shadow of *tutelas* and the Constitutional Court's expansive interpretation of the right to health. Non-PBS treatments, authorized via MIPRES or ordered via *tutelas*, are fully funded by the public budget. According to the Ministry of Health, the amount spent on treatments outside PBS in 2016 was equivalent to 10% of the total cost of PBS treatments in the same year.[50]

In 2020, in an attempt to control the increasing deficits caused (at least in part) by reimbursements, the government created a system of "maximum budgets" (*presupuestos máximos*). Under this new system, apart from the premium EPSs receive per person registered with them to cover the PBS treatments, the EPSs will also receive from ADRES a fixed amount per person insured to cover non-PBS treatments. Therefore, instead of applying for reimbursement, EPS will receive a fixed amount to pay for non-PBS treatments. Reimbursements are now only available for a few treatments, such as orphan drugs for rare diseases. This new system of maximum budgets further blurs the distinction between PBS and non-PBS treatments from the perspective of patients, EPSs, and the government. This was a foreseeable (if not intended) consequence of C-313/2014 and Law 1751/2015.

There is no guarantee that the value of the "maximum budgets" received by EPSs will suffice to cover the costs incurred by them to fund all the non-PBS treatments required by patients. Therefore, the risk that this initiative may not reduce the financial imbalance in the health system, which causes implicit rationing and obstacles for patients to access quality care, cannot be ruled out. There is also the risk that it will lead to more right to healthcare litigation if EPSs start to outspend their "maximum budgets".[51]

In sum, the Court that required more transparency, participation, accountability, and evidence in the selection of treatments in T-760/2008 was the same that ruled out positive lists and explicit rationing in C-313/2014. Only on the surface, this is a radical change in its interpretation of the right to health. C-313/2014 was the logical conclusion of a case law that has consistently ignored that the Colombian system cannot meet all health needs and, therefore, foreclosed any serious discussion about fair priority-setting in healthcare.

Important lessons can be learned from the fact that the number of *tutelas* and the amount spent on reimbursements have increased significantly after all the reforms to address the regulatory failures identified by the Court. First, it is wrong to blame the regulatory failures for the existence of unmet health needs within a population. A well-managed health system can certainly meet more health needs by improving reach and quality while reducing waste, inefficiency, and unfairness, but it will not make scarcity disappear. Second, courts that foreclose explicit

50 Ministerio de Salud y Protección Social, *Estructura del Gasto en Salud Pública*, 18.
51 Defensoría del Pueblo de Colombia, *La Tutela y los Derechos 2019*, 17.

priority-setting while giving themselves the final word on the funding of treatment increase incentives for ad hoc individual decisions that allocate resources disregarding value for money and the opportunity costs for the health system and other users. Inefficiency and unfairness deteriorate the quality of the health system, which then triggers even more individual claims that feed this continuous cycle.

The lack of explicit priority-setting informed by scientific and economic analyses, and the constant increase in ad hoc allocative decisions, are regulatory failures in the Colombian health system that the Judiciary has helped to create and aggravate. What role, if any, can HTA have under these circumstances will be discussed in the section that follows.

Health technology assessment and priority-setting

In Colombia, discussions about fair priority-setting in healthcare are complicated by the fact that a significant share of public resources is allocated through ad hoc individual decisions. In concrete cases, courts have shown neither deference to nor serious interest in engaging with the priority-setting decisions made by health authorities. Rather than scrutinizing whether priority-setting was fair, courts have preferred to find that any unmet health need is a rights violation. As discussed earlier in this chapter and previously in this book, this sort of judicial intervention rules out from the start any meaningful institutional dialogue about fairness in priority-setting.

It is important to acknowledge that POS packages were not always regularly updated, and this has been a constant cause of complaint and critique by stakeholders and analysts. It is thus fair to say that many would have not received needed care if access was restricted to POS-included treatments only.[52] Moreover, the process for evaluating new technologies for POS inclusion started with very limited technical support and public participation. Updates were mostly focused on high-cost treatments based on unclear criteria and without attention to health technology assessment (HTA) or epidemiological information.[53] On the other hand, treatments considered cost-effective were not included and items that were already in the contributory POS took too long to be included for the subsidized scheme.[54] This went in the opposite direction of the original plan to unify the POS in each scheme over time.

The high number of *tutelas* and the activist attitude of courts in right to healthcare cases in Colombia are often explained by the infrequent update to POS packages coupled with the absence of an effective system for stakeholders

52 Sourdís and Ripoll, "Hacia un sistema de priorización".

53 Grupo de Economia de Salud, "Transición en el Sistema de Salud Colombiano," *Observatorio de Seguridad Social* 15, no. 30 (June 2015): 2.

54 Giedion, Panopoulou and Gómez-Fraga, *Diseño y ajuste*, 54. Claudia González, "Plan de beneficios de colombia."

to request the inclusion of a treatment in the package or to challenge its non-inclusion.[55] Accordingly, this lack of frequent POS updates, commonly blamed on the government's omission, explains and justifies judicial decisions ordering the funding of non-POS treatments to individuals. Courts are thus seen as a mechanism to redress the regulatory failures of the health system.

However, the relationship between the content in POS packages and courts is multifaceted. It is plausible to suppose that the infrequent update to POS was, at least in part, due to the opportunity costs of reimbursing treatments following CTC or judicial decisions.[56] For instance, until 2015, the contributory system, which has sustained continuous deficits, would have had a surplus for most of its existence if the amount spent on reimbursements was excluded.[57] A health system unable to make ends meet has a much narrower margin to expand its list of treatments, particularly when it is also trying to expand the number of people covered, as was the case in Colombia. It is not accidental that some cost-effective services (e.g. diagnosis and preventive care) were not included in POS while high-cost interventions (including experimental treatments) were funded via *tutelas* or CTCs. These health needs were all competing for the same scarce healthcare resources, but those that reached courts or CTCs through individual claims have gained priority.

Reimbursements via court rulings and CTC decisions have also affected decisions about what is included in POS. This happens indirectly when the inclusion of a treatment in POS following price negotiation is a money-saving alternative to reimbursing it following each administrative or judicial claim.[58] This was possibly the case of antiretrovirals for HIV/AIDS that were included in POS following a huge number of *tutelas*, although it is difficult to be precise about whether litigation was either necessary or sufficient for this outcome.[59] Unsurprisingly, the first POS update following T-760 focused on treatments frequently provided via *tutelas* or administrative claims that had a large impact on public funds.[60] The inclusion of treatments in POS can also be directly ordered by a court, which was the case of the drug *Zometa*, despite the contrary recommendation of the health technology assessment (HTA) body.[61]

55 Rodríguez-Garavito, "La judicialización de la salud," 537.
56 Grupo de Economia de Salud, "Transición en el Sistema de Salud Colombiano," 2.
57 Grupo de Economia de Salud, 13.
58 See Giedion et al., *La priorización en salud*, 162–163; Giedion, Panopoulou and Gómez-Fraga, *Diseño y ajuste*, 83; Uprimny and Durán, *Equidad y protección judicial*, 41; Prada et al., "Higher Pharmaceutical Public Expenditure after Direct Price Control," 2.
59 Prachniak-Rincón and Onís, "HIV and the Right to Health," 161; Ana C. González and Juanita Durán, "Impact of Court Rulings on Healthcare Coverage: The Case of HIV/AIDS in Colombia," *MEDICC Review* 13, no. 3 (July 2011); Uprimny and Durán, *Equidad y protección judicial*, 50.
60 Claudia González, "Plan de beneficios de colombia."
61 Acuerdo 263 de 2004: Por el cual se da cumplimiento al fallo proferido por el Consejo de Estado, Sala de lo Contencioso Administrativo, Sección Tercera, dentro del expediente AP 2212. See also, Giedion, Panopoulou and Gómez-Fraga, *Diseño y ajuste*, 83.

Either directly or indirectly, court decisions have forced healthcare expenditure based on access to courts rather than fair priority-setting considerations. Despite the obvious benefits to some groups of patients, this limits the resources for including other services that are arguably preferable from a public health perspective.[62] Litigation and the direction in which it steered the Colombian health system resulted in the increasing emphasis on curative treatments that can be individually consumed, particularly high-cost drugs, at the expense of public health measures. According to Everaldo Lamprea, there is a correlation between increasing litigation, increasing expenditure on pharmaceuticals, the stagnation of preventive care intervention, and the deterioration in key social determinants of health.[63] It is also noticeable that a very expansive interpretation of the right to healthcare that allows access to high-cost cutting-edge technologies has coexisted with persistent healthcare inequalities and the lack of basic healthcare services, particularly in rural areas.[64]

Correlation is not causation, and it is difficult to prove that, in a counterfactual scenario where courts were more self-constrained, more decisions would have been made informed by scientific and economic evidence and based on fair principles of distributive justice. However, it is plausible to affirm that courts have limited this possibility when pushing public health expenditure towards high-cost treatments, which have opportunity courts that are most likely born by those with less voice or whose needs have less visibility in society.

In recent years, and partially in response to the decision in T760/2008,[65] POS (and later PBS) updates have become more frequent, technically robust, and procedurally more inclusive and transparent. HTA has also been strengthened as a tool for priority-setting. The Institute for Health Technology Assessment (IETS) was created through Law 1438/2011 to further institutionalize HTA in order to set priorities in Colombia in a more transparent, participatory, and systematic way.[66] According to Aurélio Mejía, (former Deputy Director of HTA at IETS) and Héctor Castro (founding Executive Director of IETS), the institute was conceived as one of the institutional responses to a context of lack of trust in the health system, irregular POS updates, and the exponential increase in the number of *tutelas* for healthcare.[67] Yet, interestingly and worryingly (but similar

62 Ana González and Durán, "Impact of Court Rulings."

63 Lamprea, "Colombia's Right to Health Litigation," 149.

64 Joe Parkin Daniels, "Colombian Protest Over Inequalities in Healthcare," *The Lancet* 397, no. 10293 (June 2021).

65 Giedion, Bitrán, and Tristao, *Health benefit plans*, 94. Mejía and Muñoz, *Institutos de evaluación de tecnologias sanitarias*; Giedion et al., *La priorización en salud*; Hawkins and Alvarez-Rosete, "Judicialization and Health Policy in Colombia."

66 See Hector E. Castro, "Advancing HTA in Latin America: The Policy Process of Setting up an HTA Agency in Colombia," *Global Policy* 8, S2 (March 2017): 99; Defensoría del Pueblo de Colombia, *La tutela y los derechos 2018.*

67 Aurélio Mejía, Interview via internet with the author, April 9, 2020; Héctor Castro, Interview via internet with the author, April 10, 2020.

to what was found in Brazil), research from 2017 (six years after its creation) show that IETS is unknown to Colombian judges and its assessments have had no role in judicial decisions, which still rely mostly on the information provided by the litigants' treating physician.[68]

IETS is primarily responsible for producing evidence-informed recommendations regarding the inclusion of a technology in POS (now PBS). After assessing a technology, IETS makes its recommendation to the Ministry of Health, which will then make the final decision about its inclusion in the benefits package. According to Law 1438/2011, IETS should assess health technologies considering their safety, efficacy, efficiency, effectiveness, impact on mortality and morbidity, and economic impact. Economic analysis, in particular cost-effectiveness analysis, has a central role in IETS's assessments and in determining the POS (PBS) content.[69] Priority-setting considering economic and public health data is certainly not an innovation brought by IETS to Colombia. It was required by Law 100/1993, Law 1438/2011, and subsequent administrative regulations that determine that the POS update should consider scientific evidence, epidemiology, cost-effectiveness, and budget impact.[70]

The role of IETS goes beyond making recommendations about the inclusion of treatments in POS (PBS). Decree 330/2017 regulates the involvement of IETS in the creation of negative lists, namely the treatments that are not eligible for funding according to the criteria established in Law 1751/2015 (treatments for cosmetic purposes only, with no evidence of safety and efficacy or effectiveness, without marketing authorization, experimental, or only available abroad). IETS's assessments are also used for price regulation. Some drugs have their prices capped in Colombia and their maximum prices are determined by INVIMA (the regulatory agency responsible for the marketing authorization and the price regulation of drugs in Colombia) informed by IETS's assessments. According to Decree 433/2018, one of the methods used by IETS to set the maximum price is to compare the safety and effectiveness of a new technology with those of alternative treatments already available in the Colombian market. It can also consider cost-effectiveness and budget impact. Given that the health system can be obliged to provide any treatment that has not been explicitly excluded from coverage, the process for marketing authorization runs in parallel with HTA for some treatments selected by the Ministry of Health.[71]

Since the health system has very limited powers to set priorities and deny the funding of treatment, there is now an emphasis on strategies for price reduction

68 Leonardo Cubillos Turriago et al., *Estudio exploratorio sobre mecanismos de asistencia técnica en asuntos de salud y tutela en Colombia: grupos focales com jueces municipales y jueces de circuito de las ciudades de Bogotá, Medellín y Barranquilla*, Papeles em Salud 9 (World Bank/ Ministerio de Salud y Protección Social, 2017).

69 Instituto de Evaluación Tecnológica em Salud, *Manual para la elaboración de evaluaciones económicas en salud* (Bogotá: Instituto de Evaluación Tecnológica em Salud, 2014).

70 Giedion, Panopoulou and Gómez-Fraga, *Diseño y ajuste*, 38, 78–79, 84.

71 Mejía and Muñoz, *Institutos de evaluación de tecnologias sanitarias*, 44.

to control healthcare costs. They include price regulation for drugs, centralized public procurement to increase the health system's bargaining power, and incentives for price competition. Despite the reduction in the price of many drugs, the emerging data seems to indicate that price control policies have been insufficient to rein in the significant increase in pharmaceutical expenditure in Colombia.[72]

The health system's deficits are also increasing and threaten the financial sustainability of the Colombian health system, which results in implicit rationing through increasing waiting lists and the shortage of essential health interventions.[73] Moreover, the more frequent update of POS (PBS) in recent years has not stopped the number of requests for the reimbursement of non-included treatments (including via *tutelas*) from growing.[74] These requests are driven by new technologies and the health system, with limited powers to set priorities, does not seem able to keep up with the speed of medical innovation. The more frequent PBS updates have not stopped the *tutela* claims for on-list treatments either. It is actually the opposite: the proportion of *tutelas* for treatments that are included in PBS over the total of healthcare-related *tutela* claims has increased dramatically over the last years (from 56% in 2003 to 85% in 2019).[75] This confirms that it is an illusion that a health system can prevent rationing by simply expanding, on paper, the list of treatments a system must formally cover. Lastly, it has also been noticed that successful litigation is not a guarantee of access either as there are problems of lack of compliance with judicial decisions ordering the provision of treatment.[76] That means even court-ordered treatments can be rationed and, therefore, it is another illusion that more litigation can prevent healthcare rationing.

In sum, the improvements in how priorities are set by the Colombian health system, which includes the more frequent POS (PBS) updates and the institutionalization of HTA, were in part driven by courts. Yet, this occurs concomitantly with the fact that PBS and HTA are currently tools of very limited importance for actual priority-setting in Colombia, which results in part from the involvement of the Judiciary in the health sector over the last decades. What started in Law 100/1993 as an attempt to make priority-setting explicit through benefits packages and HTA is now a mostly implicit rationing system.

72 Andía, *El "efecto portafolio" de la regulación de precios de medicamentos.*

73 Ursula Giedion and Pamela Góngora, "Para decir 'SÍ' a la salud, Colombia debe aprender a decir 'NO'," *IADB Blog*, November 5, 2018, https://blogs.iadb.org/salud/es/priorizar-el-gasto-en-salud/; Aurélio Mejía, interview via internet with the author, April 9, 2020; Héctor Castro, interview via internet with the author, April 10, 2020; Ornella Moreno-Mattar, interview via internet with the author, April 10, 2020.

74 Prada et al., "Higher Pharmaceutical Public Expenditure after Direct Price Control," 2.

75 Defensoría del Pueblo de Colombia, *La tutela y los derechos 2019*, 177.

76 Defensoría del Pueblo de Colombia, *La tutela y los derechos 2019*, 120.

Conclusion

Right to healthcare litigation has had an enormous impact on the Colombian health system. It is much more than just the amount spent to comply with judicial decisions ordering the provision of treatment. Courts have affected the priority-setting of healthcare from micro to macro levels. Two main reasons are frequently given to explain (and, to a large extent, justify) this very activist role of courts. The first is the arguably incompetent, corrupt, sluggish, and "neoliberal" governments that were unable or unwilling to respond to society's demands for healthcare. The second, and connected to the first, are the severe problems of functioning, accountability, representability, and popularity in Colombia's democratic system.[77]

It is beyond the scope of this book to evaluate whether these characterizations of Colombia's government and democracy are generally accurate. However, and specifically concerning the Colombian health system, the argument that the political, managerial, and regulatory failures explain or justify courts' intervention in the health system is less compelling. Litigation indeed reflects some of the very deep problems in the Colombian health system, such as underfunding, inequality, corruption, and loose regulation. However, litigation has also aggravated some of these problems by allocating a vast amount of resources ignoring evidence and fairness considerations; forcing governments to fund high-cost drugs at any cost at the expense of the needs of those with less organization, voice, and visibility; encouraging questionable behaviour by EPSs, service providers, and the pharmaceutical industry; and hence probably causing more implicit rationing through delays, red tape, or lower quality in service provision.

It is important to reiterate that behind the language of human rights protection used by courts are policy choices with enormous distributive and institutional implications. These implications are less visible when the analysis of court decisions is limited to the rights-protective rhetoric and the beneficiaries of court decisions. However, they become apparent when the opportunity costs and the impact on the fairness of priority-setting in the health system are considered.[78]

The opposition between, on one hand, rights protective courts against, on the other, incompetent and irresponsible governments and politicians is an oversimplification (if not a mis-characterization) of the last 30 years of intense healthcare reforms and right to healthcare litigation in Colombia. Governments have

77 See Lamprea and García, "Closing the Gap"; David Landau, "Political Institutions and Judicial Role in Comparative Constitutional Law," *Harvard International Law Journal* 51, no. 2 (Summer 2010): 360; Hawkins and Alvarez-Rosete, "Judicialization and Health Policy"; Alicia Ely Yamin and Oscar Parra-Vera, "How do courts set health policy? The case of the Colombian Constitutional Court," *PLoS Medicine* 6, no. 2 (2009); Alicia Ely Yamin, Oscar Parra-Vera and Camila Gianella, "Colombia Judicial Protection of the Right to Health: An Elusive Promise?" in *Litigating Health Rights: Can Courts Bring More Justice to Health?* edited by Alicia Yamin and Siri Gloppen (Harvard University Press, 2011).

78 See Chapter 2.

successfully universalized population coverage and have made several attempts to make rationing explicit and priority-setting fairer. Courts, through individual and structural remedies, have insisted on the public funding of all services prescribed to any patient (with limited exceptions), basically making explicit priority-setting unlawful. Moreover, compliance with T-760, the most ambitious judicial intervention in the Colombian health system, depended to a large extent on the willingness of the government to comply with the structural orders set by the Court. The reforms that followed T-760 were as much compliance with the Court decision as they were a policy agenda set by President Manuel Santos.

Lastly, the number of *tutelas* and the value of reimbursements are still large and growing although some of the regulatory failures identified as the causes of litigation for health treatments have been addressed, such as the inequality between the subsidized and the contributory POSs (PBS), the lack of comprehensive and frequent updates to POS (PBS) packages, and an ineffective administrative procedure for making individual claims.

Positive lists (such as POS and PBS) created through fair priority-setting, which includes HTA, can help health systems maintain their financial sustainability while promoting fair access to healthcare. They make explicit *what* is being provided and, ideally, *why* and *how* these decisions are made. Colombian courts, however, have refused to accept that positive lists could work as floodgates to control the demand for healthcare. This has increased access on paper but, when rights are duties are de-linked from resource availability, the result is more implicit rationing.

PBS keep expanding and being updated but increasing coverage on paper for an already overstretched health system leads to rationing within the PBS services, as the high proportion of *tutelas* for PBS treatments show. The number of *tutelas* keeps growing for both PBS and non-PBS treatments, but this does not guarantee access either as health systems do not always comply with judicial orders. That is, choices are being made about which court rulings to obey. Despite the implementation of measures to control the price of health products, the deficit in the health system is increasing and will have to be covered by the public budget. This has huge opportunity costs, which are normally borne by other healthcare service users.

This should be read as a reminder of the perennial mismatch between the demand for healthcare and the capacity of any health system to meet it. Regulatory changes, administrative reforms and budget increases can help narrow this gap but they will not make it disappear (at least not in the foreseeable future). Tragic choices will still have to be made and every health system will have to set priorities. The real choice then is between setting them implicitly or explicitly.[79] To a large extent, courts speaking the language of rights have made the choice for the Colombian health system.

79 See Chapter 2.

6 England

From Wednesbury unreasonableness to accountability for reasonableness

In many jurisdictions, patients have been resorting to the courts to challenge health systems' decisions which deny them the funding of specific health treatments. English[1] courts are no exception to this phenomenon as they have been judging claims against healthcare rationing decisions for over 40 years. Even so, the impact of this sort of litigation on the National Health Service (NHS) has not received much attention from the social rights literature compared with the copious scholarship on the same phenomenon in jurisdictions such as Brazil and Colombia. This lack of interest is most likely due to the absence of a justiciable right to health written in legislation and a general perception that English courts usually refrain from interfering with discretionary allocative decisions in issues of social policy.

However, this lack of attention to the case of England is a serious lapse in this literature. The English case law offers a wide spectrum of responses to the dilemma between holding decision-makers in the NHS accountable and recognizing their expertise and constitutional role. England is also a jurisdiction in which adjudication has contributed to produce incremental, but significant and enduring, changes in the way the health system sets priorities. This chapter aims at filling this gap and, by doing so, will offer contributions not only to the literature on social rights but also to public law, medical law, and socio-legal studies scholarship.

The English case law on healthcare rationing can be divided into two stages. This reflects the move from the courts' very deferential "Wednesbury unreasonableness" approach in the first stage to the heightened scrutiny of rationing decisions in the second. The case law developed during the second stage offers a counter-example to a common perception among public law and human rights scholars that English courts are generally deferential to administrative decisions that involve discretionary allocative choice, particularly in issues of socio-economic

1 I use "England" to mean "England and Wales". All but one case analysed in this research were judged by the Courts of England and Wales and the National Institute for Health and Care Excellence provides guidance for health authorities in England and Wales.

DOI: 10.4324/9781315149165-6

policies.[2] This case law actually shows a judiciary that, although still sensitive to the financial and distributive issues facing policymakers, is not easily impressed by their constitutional authority and expertise, and that is willing to scrutinize procedural fairness, policy considerations, and the scientific evidence for rationing decisions.

It has been suggested in the medical law literature that this move from a very deferential approach to a heightened scrutiny of rationing decisions is the result of the increasing explicitness of rationing in the NHS. It is, according to this argument, the awareness of the existence, scope, and processes of rationing that led to the heightened judicial control.[3] Indeed, the change in the courts' approach to the judicial review of rationing decisions was concomitant to a move towards explicit rationing in the NHS. However, correlation is not causation and a more comprehensive analysis of the case law and of the process towards explicit rationing in the NHS, as proposed in this chapter, shows a more complex relationship between courts and priority-setting in England. It also shows that the more explicit rationing in the NHS cannot adequately explain the courts' increasingly heightened scrutiny and that it is rather the latter that helps to explain the former.

Litigation and the rigorous judicial scrutiny of rationing decisions are certainly part of a context in which rationing has become more explicit. Yet, courts have also contributed to creating this same context by making rationing more visible to the public ("explicit about what") and by requiring primary decision-makers to provide clear and better reasons for denying the funding of a treatment and to decide through more transparent procedures ("explicit about why and how"). The mutually reflexive relation between how courts decide claims related to the public funding of health treatments and how priorities are set in the NHS makes the case of England relevant for the scholarship that tries to understand the roles courts can play in health policies. It is also important for socio-legal scholars interested in understanding the impact of adjudication on bureaucracies.[4]

2 See Merris Amos, "The Second Division in Human Rights Adjudication: Social Rights Claims under the Human Rights Act 1998," *Human Rights Law Review* 15, no. 3 (2015); Jeff King, "The Justiciability of Resource Allocation," *Modern Law Review* 70, no. 2 (2007); Anashri Pillay, "Economic and Social Rights Adjudication: Developing Principles of Judicial Restraint in South Africa and the United Kingdom," *Public Law* (2013). See also Atina Krajewska, "Access of Single Women to Fertility Treatment: A Case of Incidental Discrimination?" *Medical Law Review* 23, no. 4 (Autumn 2015): 627.

3 See Christopher Newdick, *Who Should We Treat: Rights, Rationing, and Resources in the NHS* (Oxford University Press, 2005), 93; Keith Syrett, "The English National Health Service and the 'Transparency Turn' in Regulation of Healthcare Rationing," *Amsterdam Law Forum* 3, no. 1 (2011); Keith Syrett, "Impotence or Importance? Judicial Review in an Era of Explicit NHS Rationing," *Modern Law Review* 67, no. 2 (March 2004): 297.

4 See e.g. Marc Hertogh and Simon Halliday, eds., *Judicial Review and Bureaucratic Impact: International and Interdisciplinary Perspectives* (Cambridge: Cambridge University Press, 2004); Maurice Sunkin, "Impact of Public Law Litigation," in *The Cambridge Companion to Public Law*, edited by Mark Elliot and David Feldman (Cambridge: Cambridge University Press, 2015).

This chapter starts by examining English courts' case law in cases that challenge the rationing of healthcare interventions by the NHS. It will then analyse the process towards explicit rationing in the NHS highlighting how courts have contributed to making healthcare rationing more explicit "about what" and "about why and how". This chapter will argue that courts' departure from "Wednesbury unreasonableness" has led to the progressive incorporation of the conditions for "accountability for reasonableness", as proposed by Norman Daniels.[5] The conclusion discusses the lesson that can be drawn from the analysis of the relationship between courts and priority-setting in the NHS to understand the potentials, limitations, and paradoxes of judicial accountability in healthcare policies.

Judicial review of healthcare rationing decisions: from "Wednesbury" to a heightened scrutiny

This section will examine English court cases in which claimants challenged a rationing decision made within the NHS,[6] namely a discretionary decision to deny public funding for a healthcare intervention that results from the need to set priorities in the allocation of scarce resources.[7] An analysis of these cases allows the division of the English case law into two distinct stages. In the first stage, from the 1980s until the mid-1990s, the courts showed enormous deference to the decisions made by the NHS for epistemic and constitutional reasons. They considered medical/scientific assessments and allocative decisions to be beyond the reach of judicial scrutiny and thus that the courts should only intervene if the

5 Norman Daniels, *Just Health: Meeting Health Needs Fairly* (Cambridge University Press, 2007). See also Norman Daniels and James E. Sabin, *Setting Limits Fairly: Learning to Share Resources for Health*, 2nd ed. (New York: Oxford University Press, 2008).

6 Some authors exclude from the definition of rationing the cases in which funding is denied because a treatment is considered not efficacious or effective for a cohort of patients or an individual (see e.g. Jonathan Herring, *Medical Law and Ethics*, 6th ed. (Oxford: Oxford University Press, 2008), 63). The definition of rationing in this chapter does not exclude these cases. When it comes to an administrative decision about the provision of a treatment, it is normally difficult to disentangle reasons of effectiveness and efficacy from those of cost. In an ideal world where resources are unlimited, it would be perfectly rational to provide treatments which have low or questionable effectiveness or efficacy. However, given the reality of any health system, every treatment carries opportunity costs and thus treatments' effectiveness, alongside their cost, has a central role in priority-setting (see Trygve Ottersen et al., *Making Fair Choices on the Path to Universal Health Coverage – Final Report of the WHO Consultative Group on Equity and Universal Health Coverage* (Geneva: World Health Organization, 2014)).

7 This section covers all the judicial review cases on this topic found in the specialist literature; among the precedents cited by the courts; and in the Bailii, Westlaw, and LexisLibrary databases. Given the scope of the chapter, cases concerning service reconfiguration that do not directly result in the denial of funding for health treatment, the provision of social care, statutory interpretation, end-of-life decisions, compensation for medical negligence, and issues related to the commissioning of products for unlicensed use were not covered.

administrative decision was so unreasonable that no reasonable authority could ever have come to it.

In the second stage, from the mid-1990s onwards, the courts started judging in a way that, during the first stage, they had affirmed they should not. They have started scrutinizing reasons and procedures to an extent that authorities were required to act "synoptically", namely to demonstrate that they did the best possible job in gathering facts, evaluating alternatives, and articulating the values that had led to their decisions.[8]

It has been suggested that this change in approach is the result of a context in which healthcare rationing was becoming more explicit. However, this section argues that this change is better understood as the result of the incorporation of the language of rights with the related recognition of authorities' duty to provide reasons in English public law.

First stage: minimal scrutiny and "Wednesbury unreasonableness"

The first cases in which a decision not to fund treatment was challenged in courts were *Hincks*,[9] *Harriott*,[10] *Walker*,[11] *Collier*,[12] and *Seale*.[13] In *Hincks*, *Walker*, and *Collier* claimants sought a declaration that the delay in the performance of surgery they needed, due to insufficient funding and long waiting lists, was a breach of the respective health authorities' duty to provide comprehensive healthcare. In *Seale*, the applicant claimed that the health authority's policy to fund in vitro fertilization (IVF) exclusively to women between 25 and 35 years old was irrational because it was based on controversial scientific opinion and established a blanket cut-off point that took no account of individual circumstances. *Harriot*, which also involved funding for IVF, was a claim against an ethical committee recommendation to remove the applicant from the waiting list for assisted reproduction due to her past criminal convictions.

In *Hincks*, *Walker*, *Collier*, and *Seale*, the courts restrained themselves to a minimal level of scrutiny of the allocative choices and trusted primary decision-makers to make the best decisions. The court's reasoning was straightforward: resources are scarce, not all health needs can be met, and thus rationing is necessary; and health authorities are best able to do this. On this basis, the courts determined that they had no reason to review rationing decisions unless they were "Wednesbury unreasonable", i.e. so absurd or outrageous in their defiance

8 On synoptic decision-making, see Martin Shapiro, "The Giving Reasons Requirement," *University of Chicago Legal Forum* (1992).

9 *R. v Secretary of State for Social Services and Ors ex parte Hincks* [1980] 1 B.M.L.R. 93.

10 *R. v Ethical Committee of St. Mary's Hospital (Manchester), ex parte Harriot* [1988] F.L.R. 512.

11 *R. v Central Birmingham Health Authority, ex parte Walker* [1988] 3 B.M.L.R. 32.

12 *R. v Central Birmingham Health Authority, ex parte Collier* [1988], 151.

13 *R. v Sheffield Health Authority, ex parte Seale* [1994] 25 B.M.L.R. 1.

of logic or morality that no reasonable person addressing the question would have come to the same conclusion.

Under such a test, a public body is placed under no obligation to explain the decision reached unless the applicant for judicial review can make a case for its irrationality. As the Court of Appeal affirmed in *Collier*, it would be desirable for health authorities to provide reasons and justification for the allocation of scarce resources, but courts were not the forum for calling into question the health authorities' reasoning: "this court and the High Court have no role of general investigators of social policy and of allocation of resources."[14] Moreover, the courts refused to adjudicate between conflicting medical evidence and did not require authorities to consider exceptional individual circumstances to a general policy. Walker L.J., in *Hincks*, stated:

> This court can no more investigate on the facts of this case than it could do so in any other case where the balance of available money and its distribution and use are concerned. Those, of course, are questions which are of enormous public interest and concern – but they are questions to be raised, answered and dealt with outside the court ... I am wholly convinced that this decision of the health authority is not justiciable ... I deprecate any suggestion that patients should be encouraged to think that the court has a role in a case of this kind.[15]

In *Harriot*, there was no deep engagement with the reasons for refusing treatment either. Lack of resources was not an issue that emerged to the forefront of the recommendation to refuse the applicant funding for IVF, although it was mentioned that in a situation of scarcity "some individuals will have a more compelling case for treatment than others".[16] Schiemann J. admitted the possibility of a policy being reviewed by courts but mentioned the absurd and outrageous decision to refuse "treatment to anyone who was a Jew or coloured" as an example of an illegal policy.[17] The High Court also refused to find illegality in the fact that the applicant was refused the opportunity to establish that her case was exceptional and that the true reason for removing her from the waiting list had not been initially given to her.

Given the courts' self-restraining understanding of their role in reviewing rationing decisions and the difficulty of showing that a decision was absurd in its defiance of logic or morality, it is not surprising that in all the aforementioned cases the rationing decisions resisted judicial review.

14 *Central Birmingham Health Authority, ex parte Collier* [1988], 151.
15 *Secretary of State for Social Services and Ors* [1980] 1 B.M.L.R 93.
16 *Ethical Committee of St. Mary's Hospital* [1988] F.L.R. 512, 514.
17 *Ethical Committee of St. Mary's Hospital* [1988] at 519.

A turning point in the courts' approach was *Child B*.[18] A child suffering from cancer had received many courses of treatment all of which failed to produce enduring results. On this basis, the doctors in the UK concluded that no further treatment could be usefully applied. However, Child B's father found an expert in the US willing to try another course of chemotherapy. The child's doctors disagreed on the basis that the treatment would cause unnecessary suffering for the child and that the chances of success were very low given the experimental nature of the treatment. Based on the medical evidence and the cost of the treatment, the local health authority decided not to fund it.

The child's family sought judicial review and the decision not to fund another course of chemotherapy was quashed by the High Court for being "Wednesbury unreasonable". The High Court judged that (1) the health authority failed to have regard for the wishes of the patient; (2) the treatment should not be considered experimental given the estimates of success presented by the American practitioners; (3) even though the prospects of success were small, the patient should enjoy a worthwhile chance of life; (4) the cost of the treatment was overestimated by the health authority; (5) the argument concerning the lack of resources consisted only of grave and well-rounded generalities; (6) when life is at risk, health authorities must do more than toll the bell of tight resources and must explain the priorities that have led them to decline to fund the treatment; and (7) in spite of the discretion given to a public authority, it should not be permitted to perpetrate an infringement of rights unless a substantial objective justification on public interest grounds could be demonstrated.

The innovations in this decision cannot be underestimated. Although still applying the language of "Wednesbury unreasonableness", the case was analysed in a way that courts had explicitly affirmed in earlier decisions that they would not: questioning the health authority's medical/scientific appraisal of the treatment; transferring the burden of proof to health authorities who were expected to provide reasons for not providing the treatment; considering that the fact that resources are scarce does not justify the denying of treatment for costs reasons only; affirming that the patient's individual circumstances should be taken into consideration; and establishing that the health authorities' level of discretion was narrower in such a case, given the important right that was being jeopardized.

The Court of Appeal, however, overturned this decision. It stated that the court was not the arbiter of the merits of cases and that no real evidence was needed to satisfy a court that no health authority was in a position to purchase everything it would wish in the interests of patients. Accordingly, courts could not shut their eyes to the real world in which health authorities were constantly pressed to make ends meet and were legally charged with making difficult and agonizing decisions. Therefore, courts could not be expected to scrutinize or review the priority-setting decisions made by health authorities unless the

18 *R. v Cambridge Health Authority, ex parte* B [1995] 2 All E.R. 129; [1995] 1 W.L.R. 898.

authorities had acted in a way that exceeded their powers or unreasonably in the sense of being absurd:

> Difficult and agonizing judgements have to be made as to how a limited budget is best allocated to the maximum advantage of the maximum number of patients. This is not a judgement which the court can make ... it is not something that a health authority can be fairly criticized for not advancing before the court.[19]

Notwithstanding the decision of the Court of Appeal, which reaffirmed the self-restraint approach that had prevailed until then, the decision of the High Court in *Child B* is a landmark. Not only was it the first case in which a healthcare rationing decision was quashed, but it also inaugurated a legal reasoning and a heightened level of scrutiny that have become prevalent in the English case law ever since.

Second stage: heightened scrutiny of reasons and procedures

After *Child B*, and despite the Court of Appeal's decision in this case, the principle that a rationing decision will withstand judicial review simply if it is not absurd was replaced by the requirement that authorities take all the relevant considerations into account when limiting access to a health treatment. In this second stage, the courts have started to require administrative decisions to be based on explicit and rational reasons, and made through transparent and fair processes. In addition, as will be shown in this section, the courts have become increasingly demanding and stringent when assessing these reasons and processes.

In *Coughlan*,[20] the decision to close a hospital where a disabled patient was living and move her to another location for financial and clinical reasons was quashed. The Court of Appeal considered, among other things, the assessment of the patient's individual circumstances, the legitimate expectation of the patient who had been promised she would be allowed to reside in that hospital "for life", whether there was an overriding public interest that would justify frustrating this expectation, and if alternative placement that would meet her needs had been identified. As affirmed by Lord Woolf: "In drawing the balance of conflicting interests the court will not only accept the policy change without demur but will pay the closest attention to the assessment made by the public body itself."[21]

In *Fisher*,[22] a treatment for multiple sclerosis was denied by reasons of lack of funds and insufficient evidence of its efficacy and cost-effectiveness, in spite of

19 *R. v Cambridge Health Authority, ex parte* B [1995] 1 W.L.R. 898, 906, per Sir Thomas Bingham.

20 *R. v North and East Devon Health Authority, ex parte Coughlan* [2001] Q.B. 213.

21 *R. v North and East Devon Health Authority, ex parte Coughlan*, para 89.

22 *R. v North Derbyshire Health Authority, ex parte Fisher* [1997] 8 Med L.R. 327.

an NHS circular asking health authorities to develop and implement arrangements to prescribe it. The High Court quashed the decision on the basis that the defendant authority had failed to give clear and rational reasons for not complying with the national policy and that it established a blanket ban that did not take into account the patient's individual circumstances. In *Elizabeth Rose*, the decision not to fund oocyte cryopreservation for a patient preparing for a cancer treatment that would make her infertile was quashed on the grounds that the commissioning group has a duty to give a reasoned explanation for why they are departing from a non-binding NICE guideline recommending the intervention in her case.[23]

A blanket ban on a treatment was also the reason for quashing a decision in *A, D and G*,[24] in which there was a challenge against a policy that gave gender reassignment surgery low priority for funding. Despite the local health authority policy mentioning that exceptional circumstances would be considered, the Court of Appeal found that the manner of considering these exceptional cases actually amounted to a blanket policy. The Court of Appeal also challenged the authorities' scientific assessment and concluded that they had not engaged with the existing evidence that this treatment was effective.

The prohibition of a blanket ban and the duty of authorities to take into account the patients' individual (and possibly exceptional) circumstances were reaffirmed in several subsequent cases in which decisions not to fund drugs for reasons of cost and lack of evidence were judged unlawful.[25] In these cases, courts accepted that a drug may not be funded for priority-setting reasons, but such a policy would only be accepted as reasonable if grounded on clear and rational reasons and envisaged exceptional circumstances.

Moreover, the concept of exceptionality cannot be too narrow to the extent that no case would be exceptional. In *Rogers*,[26] the Court of Appeal quashed a policy not to fund Herceptin except in exceptional clinical circumstances, which had been upheld by the High Court, on the grounds that the circumstances that would make a case exceptional were not clear. In *Otley*,[27] *Ross*,[28], *S*,[29] and *SB*,[30] based on divergent expert opinions, the courts also challenged the health authori-

23 *R. v Thanet Clinical Commissioning Groups, ex parte Elizabeth Rose* [2014] EWHC 1182.

24 *R. v North West Lancashire Health Authority, ex parte A, D and G* [1999] All E.R. (D) 911.

25 *R. v Swindon NHS Primary Care Trust, Secretary of State for Health, ex parte Rogers* [2006] EWCA. Civ 392; *R. v Bromley NHS Primary Care Trust, ex parte Gordon* [2006] EWCA Civ 392; *R. v Barking & Dagenham NHS PCT, ex parte Otley* [2007] EWHC 1927; *R. v West Sussex Primary Care Trust, ex parte Ross* [2008] EWHC B15; *R. v Salford Primary Care Trust, ex parte Murphy* [2008] EWHC 1908; *S (a child) v NHS England* [2016] EWHC 1395.

26 *Swindon NHS Primary Care Trust, Secretary of State for Health, ex parte Rogers* [2006] EWCA Civ 392.

27 *Barking & Dagenham NHS PCT, ex parte Otley* [2007] EWHC 1927.

28 *West Sussex Primary Care Trust, ex parte Ross* [2008] EWHC B15.

29 *S (a child) v NHS England* [2016] EWHC 1395.

30 *SB v NHS England [2017]* EWHC 2000.

ties' analysis of the scientific evidence and their conclusion that the claimant's case was not exceptional. In *Murphy*,[31] even though none of the factors brought by the patient could make her case exceptional according to the policy then in force, the court quashed the decision on the grounds that authorities had evaluated each of the factors separately rather than holistically ("in the round").

In the most recent case, the Court of Appeal also challenged the clinicians' assessment of the evidence that led to the conclusion that a child was not eligible to receive treatment with a high-cost drug (Nusinersen) for a rare condition.[32] After considering the clinical evidence and factual elements of the case, the court reached the conclusion that the decision not to fund the drug was irrational ("so unreasonable that a reasonable decision-maker, properly directing herself in law, could not have made it")[33] although it was made by two medical experts and upheld by the High Court. Interestingly, the needs of the child were also central for this decision, echoing the principle set by the High Court in *Child B* that the more a decision will impact a person's life, the more intense the judicial scrutiny should be:

> the court should be conscious when determining the appropriate intensity of review [...] of the considerable impact on this little girl of the decision. [...] [Nusinersen] has the potential significantly to delay the inevitable day when she will be rendered immobile. There is no other treatment available for her.[34]

Apart from cases against decision-makers at the local level, there have also been legal challenges to health technology appraisals made by the now-called National Institute for Health and Care Excellence (NICE) that did not recommend the funding of treatments in the NHS. In these judgments, the courts gave special attention to the fairness of the procedure through which a decision was made, which included discussions on whether NICE had the duty to release to interested parties a fully executable version of the economic model used to calculate cost-effectiveness,[35] and on the alleged bias or conflict of interest of the experts chosen by the institute to carry out the appraisals.[36]

The issue of the appropriate intensity of judicial scrutiny of the decisions made by NICE and of the reasons given by the institute was raised in *Servier*.[37] The

31 *Salford Primary Care Trust, ex parte Murphy* [2008] EWHC 1908.

32 *Basma v Manchester University Hospitals NHS Foundation Trust & Anor* [2021] EWCA Civ 278.

33 *Basma v Manchester University Hospitals NHS Foundation Trust & Anor*, para 102.

34 *Basma v Manchester University Hospitals NHS Foundation Trust & Anor*, para 83.

35 *R. v NICE, ex parte Eisai Ltd.* [2007] EWHC 1941; *R. v NICE, ex parte Bristol-Myers Squibb Pharmaceuticals Ltd.* [2009] EWHC 2722; *R. v NICE, ex parte Servier Laboratories Ltd.* [2010] EWCA Civ 346.

36 See also *R. v NICE, ex parte Fraser and Another* [2009] EWHC 452.

37 *NICE, ex parte Servier Laboratories Ltd.* [2010] EWCA Civ 346.

High Court judged that a NICE decision not to recommend a new treatment for osteoporosis had taken into consideration all the relevant data, that the reasons were explained in a sufficient, reasonable, and intelligible way, and that it was for NICE to decide on the weight to be attributed to the evidence brought.[38] The Court of Appeal disagreed with the High Court and decided that NICE should make a fresh decision. NICE had decided to reject part of the data presented by the product manufacturer due to its low scientific quality, but the Court of Appeal considered that the scientific reasons for this decision were "inadequately explained" by NICE.

There have been some exceptions to the heightened scrutiny approach of the second stage. In *Pfizer*,[39] the Court of Appeal overturned a High Court decision that had quashed the Department of Health policy restricting the funding of Viagra in the NHS. The High Court had concluded that the lack of sufficient and transparent reasons for this policy was a violation of domestic and EU law.[40] However, the Court of Appeal, echoing the judicial reasoning that had dominated the landscape in the first stage, judged that the allocation of resources was a political issue and that it would be inappropriate for each administrative decision to be subject to the detailed scrutiny and exposition of the merits and economics of particular medical products. The higher status of the defendant in this case – the Secretary of State for Health – may explain why its decision was considered "political" by the court and thus attracting greater judicial deference if compared to decisions made by NICE or at the local level. This could also explain why the majority of the Supreme Court in *A and B*[41] was not stringent in its assessment of the reasons given by the Secretary of State for Health for not making provisions to enable women resident in Northern Ireland to access abortion services in England free of charge under the NHS.[42]

Another exception, although for a different reason, was the High Court decision in *Watts*.[43] This case concerned the right of a patient under European Union Law to claim reimbursement from the NHS of a treatment performed abroad. The High Court, departing from other judgments involving the denial of funding, conceptualized the case from the perspective of individual rights and needs rather than service provision.[44] It concluded that considerations of a purely economic

38 See also *NICE, ex parte Fraser and Another* [2009] EWHC 452.

39 *R. v Secretary of State for Health, ex parte Pfizer* [2002] EWCA Civ 1566. See also *R. v North Staffordshire Primary Care Trust, ex parte Condliff* [2011] EWCA Civ 910, in which the Court of Appeal upheld the decision of the health authority made solely on the basis of the existing medical evidence and did not take into account patients' social circumstances.

40 Council Directive 89/105/EEC of 21 December 1988 relating to the transparency of measures regulating the prices of medicinal products for human use and their inclusion in the scope of national health insurance systems [1988] OJ L 40, Art. 7.

41 *R. v Secretary of State for Health, ex parte A and B* [2017] UKSC 41.

42 See, also, *BA v Secretary of State for Health and Social Care* [2018] EWCA Civ 2696.

43 *R. v Secretary of State for Health, ex parte Watts* [2003] EWHC 2228 (Adm).

44 See Jonathan Montgomery, "Law and the Demoralization of Medicine," Legal Studies 26, no. 2 (2006): 198.

nature could not itself restrict patients' right to have medical services provided abroad and rejected as "speculation unnourished by common sense"[45] that this would put at risk the public system's capacity to work efficiently. The Court of Appeal deferred the judgment on this case until a decision of the European Court of Justice, but raised concerns about the High Court judgment and questioned whether a court was in the position to conclude that attributing to the NHS the duty to fund treatments abroad would not have an economic impact or undermine the waiting lists system.[46]

In sum, an almost linear narrative can be told about how the case law has evolved from a very self-restrained review of healthcare rationing decisions towards one in which courts have constantly added new boxes that authorities had to tick for a rationing decision to withstand judicial review.[47] The assumption that primary decision-makers in the NHS are doing their work properly, and that the courts should not scrutinize their choices, has ceased to be prevalent among judges. Courts during the second stage have judged in a way that during the first stage they explicitly and unequivocally affirmed they should not: heightening the scrutiny of the reasons and procedures for policies, challenging scientific and clinical assessments based on competing expert opinions, requiring that exceptional individual circumstances be considered, and questioning the weighing up of the competing interests made by primary decision-makers. In some cases, they have confronted budgetary issues and considered, in one case, that the provision of a drug would require the allocation of relatively small resources and would not put at risk the interest of other patients[48] and, in another, that the respondent authority had funds available but decided not to use them.[49] This heightened judicial scrutiny led to several rulings against the NHS (see Figure 6.1). In a few cases, a quashing order was followed by the requirement of the immediate provision of the treatment claimed by the patient.[50]

Explaining the departure from "Wednesbury unreasonableness"

It has been argued in the medical law literature that the move from the very deferential classic "Wednesbury unreasonableness" to a heightened scrutiny of

45 *Secretary of State for Health, ex parte Watts* [2003] EWHC 2228 (Adm) 148.

46 *R. v Secretary of State for Health, ex parte Watts* [2004] EWCA Civ 166.

47 See also Keith Syrett, "Rationing in the Courts: England," chap. 6 in *Law, Legitimacy and the Rationing of Health Care: A Contextual and Comparative Perspective* (Cambridge University Press, 2007); Ellie Palmer, *Judicial Review, Socio-Economic Rights and the Human Rights Act* (Oxford: Hart, 2007), 209; Newdick, *Who Should We Treat*, 93; Syrett, "English National Health Service," 107.

48 *Barking & Dagenham NHS PCT, ex parte Otley* [2007] EWHC 1927.

49 *North Derbyshire Health Authority, ex parte Fisher* [1997] 8 Med L.R. 327.

50 *West Sussex Primary Care Trust, ex parte Ross* [2008] EWHC B15; *Bromley NHS Primary Care Trust, ex parte Gordon* [2006] *EWCA Civ 392; Barking & Dagenham NHS PCT, ex parte Otley* [2007] EWHC 1927.

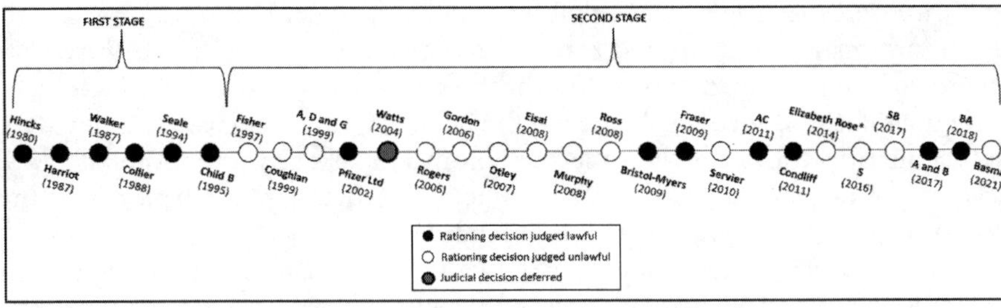

* The CCG decision for the claimant was upheld, although the policy was considered unlawful.

Figure 6.1 Timeline – judicial review of healthcare rationing decisions. Source: own creation.

rationing decisions can be explained by the increasing explicitness in the way healthcare is rationed in the NHS.[51] According to this argument, the more people know that they are being denied potentially beneficial treatment, the more they will litigate; and the more transparent the reasons and processes for priority-setting are, the stricter the judicial scrutiny will be. The following excerpt by Syrett illustrates this position well:

> Given that the environment in which rationing takes place is significantly altered from that which existed in the late 1980s – and, in particular, that awareness of the existence, scope and processes of rationing is much greater as a consequence of a general shift towards explicitness – such a transformation in judicial attitudes is perhaps unsurprising.[52]

If this argument is correct, then the case of England would have confirmed the hypothesis that explicit rationing "opens the door to attack" from dissatisfied patients and their lawyers and leads to more and more successful litigation.[53] However, by analysing the case law chronologically it is possible to observe that it is actually the rigorous judicial scrutiny of rationing decisions that have driven the NHS to be more explicit about the reasons and procedures leading to the denial of treatment, rather than the other way round.

In most cases in which decisions not to fund treatments were judged unlawful, decision-makers were unable to meet the requirements of the courts, which includes to give clear and rational reasons for a complete ban on a treatment; to take into account exceptional circumstances and analyse them as courts were

51 See Newdick, *Who Should We Treat*, 93; Syrett, "English National Health Service"; Syrett, "Impotence or Importance?" 297.

52 Syrett, "English National Health Service," 108.

53 This hypothesis was discussed by Daniels and Sabin, *Setting Limits Fairly*, 50; Daniels, *Just Health*, 122.

expecting them to do; to thoroughly consider the relevant conflicting scientific evidence; to explain the departure from national guidelines, and; to disclose relevant information to interested parties. As the case law shows, courts were willing to add new requirements to the checklist which authorities had to follow to have their decisions upheld. These requirements, as will be discussed below, were subsequently incorporated into the decision-making process at the administrative level to avoid future litigation, to discharge the burden of proof expected by the courts, or simply to comply with a judicial decision.

Given that explicit rationing cannot adequately explain the transformation in the way courts review rationing decisions, this section develops an alternative hypothesis, namely that judges' changing attitude towards healthcare rationing was part of a broader change in the English public law culture and practice that led to an increase in the courts' assertiveness with regard to their own role in judicial review in general.[54]

Traditionally, the English courts have played a marginal political role and avoided interference in "policy questions", probably due to the absence of a written Constitution and mechanisms for the control of constitutionality, and to a strong attachment to the principle of separation of powers. They had refused, on the whole, to substitute their own decisions on the merit of a policy for those of the primary decision-maker unless an administrative decision was "Wednesbury unreasonable".[55] The courts' very deferential approach when judging healthcare rationing cases before *Child B* should be understood within this broader context.

However, and particularly from the 1990s onwards, the growing use of the courts to challenge public authorities' decisions was noted, and it was certainly not restricted to access to healthcare issues.[56] This is partly explained by the increasing pressure from the European Convention on Human Rights (ECHR) upon the British Constitution and legal culture in favour of greater participation by the courts in political and economic decision-making.[57] Rights were invoked as sources of normative principles or standards of public policy even before the ECHR was introduced into domestic legislation via the Human Rights Act

54 The possibility that changes in English administrative law could impact courts' level of scrutiny and medical decision-making had been suggested by Newdick, *Who Should We Treat*, 119; Cameron Stewart, "Tragic Choices and the Role of Administrative Law," *BMJ* 321, no. 7253 (2000): 105–107.

55 See Maurice Sunkin, "The United Kingdom," in *The Global Expansion of Judicial Power*, eds. C. Neal Tate and Torbjörn Vallinder (New York: NYU Press, 1995), 67; Carol Harlow and Richard Rawlings, *Law and Administration*, 3rd ed. (Cambridge: Cambridge University Press, 2009), 95–96.

56 Government Legal Department, *The Judge Over Your Shoulder*, 5th ed. (London: Government Legal Department, 2018), 4; Sunkin, "The United Kingdom," 69; Varda Bondy and Maurice Sunkin, *The Dynamics of Judicial Review Litigation: The Resolution of Public Law Challenges Before Final Hearing* (The Public Law Project, 2009).

57 Sunkin, "The United Kingdom," 75.

(HRA).[58] The enactment of the HRA in 1998 brought to England the "politics of rights" and further increased the political power of the institutions ultimately responsible for enforcing these rights, namely the courts, vis-à-vis the political and administrative institutions responsible for making policies. The incorporation of the language of rights mitigated the barriers to judicial scrutiny, which were based on the authority of the formal source of power and on the respect for administrative discretion, and created the expectation that courts would do more than just test whether an impugned decision was absurd.[59]

In tandem with the affirmation of the language of rights, there has been an increasing tendency in English law to recognize the requirement for detailed scrutiny of public authorities' reasons. Writing in 1986, Richardson found that the duty to give reasons was starting to be developed in the UK, although in a milder version than the "hard look" doctrine of US administrative law.[60] However, the principle that the administration has a duty to give reasons started to be articulated and applied in the early 1990s in a wide variety of cases and against a long-established principle in English law that the authorities had no general duty to provide reasons.[61]

This increasing judicial demand for public authorities to provide reasons was felt by the public administration. In the different editions of *The Judge Over Your Shoulder*, a guideline prepared by the Treasury Solicitor's Office to advise various authorities about how to make decisions less vulnerable to judicial review, it can be noted that the need to provide reasons was initially seen as exceptional and relevant only in certain circumstances, but later became the rule for the administration.[62]

According to Hunt, English public law was already "feeling its way" towards a "culture of justification" and the HRA accelerated the pace of this transition.[63] The process of translating the language of rights into a demanding judicial con-

58 Harlow and Rawlings, *Law and Administration*; Anthony Lester, "Human Rights and the British Constitution," in *The Changing Constitution*, 7th ed., edited by Jeffrey Jowell and Dawn Oliver (Oxford University Press, 2011), 76–77; Thomas Poole, "Legitimacy, Rights and Judicial Review," *Oxford Journal of Legal Studies* 25, no. 4 (Winter 2005): 706.

59 T. R. S. Allan, "Human Rights and Judicial Review: A Critique of 'Due Deference'," *The Cambridge Law Journal* 65, no. 3 (November 2006): 671; Thomas Poole, "Tilting at Windmills? Truth and Illusion in 'The Political Constitution'," *Modern Law Review* 70, no. 2 (March 2007): 266; Paul Craig, *Administrative Law*, 6th ed. (London: Sweet & Maxwell UK, 2008), 620.

60 Genevra Richardson, "The Duty to Give Reasons: Potential and Practice," *Public Law* (Autumn 1986). See also Shapiro, "The Giving Reasons Requirement," 179.

61 M. Elliot, "Has the Common Law Duty to Give Reasons Come of Age Yet?" *Public Law* (2011): 58; Paul Craig, "The Common Law, Reasons and Administrative Justice," *The Cambridge Law Journal* 53, no. 2 (1994).

62 See the 1987, 1994, 2000, 2006 and 2018 editions of this document.

63 Murray Hunt, "Sovereign's Blight: Why Contemporary Public Law Needs the Concept of 'Due Deference'," in *Public Law in a Multi-Layered Constitution*, edited by Nicholas Bamforth and Peter Leyland (Oxford: Hart, 2003), 342.

trol of administrative procedures and reasons transcended the traditional frontiers of the English courts' deference and, at the same time, established new boundaries for the actions of the courts. The duty to provide reasons has become a device to allow courts to perform their enhanced supervisory function by retracing the authorities' reasoning process to ensure that decisions were made in a thoughtful and non-arbitrary way.[64]

The language of rights and the duty to provide reasons found an elective affinity in the English courts. This is perfectly translated in the words of Laws J. in a 1993 article which affirmed that courts should accord "the first priority to the right in question unless the [decision-maker] can show a substantial, objective, public justification for overriding it"[65] and that "the greater the intrusion proposed by a body possessing public power over the citizen into an area where his fundamental rights are at stake, the greater must be the justification which the public authority must demonstrate".[66] The same idea with very similar words appeared in the High Court decision in *Child B*,[67] which was judged by Laws J. himself.

The language of "Wednesbury" was not abandoned but applied in a "heightened" form. For instance, the High Court in *Otley*[68] concluded that the health authority's policy was "Wednesbury unreasonable", but only after carrying out detailed scrutiny of the choices, scientific evidence, and values underpinning the administrative decision.[69] The departure from an approach in which deference on the part of courts was not warranted by simply mentioning administrative discretion or constitutional authority, but had to be earned by authorities able to justify their decisions, was reiterated in a recent case regarding the funding of a health treatment:

> Irrationality *simpliciter* is a very high hurdle to surmount, and in its most straightforward sense entails the Court coming to the conclusion that the decision under scrutiny was so unreasonable as to be perverse. That assessment does not necessarily entail any evaluation of the reasons given by the decision-maker or the reasoning process displayed thereby. [...] it is certainly possible to advance what may be seen as a somewhat narrower irrationality challenge which focuses on the quality and logicality of the reasons actually given by the decision-maker in the particular case.[70]

64 Craig, *Administrative Law*, 283. See also Shapiro, "The Giving Reasons Requirement," 186.
65 John Laws, "Is the High Court the Guardian of Fundamental Constitutional Rights?" *Commonwealth Law Bulletin* 18, no. 4 (1992): 1392.
66 Laws, 1389. See also *R. v Ministry of Defence, ex parte Smith* [1995] EWCA Civ 22.
67 *Cambridge Health Authority, ex parte B* [1995] 2 All E.R. 129; [1995] 1 W.L.R. 898; see also *North and East Devon Health Authority, ex parte Coughlan* [2001] Q.B. 213, 93.
68 *Barking & Dagenham NHS PCT, ex parte Otley* [2007] EWHC 1927.
69 See *SB v NHS England* [2017] EWHC 2000.
70 *Thanet Clinical Commissioning Groups, ex parte Elizabeth Rose* [2014] EWHC 1182, 95.

It is important to note that human rights were used by claimants in challenges to healthcare rationing decisions and rights have been discussed and mentioned in judgments to justify a heightened judicial scrutiny. However, human rights did not come to the forefront of judges' legal analysis and have not been determinant for the outcome of the cases.[71] This finding is consistent with what Poole observed when analysing human rights cases decided by the English courts: even though in most cases there was some preliminary consideration of the importance of the rights affected by the administrative or political decision being challenged, these were not the primary centre of attention or discussion. Rather, according to Poole, cases were decided mainly on the basis of an analysis of the authorities' expertise and the legitimacy of the judicial review in the constitutional balance.[72]

It is also important to remark that English courts, unlike their counterparts in Brazil and Colombia, have never recognized a judicially enforceable individual human right to receive any medical treatment. The ECHR and the domestic statutory law have never been interpreted as creating an individual right to healthcare that can trump rationing decisions made by the NHS. The quote below makes this point clear:

> There is no enforceable individual entitlement to a particular level or location of care from the NHS ... That is consistent with article 8 of the European Convention on Human Rights (ECHR), which does not give a patient a right to any particular type of medical treatment from the State, given the fair balance that has to be struck between the competing interests of the individual and society as a whole and the wide margin of appreciation enjoyed by States especially in the assessment of the priorities in the context of allocation of limited state resources.[73]

Lastly, the findings of the case-law analysis in this section contradict the idea that English courts tend to be deferential to authorities when it comes to reviewing administrative decisions involving discretionary allocative decision-making and social policies.[74] The decision of the Court of Appeal in *Child B*, which is often cited as a leading authority of this deferential doctrine,[75] is actually one of the last examples of such a self-restrained approach by courts in the review of

71 The High Court decision in *Secretary of State for Health, ex parte Watts* [2003] EWHC 2228 (Adm) can be seen as an exception given the court's individual-centred and rights-based approach.

72 Poole, "Tilting at Windmills?" 709.

73 *R (Dyer) v The Welsh Ministers and others* [2015] EWHC 3712 (Admin) at 17. See, also, *University College London Hospitals NHS Foundation Trust v MB (Rev 1)* [2020] EWHC 882 at 55.

74 See Amos, "Second Division"; King, "Justiciability of Resource Allocation," 197; Pillay, "Economic and Social Rights Adjudication." See also Krajewska, "Access to Fertility Treatment," 627.

75 See King, 199.

healthcare rationing decisions. What followed next was the vindication of what it had overturned.

In sum, the changes in the courts' approach when judging healthcare rationing decisions are better understood when they are put in the broader context of the transformations in English public law in recent decades. Therefore, using explicit rationing as an explanatory variable offers a very limited account of the changes in the case law. It also prevents the full understanding of the influence litigation had in shaping the institutions and procedures for priority-setting in the NHS. This sets the scene for what follows.

Priority-setting in the NHS: from implicit rationing to "accountability for reasonableness"

Not only has the way the courts decide claims for the provision of healthcare changed significantly over the last 30 years, but healthcare rationing in the NHS has also evolved from implicit to being increasingly explicit "about what" and "about why and how" during the same period.

The distinction between the two aspects of explicit rationing – "about what" and "about why and how" – is important (although not always clearly made in the literature) because both aspects of explicitness do not necessarily come together. The public may be aware of which treatments are not being provided to patients ("explicit about what"), but without the reasons or the procedure through which these decisions are reached being disclosed ("explicit about why and how").[76] As will be seen in this section, explicit rationing "about what" is not immediately or necessarily followed by explicitness "about why and how". Being explicit "about why and how" is a policy choice. This distinction also allows a more precise account of the different stages in the process from implicit to explicit rationing in the NHS and of the role played by the heightened judicial scrutiny in making rationing more explicit – in both senses – in the NHS.

The impact of the courts on administration is not always easy to establish. Whilst it can be clear when certain bureaucratic changes are ordered by a court or when a policy is admittedly aimed at responding to a judicial decision or a group of decisions, there are other forms of impact that are more difficult to determine. Some changes are not provoked by the outcome of a judicial decision per se, but by what the courts say and the publicity brought by a particular case.[77] Moreover, the impact can also be diffuse and influence the less accessible aspects of an administration learning to live with the shadow of judicial review, such as

76 See Daniels, *Just Health*, 109.

77 Maurice Sunkin and Genevra Richardson, "Judicial Review: Questions of Impact," *Public Law* (1999): 90; César Rodríguez-Garavito, "Beyond the Courtroom: the Impact of Judicial Activism on Socioeconomic Rights in Latin America," *Texas Law Review* 89 (2011).

the internal and informal working practices of departments and their decision-making culture.[78]

Most of the impact courts have had on priority-setting in the NHS is of the kind that is more difficult to determine. However, by focusing on two landmarks cases – *Child B*[79] and *Pfizer*[80] – it is possible to show that the impact exists and that it is relevant. *Child B* contributed to bringing the public's attention to the fact that rationing was occurring in the NHS and it also made health authorities aware that they now had to set priorities with the judges over their shoulders. *Pfizer* alerted the NHS that it needed a national system for making the assessment of health technologies more informed and consistent in order to avoid and respond to litigation. These two landmark cases, coupled with subsequent judicial decisions, created incentives for important institutional reforms and there is evidence that the courts' rulings have been shaping the decision-making process in the NHS.

It is important to clarify that this chapter is not claiming any strong causal relation in the sense of arguing that litigation has been a sufficient or a necessary condition for the changes in priority-setting in healthcare in England. As previous research on the impact of litigation on bureaucracies has indicated, it is very difficult to isolate the role of courts and estimate their independent impact because policymakers are continuously reacting to multiple pressures.[81] What is possible to show, however, is that courts were an ingredient within the "soup of influences" that created a context that made rationing more explicit "about what" and that, through their rulings, they established a continuous dialogue with decision-makers in the NHS that contributed to making rationing explicit "about why and how".

From implicit to explicit "about what"

The NHS, like any other healthcare system in the world, has always had to set priorities and restrict access to healthcare for cost reasons. For many years, this restriction took the form of implicit rationing. Rationing decisions were mostly hidden in clinical appraisals made by practitioners who, aware of the budgetary

78 See Genevra Richardson, "Impact Studies in the United Kingdom"; Peter Cane, "Understanding Judicial Review and its Impact"; and Maurice Sunkin, "Conceptual Issues in Researching the Impact of Judicial Review on Government Bureaucracies," in *Judicial Review and Bureaucratic Impact*, eds. Marc Hertogh and Simon Halliday (Cambridge: Cambridge University Press, 2009); Harlow and Rawlings, *Law and Administration*, 95–96, 713; Maurice Sunkin and Kathryn Pick, "The Changing Impact of Judicial Review: The Independent Review Service of the Social Fund," *Public Law* (Winter 2001): 760; Government Legal Department, *The Judge Over Your Shoulder*.

79 *Cambridge Health Authority, ex parte B* [1995] 2 All E.R. 129; [1995] 1 W.L.R. 898.

80 *Secretary of State for Health, ex parte Pfizer* [2002] EWCA Civ 1566.

81 See Sunkin and Richardson, "Judicial Review". See also *Oxford Research Encyclopedias*, Politics, s.v. "Courts and Social Policy," by Jeb Barnes, http://politics.oxfordre.com/view/10.1093/acrefore/9780190228637.001.0001/acrefore-9780190228637-e-90.

constraints, have told patients that nothing more could be done to benefit their health, rather than saying explicitly that a treatment could not be provided because resources were not available or were to be allocated for other priorities.[82] Thus, for many years, through a technocratic paternalism grounded in a "deep reservoir of deference to doctors", the NHS managed to dampen down patients' expectations and maintain rationing implicit.[83]

This implicit rationing scheme started to become unsustainable in the 1990s. One of the reasons was the health reform that created a provider–purchaser split and introduced an internal market into the NHS. This led to an uneven provision of care as the access to some treatments depended on the patients' catchment area rather than on their needs alone – the so-called "postcode lottery". This made the public aware that the basket of treatments available to patients was not based solely on clinical reasons, but was also a matter of policy choice and priority-setting.[84]

In addition, the menu of technological possibilities in healthcare began expanding exponentially in recent decades. Health conditions that were once considered untreatable are now finding suitable treatments as a result of the development of costly new medical technologies.[85] This scientific progress, coupled with its marketing and media coverage, has coincided with an ageing society of more educated and better-informed citizens (notably with the advent of the internet) with higher expectations of being treated with the latest and best that the medical science can offer.[86] In England, the role of the media has also been particularly

82 See Bill New and Julian Le Grand, *Rationing in the NHS: Principles and Pragmatism* (London: King's Fund, 1996); Joanna Coast, "Rationing within the NHS Should Be Explicit – The Case Against"; Rudolf Klein, "Defining a Package of Healthcare Services the NHS Is Responsible for – The Case Against"; and Len Doyal, "Rationing within the NHS Should Be Explicit – The Case For," in *Rationing: Talk and Action in Health Care*, ed. Bill New (London: BMJ/King's Fund, 1997); Henry J. Aaron and William B. Schwartz, *The Painful Prescription: Rationing Hospital Care* (Washington, DC: The Brookings Institution, 1984); Rudolf Klein, Patricia Day and Sharon Redmayne, *Managing Scarcity* (Buckingham: Open University Press, 1996), 42.

83 New and Le Grand, *Rationing in the NHS*, 6.

84 See Rudolf Klein, *The New Politics of the NHS: From Creation to Reinvention* (Abingdon: Radcliffe, 2006), 213; A. Coulter, "NICE and CHI: Reducing Variations and Raising Standards," *Health Care UK 1999/2000* (London: King's Fund, 1999), 122–123; Klein, Day and Redmayne, *Managing Scarcity*, 68; Louise Locock, "The Changing Nature of Rationing in the UK National Health System," *Public Administration* 78, no. 1 (Spring 2000).

85 Andrew Stevens and Ruairidh Milne, "Health Technology Assessment in England and Wales," *International Journal of Technology Assessment in Health Care* 20, no. 1 (Winter 2004): 12; Daniel Callahan, "End-of-Life Care: A Philosophical or Management Problem," *Journal of Law, Medicine and Ethics* 39, no. 2 (Summer 2011); Corinna Sorenson, Michael Drummond, and Panos Kanavos, *Ensuring Value for Money in Health Care: The Role of Health Technology Assessment in the European Union*. Observatory Studies Series 11. (Copenhagen: European Observatory on Health Systems and Policies, 2008).

86 Callahan, 115; Dan Crippen and Amber E. Barnato, "The Ethical Implications of Health Spending: Death and Other Expensive Conditions," *The Journal of Law, Medicine & Ethics* 39, no. 2 (Summer 2011); Albert A. Okunade and Vasudeva N. R. Murthy, "Technology as

relevant with stories of healthcare rationing presented in a "melodramatic style", which, whilst very rare in the 1980s, started to represent a constant source of public pressure on the NHS from the 1990s onwards.[87]

In sum, patients have become more aware of what they could have and of what they were denied by the NHS. They have also become more assertive in demanding that doctors and the health system make use of these new technologies, including through litigation.[88]

However, courts have not been merely reflecting the change in the way rationing has been carried out in the NHS. As already suggested by the socio-legal literature, judicial decisions are influenced by the very context that they help to create[89] and, if there is a court case to be singled out in this respect, it is *Child B*.[90]

Child B was the first healthcare rationing case to receive the attention of the mass media and this gave explicit rationing "about what" extraordinary visibility. *Child B* contributed to lifting the veil of implicit rationing for the public and started an unprecedented national debate about rationing, which greatly increased the pressure on authorities and politicians. Without the judicial dispute, the child's drama would arguably have passed unnoticed by the media and public opinion. Instead, the legal case was on the front pages of all the national newspapers, was the subject of many editorial comments, and was also covered prominently on television.[91] The fact that the media coverage was often critical of the health authority also contributed to weakening the public's trust in the decisions made by the health system.[92] Commentators have also noticed that

a 'Major Driver' of Health Care Costs: A Cointegration Analysis of the Newhouse Conjecture," *Journal of Health Economics* 21, no. 1 (January 2002).

87 Bill New, "Introduction," in *Rationing: Talk and Action in Health Care*, ed. Bill New (London: King's Fund/BMJ, 1997), 4; see also Jo Lenaghan, "Central Government Should Have a Greater Role in Rationing Decisions – The Case For" in *Rationing*, ed. New; Penelope Mullen and Peter Spurgeon, *Priority Setting and the Public* (Boca Raton, FL: Radcliffe, 1999), 3; New and Le Grand, *Rationing in the NHS*, 29; Aaron and Schwartz, *The Painful Prescription*, 110.

88 Klein, *The New Politics of the NHS*, 214; Daniels, *Just Health*, 134; John Spiers, "The Realities of Health Care Rationing in the NHS" in *The Realities of Rationing: 'Priority Setting' in the NHS* (London: Institute of Economic Affairs Health & Welfare Unit, 1999), 5; Chris Ham and Susan Pickard, *Tragic Choices in Health Care: The Case of Child B* (King's Fund, 1998), 33.

89 See Sunkin, "Conceptual Issues," 67.

90 *Cambridge Health Authority, ex parte B* [1995] 2 All E.R. 129; [1995] 1 W.L.R. 898.

91 Ham and Pickard, *Tragic Choices*, 49; V. Entwistle et al., "The Media and the Message: How Did the Media Cover the Child B Case," in *Sense and Sensibility in Health Care*, edited by Marshall Marinker (London: BMJ, 1996); Sarah Barclay, *Jaymee: The Story of Child B* (London: Viking, 1996); David Price, "Lessons for Health Care Rationing from the Case of Child B," *BMJ* 132, no. 7024 (1996): 167.

92 Ham and Pickard, 52; I. Watt and V. Entwistle, "What Are the Implications of the Child B Case for the Debate on Health Care Policies?" in *Sense and Sensibility in Health Care*, edited by Marshall Marinker (London: BMJ, 1996), 153; Lenaghan, "Central Government," 125–26.

the repercussion of this court case made rationing more visible to the public and increased the interest of the media in broader discussions about priority-setting and the allocation of resources within the NHS.[93] Moreover, *Child B* sparked an academic debate on rationing and priority-setting in the NHS, including a vast health-policy literature focusing on understanding this case and its repercussions, and trying to draw lessons from it. After the end of the legal dispute, and in contrast with the then usual reluctance to admit the existence of rationing, the defendant authority justified its decision stating that rationing is "necessary" and "legitimate", and that it should be done explicitly rather than behind closed doors.[94]

Child B not only made rationing "about what" more evident to the public, but it also made patients more aware that rationing decisions can be challenged through judicial review. Qualitative research into cases of contested funding decisions soon after *Child B* showed that not only were decision-makers in the NHS concerned about the possibility of judicial review, but also patients had become more willing to go to court or at least to invoke the threat of legal action to put pressure on health authorities to reconsider their decisions not to fund a treatment.[95] One interesting example is a letter sent by a solicitor to a health authority informing that she/he had advised the patient to apply for judicial review against the decision not to fund a treatment, and mentioning that similar cases had already been granted leave.[96]

Child B shows that the impact of a court case can go way beyond the judgment per se. The final decision by the Court of Appeal was overshadowed by the wide public, academic, and political debate about rationing in the NHS that this case provoked. It has also made health authorities aware that their priority-setting decisions have become more visible and thus were more likely to be scrutinized both inside and outside the courtroom.

From explicit "about what" to explicit "about why and how"

The visible mismatch between patients' expectations and the level of care the NHS is capable of providing has undermined the equilibrium that had previously sustained an implicit rationing system. Authorities and politicians began to face the dilemma of choosing between the ever-heavier financial costs of providing

93 Klein, *The New Politics of the NHS*, 78; Mullen and Spurgeon, *Priority Setting*, 3; Jack Kneeshaw, "What Does the Public Think about Rationing," in *Rationing*, ed. New, 58; New and Le Grand, *Rationing in the NHS*, 1; Entwistle et al., "The Media and the Message."

94 Barclay, *Jaymee*, 139–140.

95 Chris Ham and Shirley McIver, *Contested Decisions: Priority Setting in the NHS* (King's Fund, 2000), 20, 61.

96 Ham and McIver, 30.

new and expensive treatments or the ever-greater political costs of not providing them, or perhaps having to bear both costs at the same time.[97]

The NHS response to the challenges brought about by explicit rationing "about what" was to make healthcare rationing "explicit about why and how". Explicit rationing about "why and how" started with the efforts of health authorities at the local level to demonstrate that they had been rigorous and fair in arriving at their priority-setting decisions. This led to greater involvement of external advisors, the establishment of scientific committees to provide better scientific evidence, and attempts to apply an explicit priority-setting framework with clear and standardized criteria against which services and treatments could be assessed.[98] The Department of Health also showed a growing enthusiasm for using evidence-based medicine to identify and exclude procedures and treatments that were not cost-effective.[99] In 1994, the NHS Management Executive's Value for Money Unit urged health authorities to base their purchasing decisions on evidence of clinical effectiveness.[100]

The case of *Child B* made it even clearer for health authorities that they were likely to be severely scrutinized by courts and the public and, hence, that they had to show that their priority-setting decisions had been fair, transparent, and based on a rigorous assessment of the evidence. It also indicated that the NHS needed improvements in the existing procedures for priority-setting in order to deal with future cases.

Ham and McIver[101] interviewed health authorities involved in rationing decisions after *Child B* to assess the changes in their decision-making process following this case. The conclusion was that *Child B*, the then-recent judgment in *Fisher*,[102] and the constant threat of judicial review have contributed to making authorities aware that they were expected to provide better reasons to justify their decisions. In some of the cases discussed in their research, the more frequent involvement of lawyers in disputes about funding and the threat of judicial review resulted in authorities reconsidering their policy and occasionally revising their decision to avoid litigation.[103] Authorities have also realized that, to be able to

97 See Rudolf Klein, "Has the NHS a Future?" *Health Care UK 1999/2000* (London: King's Fund, 1999), 1.

98 Trevor A. Sheldon and Alan Maynard, *Rationing in Action* (London: BMJ, 1993), 13; Chris Ham, "Tragic Choices in Health Care: Lessons from the Child B Case," in *The Global Challenge of Health Care Rationing*, eds. Angela Coulter and Chris Ham (Buckingham: Open University Press, 2000), 113; Ham and McIver, *Contested Decisions*, 55–56.

99 Klein, "Defining a Package," 53.

100 National Institute for Health and Care Excellence, *The Patient's Progress towards a Better Service* (London: NHS Executive's Value for Money Unit, 1994).

101 Ham and McIver, *Contested Decisions*; see also Shirley McIver and Chris Ham, "Five Cases, Four Actors and a Moral: Lessons from Studies of Contested Decisions," *Health Expectations* 3, no. 2 (June 2000).

102 *North Derbyshire Health Authority, ex parte Fisher* [1997] 8 Med L.R. 327.

103 Ham and McIver, *Contested Decisions*, 34, 61, 66; see also McIver and Ham, "Five Cases," 120.

provide better reasons, they needed an evidence-informed, transparent, and consistent decision-making process. This, according to the interviewees, resulted in the establishment of committees for dealing with rationing decisions, the advice of independent external specialists, the search for more evidence and a more detailed look at it, a deeper understanding of the ethical issues involved, the adoption of administrative appeal procedures, and more clarity about the criteria against which the treatments demanded should be assessed. In sum, finding reasons that would be acceptable to both the courts and the public to safeguard their priority-setting decisions from legal challenge had become a permanent concern among health authorities after *Child B*.

This case also prompted an academic debate about the role of the courts in assessing this kind of case. Many commentators criticized the Court of Appeal's decision for not demanding from the health authority better reasons for not funding a lifesaving treatment and for not engaging with the High Court's argument that a reported scarcity of resources was not enough to justify a rationing decision.[104]

Child B, and the court cases that followed it, showed health authorities at the local level that rationing had to be more explicit "about why and how", but also that they needed support from the central government to do so in the form of expertise and guidelines to make complex priority-setting decisions. At that time, health authorities at the local level did not have much information available on the cost-effectiveness of treatments and they lacked expertise in producing evidence-informed priority-setting decisions. This resulted in inconsistent decisions, in the failure to provide sufficient evidence for restricting access to treatments, or in the unsatisfactory quality of the evidence provided.[105] For instance, the then Chief Executive of the Cambridge Health Authority (the defendant authority in *Child B*) complained about the "invidious position" of having to make difficult decisions without any guideline.[106]

A sophisticated health technology assessment to inform priority-setting decisions requires high levels of scientific and economic expertise. It also consumes time and resources. It would be too burdensome for each local health authority to provide a comprehensive and well-documented assessment of each new health technology. This would lead to unnecessary duplication of efforts and overall confusion and inefficiency in the system. The use of ambiguous, obscure, or conflicting criteria by different health authorities when assessing competing

104 See, e.g. Newdick, *Who Should We Treat*, 170–71; R. James and D. Longley, "Judicial Review and Tragic Choices: *Ex parte* B," *Public Law* (Autumn 1995): 367–373; Alan Parkin, "Allocating Health Care Resources in an Imperfect World," *Modern Law Review* 58, no. 6 (1995).

105 Susan Pickard and Rod Sheaff, "Primary Care Groups and NHS Rationing: Implications of the Child B Case," *Health Care Analysis* 7 (1999): 48, 54; Klein, "Defining a Package," 123; Ham and Pickard, *Tragic Choices*, 93–98; Chris Ham, "Tragic Choices in Health Care: Lessons from the Child B Case," *BMJ* 319, no. 7219 (1999): 1261.

106 Pickard and Sheaff, "Primary Care Groups," 48.

claims on resources did not help to avoid financial, political, or judicial pressure on the health system caused by explicitness "about what". The fact that treatments were unevenly purchased by different but adjacent health authorities not only showed that healthcare was being rationed but also that health authorities lacked consistent criteria for priority-setting.[107] The NHS needed a stronger lead from the centre to make priority-setting decisions, coordinate technology information analysis, and create nationally agreed standards.[108]

The first case in which the Department of Health attempted to lead from the centre was the decision not to fund Viagra in the NHS other than in exceptional circumstances. The effectiveness of Viagra was not in doubt and the Department of Health justification for restricting the provision of this drug was the cost of the treatment and its affordability for the public health system. This was considered an important landmark in the history of the NHS because it showed for the first time that the central government recognized the inevitability of rationing and that it was grappling publicly with the problem.[109]

This policy, however, was criticized because there was no clear set of evidence-based reasons for rationing Viagra, and the pharmaceutical company Pfizer filed a lawsuit on this same ground.[110] The High Court required reasons in the form of objective and verifiable criteria for restricting the provision of this treatment, which the Government could not provide. The controversy around this case and the decision of the High Court in favour of the claimant showed that rationing decisions at the national level also had to be grounded on a fair procedure, solid evidence, and consistent policy reasons.[111] In other words, the "lead from the centre" required not only central decisions being explicit "about what", but also "about why and how". Arguably, a "NICE-like" procedure was then necessary to justify the ban on Viagra, although at that time NICE was "still nothing more than a policy dream".[112]

At the end of the 1990s, the Department of Health issued two consultation documents putting forward a strategy to deal with the need to improve the

107 Klein, "Defining a Package," 124; New and Le Grand, *Rationing in the NHS*, 12; Lenaghan, "Central Government," 125–26; Spiers, "Realities of Health Care," 59.

108 Sheldon and Maynard, *Rationing in Action*, 12; Frank Honigsbaum, Stefan Holmström, and Johan Calltorp, *Making Choices for Health Care* (London: CRC Press, 1997), 68.

109 S. Dewar, "Viagra: The Political Management of Rationing" *Health Care UK 1999/2000* (London: King's Fund, 1999), 139; Kamran Abbasi, "Viagra, Rationed," *BMJ* 318, no. 7179 (1999).

110 *Secretary of State for Health, ex parte Pfizer* [2002] EWCA Civ 1566.

111 Locock, "The Changing Nature of Rationing," 91; Dewar, "Viagra," 149; John Crisholm, "Viagra: A Botched Test Case for Rationing," *BMJ* 318, no. 7179 (January 30, 1999); Richard Smith, "NICE: A Panacea for the NHS?," *BMJ* 318, no. 7187 (1999); Elias Mossialos and Martin McKee, "Rationing Treatment on the NHS – Still a Political Issue," *Journal of the Royal Society of Medicine* 96, no. 8 (2003): 372.

112 Dewar, "Viagra," 148. See also John Appleby, "Appraising NICE Appraisals," in *Health Care UK: The King's Fund Review of Health Policy*, edited by John Appleby and Anthony Harrison (Autumn 2000).

quality of care and the challenges raised by an increasingly explicit rationing: *The New NHS: Modern and Dependable*[113] and *A First Class Service: Quality in the New NHS.*[114] These documents affirmed that the NHS was "facing more challenges than ever", resulting from, amongst other things, greater and faster medical advances; a better-informed and more demanding public; an ageing population; low public confidence in the NHS prompted by the "postcode lottery"; a lack of any coherent assessment of which treatments worked best for patients; and the NHS having never been sufficiently open or accountable about the quality of its services. These documents proposed that decisions should be based on the best possible evidence and that the Government should provide new tools for tackling these challenges.

The proposal for the creation of the then-called National Institute for Clinical Excellence (NICE) was set out in these documents based on the idea that high-quality care and cost-effectiveness are two sides of the same coin.[115] NICE was aimed at creating a coherent national system for the assessment of new technologies in substitution for the plurality of bodies that were then carrying out this kind of analysis with different methods, variable quality, and sometimes duplicating each other's efforts while creating confusing evidence unlikely to be helpful to clinicians or authorities.

NICE was eventually established in 1999. It was a political recognition that a centralized, national, rational, and transparent mechanism for setting priorities was necessary in the face of the increasing financial pressure the NHS was experiencing due to the introduction of new and expensive health technologies in the market.[116] NICE is responsible, among other things, for carrying out health technology appraisals – guidelines on the use of health technologies based on clinical and cost-effectiveness analysis.

This task, due to its complexity, frequently generates scientific and moral disagreement. The institute is also frequently under political pressure from stakeholders. A NICE appraisal recommending a treatment creates a legal duty for authorities to fund it. On the other hand, although decision-makers at the local level can still fund treatments not recommended by NICE, a technology appraisal not recommending a treatment will likely restrict patients' access to it in the NHS. NICE can also make non-binding guidelines that, to a certain extent, limit the discretion of decision-makers at the local level as courts have expected them to justify the non-compliance with NICE recommendations.[117]

113 Department of Health (London: 1997).
114 Department of Health (London: 1998).
115 Department of Health (London: 1997), 3.
116 Coulter, "NICE and CHI"; Rudolf Klein and Heidrun Sturm, "Viagra: A Successful Story for Rationing?," *Health Affairs* 21, no. 6 (November/December 2002): 182; Keith Syrett, "A Technocratic Fix to the 'Legitimacy Problem'? The Blair Government and Health Care Rationing in the United Kingdom," *Journal of Health Politics, Policy and Law* 28, no. 4 (August 2003): 729.
117 *R. v Thanet Clinical Commissioning Groups, ex parte Elizabeth Rose* [2014] EWHC 1182.

It is thus necessary that NICE appraisals be legitimate. This was intended to be achieved by an emphasis on "procedural justice" in NICE, which means that "the processes by which healthcare decisions are reached are transparent, and that the reasons for the decisions are explicit".[118] According to Michael Rawlins[119] (NICE's first chairman) and to NICE itself,[120] procedural justice in NICE follows Norman Daniels' idea of "accountability for reasonableness"[121] and explicitly encompassed its four conditions:

(1) Publicity: decisions on the allocation of resources and the grounds for reaching them must be made public;
(2) Relevance: the grounds for the decisions must be relevant and acceptable by fair-minded people;
(3) Challenge and revision: the procedure should offer opportunities for challenging decisions and a transparent system should be available for revising decisions if new evidence becomes available;
(4) Regulation/enforcement: NICE has to be accountable to the public for its reasonableness in order to guarantee that the first three conditions are met.

Procedural justice in NICE is reflected in the transparency of the decisions and of the reasons that back them up (publicity); the scientific rigour in the analysis of the evidence and consideration of social values and policy (relevance); and the right of stakeholders to be consulted and to challenge the decisions, which can then be revised to incorporate new evidence (challenge and revision). In addition, as shown in the previous section, courts have scrutinized the decision-making process in NICE to guarantee that the first three conditions are met (regulation/enforcement).

In a context in which fair-minded people may disagree about which principles of justice should guide the allocation of healthcare resources, "accountability for reasonableness" offers a solution of procedural justice to the problem of making rationing decisions fair and legitimate from the perspective of those whose health needs were not met, as well as the public and (in countries such as England) the courts.

118 National Institute for Health and Clinical Excellence, *Social Values Judgements: Principles for Development of NICE Guidance*, 2nd ed. (London: National Institute for Health and Clinical Excellence, 2008), 9; see also National Institute for Health and Care Excellence, *Guide to the Methods of Technology Appraisal 2013* (National Institute for Health and Care Excellence, 2013); National Institute for Health and Excellence, "Our Charter," 2–3, https://www.nice.org.uk/about/who-we-are/our-charter.

119 Michael Rawlins, "Playing Fair on Treatments," *Health Service Journal*, 26 July 2012, https://www.hsj.co.uk/comment/michael-rawlins-playing-fair-on-treatments/5047276.article/.

120 NICE, *Social Values Judgements.*

121 See Daniels, *Just Health*; see also Daniels and Sabin, *Setting Limits Fairly.*

The decision of the High Court in *Pfizer* was almost concurrent to the establishment of NICE and some commentators suggest a direct association between this court case and the creation of the institute.[122] NICE itself has identified *Pfizer* as one of the main drivers for its creation because the case showed that the Government was vulnerable to questions about the "ad hoc and opaque fashion in which decisions were made" at the same time as it was trying to centralize priority-setting decisions to attempt to avoid the problem of the "postcode lottery".[123]

NICE had come into existence by the time of the Court of Appeal decision in *Pfizer* but, interestingly, the Government did not refer Viagra for its assessment. Arguably, this was because the Government was afraid that a favourable appraisal by NICE would increase the pressure to fund Viagra.[124] Instead, the Government's litigation strategy was to insist that this case was a problem of affordability rather than of cost-effectiveness and, successfully, relied on a more deferential attitude from the Court of Appeal. The pharmaceutical company, on the other hand, argued that decisions about the funding of drugs should be based on "cost-utility analysis", which the Government had not carried out. Whilst the Court of Appeal mentioned NICE in its decision as offering a comprehensive and empirically based framework for the adequate analysis of new technologies, it accepted the arguments of the Government without close scrutiny of this particular policy.

As in *Child B*, even though the High Court's heightened scrutiny was eventually overturned by the Court of Appeal, the *Pfizer* case had an impact that went far beyond the final outcome of the litigation. In most of the subsequent judgments, courts were willing to scrutinize the process and the reasons for a rationing decision, including those made by NICE.

In this section, the cases *Pfizer* and *Child B* were singled out for a deeper analysis, but this is far from meaning that these are the only relevant cases for understanding the impact of litigation on rationing. The continuous use of litigation to challenge rationing decisions and the increasingly heightened scrutiny by courts over the years have contributed to creating enduring changes in the way rationing decisions are made in the NHS.

The courts' requirements in judicial review are now integrated into the NHS decision-making processes for deciding on the provision of healthcare.[125] A survey of how health authorities make allocative decisions and set priorities identified

122 See Kalipso Chalkidou, "Comparative Effectiveness Review within the U.K.'s National Institute for Health and Clinical Excellence," *The Commonwealth Fund* 59 (July 2009): 3; Gardiner Harris, "The British Balance Benefit vs. Cost of Latest Drugs," *New York Times*, December 2, 2018.

123 Nicky Collum et al., *The Evaluation of the Dissemination, Implementation and Impact of NICE Guidance: Final Report* (National Institute for Health and Care Excellence, 2004).

124 Syrett, "Impotence or Importance?" 300.

125 See Rudolf Klein and Jo Maybin, *Thinking about Rationing* (London: The King's Fund, 2012), 9; Syrett, "English National Health Service."

the risk of judicial review as one of the reasons that justify the effort of making priority-setting decisions more explicit.[126] According to the preface to this research:

> The exacting nature of the financial challenge facing the National Health Service (NHS), combined with increasing demand for NHS services, means that commissioners will have to make difficult decisions about how NHS resources are used. Processes for reaching and enacting these priorities will need to be robust and transparent, and capable of withstanding judicial review.[127]

It has also become common for lawyers and legal scholars to give presentations and write papers aimed at NHS staff explaining what judicial review is, helping to interpret judicial decisions, and providing guidance on how decisions should be made to prevent litigation or to avoid having decisions quashed by the courts. The advice includes recording and providing reasons so as to show that each case has been considered in a comprehensive and attentive way.[128]

Following judgments quashing the blanket ban of treatments and requiring exceptional individual circumstances to be considered, health authorities at the local level have established Exceptional Case Panels to assess individual funding requests (IFRs) for treatments that are not routinely funded for all patients.[129] In the document that provides guidelines for the health authorities' analysis of IFRs, it is stated that authorities "must be able to explain coherently their decisions to clinicians, patients, the public, and the courts".[130] Additionally, throughout the document, there are concerns about what the courts might think of decisions made by health authorities and how to proceed in such a way as to lessen the risk of having decisions reviewed by judges. It is even recommended that the NHS act in a judicial-like way when analysing administrative appeals, using the same tests that courts apply to scrutinize their decisions.[131]

The Department of Health recommended health authorities give written justification to patients who are denied a certain treatment, clarifying the reasons

126 Suzanne Robinson et al., *Setting Priorities in Health: A Study of English Primary Trusts* (London: Nuffield Trust, 2011).

127 Robinson et al., 7.

128 See e.g. Cristopher Newdick, *Priority Setting: Legal Considerations* (London: NHS Confederation, 2008); David Lock, *Local Decision Making Judicial Script: What It Is; What It Is Not; When It Is Used and How It Works* (London: Department of Health, 2009).

129 Amy Ford, "The Concept of Exceptionality: A Legal Farce?" *Medical Law Review* 20, no. 3 (Summer 2012); Klein and Maybin, *Thinking about Rationing*, 24; NHS Confederation, *Priority Setting: Managing Individual Funding Requests* (London: NHS Confederation, 2008); National Health Service, *Directions to Primary Care Trusts and NHS Trusts Concerning Decisions About Drugs and Other Treatments* (London: National Health Service, 2009).

130 NHS Confederation, *Priority Setting*, 3.

131 NHS Confederation, 7–8.

for the decisions; that these decisions be grounded on robust evidence and consistent criteria; and that the procedure and rationale for each decision be documented.[132] Moreover, the primary decision-makers' duties of transparency, fairness, and justification, which were imposed by the courts, have become rights to which the NHS itself states that patients are entitled.[133] The NHS Constitution, which Newdick considers the reflection of principles developed by a decade of judicial review,[134] declares that patients have the right to expect local decisions on funding to be made rationally following a proper consideration of the evidence and that decisions not to fund a drug or treatment must be justified.

In conclusion, a heightened judicial scrutiny has pushed the NHS to ration healthcare in a way that is along the lines of "accountability for reasonableness" in order to avoid, respond to, and comply with judicial review. These changes in the administrative decision-making reflect the fact that the denial of funding for a health intervention will hardly ever be upheld by courts if the decision and the grounds for it are not made public ("publicity"), based on sound evidence and reasonable policy considerations ("relevance") and if the opportunity for challenging the policy or presenting a case for an exception is not given ("challenge"). Accordingly, the courts are guaranteeing that healthcare rationing decisions in the NHS will comply with the first three conditions for "accountability for reasonableness" and are thus materializing the last condition ("regulation/enforceability").[135]

Conclusion

This chapter has argued that the heightened scrutiny applied by courts has made healthcare rationing more visible in England and has contributed to shaping the decision-making process in the NHS. This relationship between litigation and

132 *Defining Guiding Principles for Processes Supporting Local Decision-Making about Medicines* (London: Department of Health, 2009); *Supporting Rational Local Decision-Making about Medicines (and Treatments): A Handbook of Practical Guidance* (London: Department of Health, 2009).

133 National Health Service, *Directions Concerning Decisions about Drugs*. The duties to provide reasons for not funding a health care intervention and to consider exceptional circumstances were also set out in the National Health Service Commissioning Board and Clinical Commissioning Groups (Responsibilities and Standing Rules) Regulations 2012.

134 Christopher Newdick, "Rebalancing the Rationing Debate: Tackling the Tensions between Individual and Community Rights," in *Prioritization in Medicine: An International Dialogue*, edited by Eckhard Nagel and Michael Lauerer (Heidelberg: Springer, 2015), 125.

135 Some authors argue that this is the role of judicial accountability in issues of resource allocation in healthcare, see Norman Daniels et al., "Role of the Courts in the Progressive Realization of the Right to Health: Between the Threat and the Promise of Judicialization in Mexico," *Health Systems & Reform* 1, no. 3 (April 2015); Syrett, *Law, Legitimacy and the Rationing of Health Care*; Keith Syrett, "Health Technology Appraisal and the Courts: Accountability for Reasonableness and the Judicial Model of Procedural Justice," *Health Economics, Policy and Law* 6, no. 4 (September 2011).

explicit rationing "about what" and, in particular, "about why and how" has been surprisingly underemphasized in the literature.

By bridging this gap, this chapter offers important contributions to the scholarship in public law, socio-legal studies, medical law, and social rights. First, a comprehensive account of the judicial decisions in cases related to healthcare rationing in this chapter challenges the idea that English courts tend to be deferential to authorities when it comes to administrative decisions involving discretionary allocative decisions in social policies. Whilst it is true that courts have very rarely interfered directly with the outcome of a policy by, for instance, ordering the provision of a treatment, they have definitely not shied away from holding authorities to account by continuously requiring better reasons and procedural fairness.

Second, this chapter provides evidence of the impact of the English Judiciary on a social policy. This was done by showing that the standards and requirements established by courts have been incorporated in the decision-making process in the NHS, by investigating published documents by NHS bodies, and by reviewing the literature on the policy implications of specific court cases. The landmark decisions in *Child B* and *Pfizer* also confirm that the policy impact of a decision is not necessarily linked to the legal success of the challenge.[136]

Even though it is not possible to affirm that litigation was necessary or sufficient for making rationing explicit (in both senses) in the NHS, or for the creation of NICE, in particular, it is plausible to say that courts, by responding to a context of transformations in public law and in the health system in England, have contributed to changing the way in which the decisions about priority-setting in healthcare are made. In other words, an account of the changes in the way the NHS set priorities in healthcare is incomplete without considering the role of litigation and judicial review.

Lastly, the analysis in this chapter vindicates the idea that authorities who are required by the courts to give reasons will make decisions more carefully and in a way that is publicly justifiable, grounded on evidence, and taking into account different views.[137] However, one should be cautious not to jump too quickly to conclusions about whether this impact has been, overall, positive or to normative recommendations regarding how courts in England or elsewhere should judge cases related to the provision and funding of healthcare treatments. It is important to look at the findings of this chapter in light of the paradox suggested by Mashaw, namely that "judicial review both supports political accountability

136 Sunkin, "Conceptual Issues," 52; Diana Kapiszewski and Matthew M. Taylor, "Compliance: Conceptualizing, Measuring, and Explaining Adherence to Judicial Rulings," *Law & Social Inquiry* 38, no. 4 (Fall 2013).

137 Jodi L. Short, "The Political Turn in American Administrative Law: Power, Rationality and Reasons," *Duke Law Journal* 61, no. 8 (2012); see also Lucinda Platt, Maurice Sunkin, and Kerman Calvo, "Judicial Review Litigation as an Incentive to Change in Local Authority Public Services in England and Wales," *Journal of Public Administration Research and Theory* 20, no. S2 (July 2010).

and impairs it, demands administrative competence and undermines bureaucratic capacities".[138]

Policymakers who have the judges looking over their shoulders and are expected to act synoptically (i.e. to show that they did the best possible job given the circumstances in terms of gathering facts, evaluating alternatives, and articulating the values that led to the decision)[139] will spend a significant amount of time and resources that could have been used for other purposes to make sure that each aspect of their policy can resist judicial review. This is particularly true if, as happens in the NHS, they feel compelled to carry out at the administrative level the same tests that they expect to be applied in judicial review.[140] The opportunity costs of making decisions less vulnerable to judicial review are difficult to measure but should not be ignored.

The increasingly heightened judicial scrutiny can also create uncertainty about what courts are expecting in terms of justification to uphold a decision. The consequence could be that decisions are based not on the best policy judgment but on the assessment of a policy's capacity to avoid judicial review. Those responsible for making allocative decisions in a health system may decide, for example, to avoid rationing care where it is most visible or which affects groups who are more disposed to litigate. They may also be likely to settle cases before they reach courts to avoid bad publicity, litigation costs, and a possible unfavourable precedent, even when the rationing decision would be reasonable and consistent from a policy perspective.[141] A concrete example of the threat of litigation influencing priority-setting is arguably the NICE decision to recommend the drug Brineura for use by the NHS following a successful application for judicial review against the institute's initial decision not to recommend it for cost-effectiveness reasons.[142] In sum, fear of litigation may lead to what decision-makers would see as second-best policies.

Furthermore, judicial oversight will not necessarily prevent inconsistent priority-setting decisions from being made. For example, English courts require that a policy to not fund a treatment must consider exceptional circumstances. However, there are no clear directions about what would count as an exception. Apart from the costs for authorities to consider the evidence related to a treatment for each individual funding request, this may result in patients with similar clinical conditions receiving different levels of care depending on how "exceptionality" is being interpreted by decision-makers in each location.[143]

138 Jerry L. Mashaw, "Bureaucracy, Democracy, and Judicial Review," in *The Oxford Handbook of American Bureaucracy*, edited by Robert F. Durant (Oxford University Press, 2010).
139 Shapiro, "The Giving Reasons Requirement."
140 See Harlow and Rawlings, *Law and Administration*, 671.
141 See Marc Gallanter, "Why the 'Haves' Come Out Ahead: Speculations on the Limits of Legal Change," *Law & Society Review* 9, no. 1 (Autumn 1974).
142 See Victoria Charlton, "Does NICE Apply the Rule of Rescue in Its Approach to Highly Specialised Technologies?" *Journal of Medical Ethics* (March 8, 2021).
143 See Ford, "The Concept of Exceptionality."

Lastly, there is also no guarantee that policy decisions following judicial review will be better informed or reasoned. Courts, depending on how heightened their scrutiny is, may be putting themselves in a position to second-guess policy decisions and thus reduce administrators' discretion to an extent that the outcome of a policy is practically predetermined based on the courts' assessment of the facts and of the policy considerations in a case.[144] This would result in the overriding of the administrative procedure by a judicial one that offers fewer of the virtues that courts require from primary decision-makers.

In sum, this chapter has argued that the heightened scrutiny applied by English courts has contributed to shaping the decision-making process in the NHS. Courts have forced decision-makers to take procedural justice seriously and to incorporate the conditions for "accountability for reasonableness" in their priority-setting decisions. However, what this means in terms of efficiency and reduction of inequalities in the access to healthcare for the population is yet to be fully understood.[145]

144 Ford, 188; Harlow and Rawlings, *Law and Administration*, 124.

145 See, e.g. Katharina Kieslich and Peter Littlejohns, "Does Accountability for Reasonableness Work? A Protocol for a Mixed Methods Study Using an Audit Tool to Evaluate the Decision-Making of Clinical Commissioning Groups in England," *BMJ Open* 5, no. 7 (July 10, 2015).

7 Conclusion

Institutionalizing, controlling, limiting, and circumventing HTA via courts

Institutionalizing HTA via courts

Scholarly discussions about priority-setting in healthcare have focused mostly on how these decisions should be made – principles, methods, and processes – but less emphasis has been given to discussions about which institution should make these decisions. Yet, institutions matter, not least because who decides will, to a large extent, determine how these decisions are made and, by consequence, the outcome (namely, who gets what and when).

This book has focused on two institutions – health technology assessment (HTA) bodies and courts – that have increasingly become part of the ecosystem of institutions involved in decisions about the allocation of scarce resources in healthcare. The fact that allocative decisions – that in the past were left to the almost unfettered discretion of politicians, health professionals, and health authorities – are now also being made by independent and arm's-length institutions can be understood within the broader context described by the French scholar Pierre Rosanvallon.

Rosanvallon argues that the legitimacy that the vote in the electoral processes renders to elected politicians and that technical expertise renders to bureaucrats in the public administration have been increasingly called into question. This has opened the space for the decentralization of decision-making powers to other institutions that derive their legitimacy from different sources, namely their impartiality, reflexivity, and proximity. *Impartiality* means the capacity to apply expertise with independence in relation to different interested parties (including the government). *Reflexity* is the deliberative capacity that allows an institution to uphold the principles valued by a political community, promote rationality, and consider perspectives and interests that would have otherwise been overlooked. Lastly, *proximity* includes the attention to procedural justice, in particular the openness and responsivity to the public and stakeholders' participation and engagement.[1]

1 Pierre Rosanvallon, *La Legitimité Démocratique* (Paris: Seuil, 2008).

DOI: 10.4324/9781315149165-7

Impartiality (independence), reflexivity (justification and deliberation), and proximity (procedural justice) tend to be emphasized, in different degrees, to justify the involvement of courts and HTA bodies in priority-setting decisions in healthcare. This is an area that has become increasingly visible, controversial, and politically sensitive. The tension between users' expectations and health systems' capacity to meet them is more likely to generate grievance and distrust if the public or those negatively affected by rationing decisions do not accept the legitimacy of the system through which priorities are set and of those making these decisions. In jurisdictions where legal rights to healthcare are recognised, this grievance and distrust have resulted in the right to healthcare litigation, namely in judicial claims related to the funding or provision of health treatments. Moreover, distrust in "priority-setters" makes courts more willing to review rationing decisions and order the funding of treatment to litigants.

In response to the growing litigation for health treatments, many have suggested that health systems should institutionalize HTA.[2] It is expected that priority-setting issues are less likely to be taken to and resolved by courts when health systems' decisions are informed by HTA and are thus perceived as fair and more legitimate. Accordingly, a functioning HTA system will allow health authorities to make more informed decisions and provide more coherent justifications for the funding or rationing of health technologies. Moreover, HTA bodies that make their decisions/recommendations through an inclusive, accountable, and transparent process should give courts more reasons to trust and rely on the government's reasons and decisions in priority-setting. This strategy was attempted in Brazil, Colombia, and England.

In Brazil, HTA was not directly required by courts. Yet, a new HTA system was created under the expectation that funding decisions informed by HTA could reduce the need for litigation to access treatment and that rationing decisions informed by HTA would be more likely to be upheld in court. In Colombia, a better process for assessing technologies was also intended to build courts' trust in the health system and expand the packages available for users, and thus reduce the need for patients to litigate. In Colombia, HTA was also indirectly required

2 See, Tania Dmytraczenko and Gisele Almeida, eds., *Toward Universal Health Coverage and Equity in Latin America and the Caribbean: Evidence from Selected Countries*, Directions in Development – Human Development (Washington, DC: World Bank Publications, 2015), 190. Kalipso Chalkidou et al., "Health Technology Assessment: Global Advocacy and Local Realities Comment on 'Priority Setting for Universal Health Coverage: We Need Evidence-Informed Deliberative Processes, Not Just More Evidence on Cost-Effectiveness'," *International Journal of Health Policy and Management* 6, no. 4 (April 2017): 234; Leonardo Cubillos et al., "Universal Health Coverage and Litigation in Latin America," *Journal of Health Organization and Management* 26, no. 3 (June 15, 2012): 393; PAHO "Health Technology Assessment and Incorporation into Health Systems" (September 19, 2012) CSP28.R9. Rebecca Dittrich et al., "The International Right to Health: What Does It Mean in Legal Practice and How Can It Affect Priority Setting for Universal Health Coverage?" *Health Systems & Reform* 2, no. 1 (2016): 28–29.

by the Constitutional Court in a structural ruling that demanded a more transparent, inclusive, and informed system for updating POS packages. In England, courts contributed to making rationing explicit "about what" and "about why and how", and set standards that have been progressively adopted by the NHS. This helped to create the context in which NICE became necessary to allow authorities to avoid and better respond to judicial review claims.

This is an interesting finding per se. There is a vast literature on the impact of social rights adjudication on social policy. Rodríguez-Garavito, for instance, has brought our attention to the fact that the effects of structural court cases can be direct (actions in compliance with a court order that affect the participants in a case), indirect (consequences that derive from the decision but that it did not stipulate for), material (concrete changes in the conduct of groups or individuals), and symbolic (changes in ideas, perceptions, and collective social constructs in issues related to the case). These effects can also be combined: direct and material, direct and symbolic, indirect and material, or indirect and symbolic.[3]

Brinks and Gauri have also expanded our understanding of the impact of courts in social rights cases by looking at how judicial decisions in individual cases may have collective effects and impact those not directly involved in the litigation. This includes, for instance, authorities making policy decisions in anticipation of litigation. They use the example of a health system that is ordered by a court to provide a specific treatment to an individual patient and then decides to fund this treatment for all eligible patients to avoid future individual claims.[4]

Building on this literature, the present book shows that the right to healthcare litigation can indeed have an enormous direct impact on access to treatment to litigants and healthcare spending due to the costs of complying with a high number of judicial decisions, such as in Brazil and Colombia. Moreover, there is also evidence that the threat of judicial control and review will affect funding decisions and thus indirectly benefit those that were not necessarily part of a judicial dispute. The inclusion in POS (PBS) of treatments that are frequently funded via reimbursements in Colombia, the individual funding requests (IFRs) decided observing standards that are likely to be considered by courts in England, and the fact that the agenda-setting at CONITEC in Brazil takes into account what is being decided by courts are just a few examples.

Rodríguez-Garavito and Brinks and Gauri have focused on the effects of specific court cases and of judicial commands on the policies they seek to change – for instance, how a court case claiming A will impact the access to A for the litigants or for the entire population that may benefit from it. This book, however, also sheds light on a kind of impact that does not fit exactly in what was described by them. It is the impact on institutions and processes that result from a high number

3 César Rodríguez-Garavito, "Beyond the Courtroom: the Impact of Judicial Activism on Socioeconomic Rights in Latin America," *Texas Law Review* 89 (2011): 1679–1680.

4 Daniel M. Brinks and Varun Gauri, "The Law's Majestic Equality? The Distributive Impact of Judicializing Social and Economic Rights," *Perspectives on Politics* 12, no. 2 (June 2014).

of cases spread over a long period. Courts and litigation can have a disruptive effect as it may force health systems to modify the way they set priorities to comply with previous decisions and to avoid or better respond to future judicial claims. Maintaining the priority-setting systems or practices that result in allocative decisions that are frequently overturned by courts ceases to be an attractive option. Right to healthcare cases thus constrain and shape policy-making and contribute to long-term and enduring changes in healthcare policy at the organizational level. One of these effects discussed in this book is the institutionalization of HTA.

To be clear, I by no means claim that litigation and judicial decisions were necessary or sufficient for the institutionalization of HTA. Even in the case of Brazil, where there is strong documented evidence that right to healthcare litigation was at the forefront of the debates about the creation of a new HTA system, it is implausible to argue that HTA would not have been institutionalized in the absence of litigation. It is often difficult to isolate the role of courts for a policy as their decisions may have radiating effects that are difficult to track and they are embedded in a context where multiple actors and institutions are acting and interacting.[5] This book thus does not offer a comprehensive explanation for why HTA was institutionalized in Brazil, Colombia, and England. Yet, it will have achieved its aim if it succeeds in showing that any explanation for this phenomenon needs to take the courts into account.

Controlling, limiting, and circumventing HTA via courts

The cases of Brazil, Colombia, and England are interesting not only because the courts there contributed to institutionalizing HTA. These three jurisdictions also present different ways in which courts can decide right to healthcare claims against health systems in which HTA is used to make or inform priority-setting decisions.

First, courts can guarantee that HTA is actually relevant to the priority-setting within a health system when they demand that rationing decisions are informed by the analysis of comprehensive evidence, follow clear and rational criteria, and are made through a fair process. Courts can also guarantee that decisions/recommendations by HTA bodies are followed or taken into account by allowing stakeholders to file legal challenges if health systems fail to do so. This can reduce the risk of health systems avoiding, ignoring, or unduly interfering in HTA.

Judicial oversight is also an important tool to guarantee that HTA bodies' procedures are lawful, non-discriminatory, informed by evidence, transparent, inclusive, consistent, and unbiased. It also offers an opportunity to question the principles and criteria adopted by HTA bodies when appraising a technology. In sum, courts can hold HTA bodies accountable, which becomes more important

5 *Oxford Research Encyclopedias*, Politics, s.v. "Courts and Social Policy," by Jeb Barnes, accessed 20 July 2017, http://politics.oxfordre.com/view/10.1093/acrefore/9780190228637.001.0001/acrefore-9780190228637-e-90.

as HTA gains centrality in priority-setting decisions that impact the life and health of many and involve the allocation of large sums of money.

Among the three jurisdictions covered in this book, England is the one that best exemplifies this kind of relationship between courts and HTA systems. English courts have scrutinized the reasons and processes for NICE technology appraisals[6] and have quashed decisions that misread or departed from NICE non-binding recommendations without clear and compelling justifications,[7] and litigation is a credible threat when access to NICE-approved treatments is denied. The judicial control of NICE assessments and of the authorities' and service providers' compliance with NICE technology appraisals and guidance reinforces the centrality of HTA in the priority-setting in the NHS. In several cases, courts have also reiterated the importance of NICE and HTA, including the use of economic analysis, which strengthens the credibility and legitimacy of the institute.[8] The Judiciary has also always admitted that priority-setting is necessary and that courts should hesitate to second-guess policy decisions that will impact the healthcare system and other users.

Accepting that resources are scarce and hence there are financial limits to what health systems can provide is what distinguishes English courts from their Brazilian and Colombian counterparts. There are decisions by the Federal Supreme Court in Brazil and the Constitutional Court of Colombia that accept, in abstract, that priorities need to be set fairly. However, in concrete individual cases, they still refuse to uphold rationing decisions, which are almost always judged as breaches of the right to health no matter how these decisions were made by the health systems. Moreover, implicitly or explicitly, they have considered that economic analyses and distributive considerations, which are key to HTA, as incompatible with the right to healthcare.

In Brazil, courts tend to ignore CONITEC's HTA reports and still decide based on the information provided by the litigant patients' physician and without considering the policy implications and opportunity costs of their judgments.[9] In other words, a rationing decision informed by HTA is treated in the same way as one that is not, which creates no incentive for better HTA or even for relying on HTA for priority-setting. This diminishes and undermines the authority

6 *R. v NICE, ex parte Eisai Ltd.* [2007] EWHC 1941; *R. v NICE, ex parte Bristol-Myers Squibb Pharmaceuticals Ltd.* [2009] EWHC 2722; *R. v NICE, ex parte Servier Laboratories Ltd.* [2010] EWCA Civ 346; *R. v NICE, ex parte Fraser and Another* [2009] EWHC 452.

7 *R. v Thanet Clinical Commissioning Groups, ex parte Elizabeth Rose* [2014] EWHC 1182; *R v Barking & Dagenham NHS PCT ex parte Otley* [2007] EWHC 1927 (Admin); *R v Salford Primary Care Trust ex parte Murphy* [2008] EWHC 1908 (Admin).

8 See, for instance, *R. v Secretary of State for Health, ex parte Pfizer* [2002] EWCA Civ 1566; *R v National Institute for Health and Clinical Excellence ex parte Bristol-Myers Squibb Pharmaceuticals Ltd* [2009] EWHC 2722.

9 Daniel Wei Liang Wang et al., "Health technology assessment and judicial deference to priority-setting decisions in healthcare: Quasi-experimental analysis of right-to-health litigation in Brazil," *Social Science & Medicine* 265 (November 2020): 6.

of CONITEC as priority-setting decisions can be easily bypassed via courts to allow individuals access to treatments that were not assessed or not recommended by the HTA body for regular and universal provision in SUS. In sum, there is the regular pathway for making decisions about the funding of treatment, which includes HTA, and one via courts, in which HTA seems to be irrelevant. This may change soon depending on the binding precedent set by the Supreme Court in case RE 566471, which may recognize the authority of priority-setting decisions informed by HTA.

In Colombia, courts have also been used to bypass priority-setting decisions made by the health system. Courts have constantly insisted that patients' right to access health treatments cannot be limited by the content of the packages that insurers are obliged to cover. They have also forced the creation of administrative mechanisms for the claiming of treatments not included in these packages. The institutionalization of HTA did not give it centrality in priority-setting as HTA plays a very limited role in determining who gets what, when, and why. Furthermore, the Constitutional Court, in 2014, issued a decision that has confirmed that cost-effectiveness and budget considerations do not justify the rationing of healthcare.[10] This puts severe constraints on the use of HTA for priority-setting. Moreover, it is unlikely that the situation will change in the near future as the Constitutional Court decision will be an obstacle for any legislative or administrative reform that tries to include efficiency and distributive considerations in priority-setting.

In Brazil and Colombia, there is an interesting paradox: the right to healthcare litigation was relevant for the institutionalization of HTA bodies but, at the same time, they are used to circumvent priority-setting decisions informed by HTA and to limit its scope. Litigation has brought HTA to the forefront of debates about how to allocate scarce healthcare resources and forced health systems to be more transparent about the criteria and methods for setting priorities. This includes addressing explicitly politically sensitive issues of cost and budget. Yet, at the same time, courts and litigation diminish the relevance of HTA in priority-setting when they refuse to uphold rationing decisions even when they are informed by HTA.

In these two South American countries, the tensions and synergies between the justiciable right to healthcare and fair priority-setting become even more noticeable. But how to explain that the same courts that demand fair priority-setting are still unwilling to uphold rationing decisions even when they are informed by HTA? I have two hypotheses.

First, maybe there is the expectation that fair priority-setting and HTA should make rationing and litigation unnecessary by filtering out treatments that will not benefit patients (e.g. those without evidence that they are safe and effective) while leading to the incorporation and provision of those that will be beneficial to them. The case studies in this book show, unsurprisingly, that this is an unrealistic

10 *Sentencia C-313/14*, CCC, 29/05/2014.

expectation. The purpose of HTA is not to make rationing disappear but rather to make these tragic choices in a more rational, evidence-informed, transparent, inclusive, and accountable way. Unfortunately, resources will remain scarce even when priorities are properly set. Ignoring this fact will only force rationing to remain implicit and made through ad hoc decisions and obscure criteria by managers and service providers coping with a large demand that cannot be matched by the existing resources, or by courts with limited capacity to understand the needs and priorities of other service users.

Another hypothesis is that in Brazil and Colombia there is the combination of, on one hand, the neo-constitutionalist doctrine[11] that is highly influential on the legal culture and the judicial practice there and, on the other, a civil law legal system. In general, judgments do not set precedents and do not create binding *stare decisis.* Therefore, judges may not see their decisions as actually making or changing policy but as one-off exceptions for individual patients. Accordingly, there is no burden on them to consider whether their ruling to "rescue" an identified litigant can be universalized for all others in the same condition. However, as the analysis in this book shows, this is a misguided understanding of the role these courts have been playing in the allocation of healthcare resources. Hundreds of thousands of such one-off decisions will have an enormous impact on policy. They will directly and indirectly, and for better or worse, allocate a significant part of the public budget for health and will force changes in how priorities are set by health systems.

In conclusion, there are many ways in which courts can induce fair priority-setting and give centrality to HTA in health systems' decisions about the funding of treatment. However, applying the right to healthcare to limit HTA or circumvent HTA creates obstacles for fair priority-setting and rules out from the start any meaningful discussion about how health systems can, within the available resources, reduce inequalities and maximize health benefits. Therefore, right to healthcare litigation may well be pushing health systems in the opposite direction of realizing the right to health and achieve UHC.[12]

Hopefully, this book, although focusing on a limited number of jurisdictions, has been able to show the importance of analysing the impact of litigation on priority-setting (and on HTA in particular) in discussions about if, when, and how courts should be involved in the priority-setting of healthcare

11 See Introduction.

12 See Chapter 2.

Bibliography

Aaron, Henry J. and William B. Schwartz. *The Painful Prescription: Rationing Hospital Care*. Washington, DC: The Brookings Institution, 1984.

Abbasi, Kamran. "Viagra, rationed." *BMJ* 318(7179) (1999): 338. https://doi.org/10.1136/bmj.318.7179.338.

Abiiro, Gilbert Abotisem and Manuela De Allegri. "Universal health coverage from multiple perspectives: A synthesis of conceptual literature and global debates." *BMC International Health and Human Rights* 15 (2015): 1–7. https://doi.org/10.1186/s12914-015-0056-9.

Administradora de los Recursos del Sistema General de Seguridad Social en Salud – ADRES. Ejecución presupuestal URA. 2020. https://www.adres.gov.co/La-Entidad/Informaci%C3%B3n-financiera/URA/Ejecuci%C3%B3n-presupuestal-URA.

Aggarwal, A., T. Fojo, C. Chamberlain, C. Davis and R. Sullivan. "Do patient access schemes for high-cost cancer drugs deliver value to society? – Lessons from the NHS cancer drugs fund." *Annals of Oncology* 28(8) (August 2017): 1738–1750. https://doi.org/10.1093/annonc/mdx110.

Akehurst, Ronald L., Eric Abadie, Noël Renaudin and François Sarkozy. "Variation in health technology assessment and reimbursement processes in Europe." *Value in Health* 20(1) (January 2017): 67–76. https://doi.org/10.1016/j.jval.2016.08.725.

Albert, Carla Estefânia. "Análise sobre a judicialização da saúde nos municípios." *Revista técnica CNM* (2016): 151–175. https://www.cnm.org.br/cms/biblioteca_antiga/An%C3%A1lise%20sobre%20a%20Judicializa%C3%A7%C3%A3o%20da%20Sa%C3%BAde%20nos%20Munic%C3%ADpios.pdf.

Allan, T. R. S. "Human rights and judicial review: A critique of 'due deference'." *Cambridge Law Journal* 65(3) (November 2006): 671–695. http://doi.org/10.1017/S0008197306007264.

Alvarez-Rosete, Arturo and Benjamin Hawkins. "Advocacy coalitions, contestation, and policy stasis: The 20 year reform process of the Colombian health system." *Latin American Policy* 9(1) (June 2018): 27–54. https://doi.org/10.1111/lamp.12141.

Amos, Merris. "The second division in human rights adjudication: Social rights claims under the Human Rights Act 1998." *Human Rights Law Review* 15(3) (2015): 549–568. https://doi.org/10.1093/hrlr/ngv015.

Andía, Oscar. "La regulación de precios de medicamentos: Insuficiente y neutralizada. ¿Tiene alguna salida el sistema de salud colombiano?" *El Pulso*, http://www.periodicoelpulso.com/2019_agosto/monitoreo-1.html.

El Andía, Tatiana S. "efecto portafolio. " *de la regulación de precios de medicamentos: La respuesta de la industria farmacéutica a la regulación de precios de medicamentos en Colombia*. Nota Técnica IDB-TN-1507. Washington, DC: Interamerican Development Bank, 2018. http://doi.org/10.18235/0001305.

Angelis, Aris and Panos Kanavos. "Value-based assessment of new medical technologies: Towards a robust methodological framework for the application of multiple criteria decision analysis in the context of health technology assessment." *Pharmacoeconomics* 34(5) (May 2016): 435–446. https://doi.org/10.1007/s40273-015-0370-z.

Angelis, Aris, Ansgar Lange and Panos Kanavos. "Using health technology assessment to assess the value of new medicines: Results of a systematic review and expert consultation across eight European countries." *European Journal of Health Economics : HEPAC: Health Economics in Prevention and Care* 19(1) (January 2018): 123–152. https://doi.org/10.1007/s10198-017-0871-0.

Appleby, John. "Appraising NICE appraisals." In: *Health Care UK: The King's Fund Review of Health Policy* Vols. 24–26, edited by John Appleby and Anthony Harrison, Autumn 2000. https://archive.kingsfund.org.uk/concern/published_works/000024662?locale=en.

Araújo, Denizar Vianna, Marcella de Souza, Cruz Distrutti and Flávia Tavares Silva Elias. "Health technologies prioritization: The Brazilian case." *Jornal Brasileiro de Economia da Saúde* 9(S1) (2017): 4–40. https://doi.org/10.21115/JBES.v9.suppl1.4-40.

Ayala, Ana and Benjamin Mason Meier. "A human rights approach to the health implications of food and nutrition insecurity." *Public Health Reviews* 38 (March 2017). https://doi.org/10.1186/s40985-017-0056-5.

Baltussen, Rob, Maarten P. Jansen, Evelinn Mikkelsen, Noor Tromp, Jan Hontelez, Leon Bijlmakers and Gert Jan Van der Wilt. "Priority setting for universal health coverage: We need evidence-informed deliberative processes, not just more evidence on cost-effectiveness." *International Journal of Health Policy and Management* 5(11) (November 2016): 615–618. https://doi.org/10.15171/ijhpm.2016.83.

Banta, David. "The development of health technology assessment." *Health Policy* 63(2) (February 2003): 121–132. https://doi.org/10.1016/s0168-8510(02)00059-3.

Barclay, Sarah. *Jaymee: The Story of Child B.* London: Viking, 1996.

Barnieh, Lianne, Braden Manns, Anthony Harris, Marja Blom, Cam Donaldson, Scott Klarenbach, Don Husereau, Diane Lorenzetti and Fiona Clement. "A synthesis of drug reimbursement decision-making processes in Organisation for Economic Co-Operation and Development countries." *Value in Health* 17(1) (January-February 2014): 98–108. https://doi.org/10.1016/j.jval.2013.10.008.

Barón-Leguizamón, Gilberto. *Cuentas de salud de Colombia 1993–2003: El gasto nacional en salud y su financiamento*. Bogotá: Ministerio de la Protección Social/Departamento Nacional de Planeación, 2007. https://www.minsalud.gov.co/Documentos%20y%20Publicaciones/CUENTAS%20DE%20SALUD.pdf.

Belloni, Annalisa, David Morgan and Valérie Paris. *Pharmaceutical Expenditure and Policies: Past Trends and Future Challenges*. OECD Health Working Papers 87. Paris: OECD Publishing, 2016. https://doi.org/10.1787/5jm0q1f4cdq7-en.

Bertram, Melanie Y., Jeremy A. Lauer, Kees De Joncheere, Tessa Edejer, Raymond Hutubessy, Marie-Paule Kieny and Suzanne R. Hill. "Cost–effectiveness thresholds: Pros and cons." *Bulletin of the World Health Organization* 94(12) (2016): 925–930. https://doi.org/10.2471/blt.15.164418.

Biehl, João, Joseph J. Amon, Mariana P. Socal and Adriana Petryna. "Between the court and the clinic: Lawsuits for medicines and the right to health in Brazil." *Health and Human Rights Journal* 14(1) (June 2012): E36–E52. https://www.hhrjournal.org/2013/08/between-the-court-and-the-clinic-lawsuits-for-medicines-and-the-right-to-health-in-brazil/.

Biehl, João, Mariana P. Socal and Joseph J. Amon. "The judicialization of health and the quest for state accountability: Evidence from 1,262 lawsuits for access to medicines in Southern Brazil." *Health and Human Rights Journal* 18(1) (June 2016): 209–220. https://www.ncbi.nlm.nih.gov/pubmed/27781011.

Bilinski, Alyssa, Peter Neumann, Joshua Cohen, Teja Thorat, Katherine McDaniel and Joshua A. Salomon. "When cost-effective interventions are unaffordable: Integrating cost-effectiveness and budget impact in priority setting for global health programs." *PLOS Medicine* 14(10) (October, 2017): e1002397. https://doi.org/10.1371%2Fjournal.pmed.1002397.

Boerma, Ties, Carla AbouZahr, David Evans and Tim Evans. "Monitoring intervention coverage in the context of universal health coverage." *PLOS Medicine* 11(9) (September 22, 2014): e1001728. https://doi.org/10.1371/journal.pmed.1001728.

Bognar, Greg and Iwao Hirose. *The Ethics of Health Care Rationing*. London: Routledge, 2014.

Bondy, Varda and Maurice Sunkin. *The dynamics of judicial review litigation: The resolution of public law challenges Before final hearing*. The Public Law Project, 2009. https://publiclawproject.org.uk/resources/the-dynamics-of-judicial-review-litigation/.

Brinks, Daniel M. and Varun Gauri. "The Law's majestic equality? The distributive impact of judicializing social and economic rights." *Perspectives on Politics* 12(2) (June 2014): 375–393. https://doi.org/10.1017/S1537592714000887.

Brinks, Daniel M., Varun Gauri and Kyle Shen. "Social rights constitutionalism: Negotiating the tension Between the universal and the particular." *Annual Review of Law and Social Science* 11(1) (November 2015): 289–308. https://doi.org/10.1146/annurev-lawsocsci-110413-030654.

Brock, Dan W. and Daniel Wikler. "Ethical issues in resource allocation, research, and new product development." In: *Disease Control Priorities in Developing Countries*, 2nd ed., edited by Dean T. Jamison, Joel G. Breman, Anthony R. Measham, George Alleyne, Mariam Claeson, David B. Evans, Prabhat Jha, Anne Mills and Philip Musgrove, 259–270. Washington, DC: World Bank, 2006. http://hdl.handle.net/10986/7242.

Brockis, Emma, Grace Marsden, Amanda Cole and Nancy Devlin. *A Review of NICE Methods Across Health Technology Assessment Programmes: Differences, Justifications and Implications*. The Office of Health Economics Research Paper 16/03. London: The Office of Health Economics, April 2016. https://www.ohe.org/publications/review-nice-methods-across-health-technology-assessment-programmes-differences.

Brownlee, Shannon, Kalipso Chalkidou, Jenny Doust, Adam G. Elshaug, Paul Glasziou, Iona Heath, Somil Nagpal et al. "Evidence for overuse of medical services around the world." *The Lancet* 390(10090) (July 2017): 156–168. https://doi.org/10.1016/s0140-6736(16)32585-5.

Bryan, S. and I. Williams. "Adoption of new technologies, using economic evaluation." In: *Encyclopedia of Health Economics* Vol. 1, edited by Anthony J. Culyer, 26–31. San Diego, CA: Elsevier, 2014.

Bump, Jesse, Cheryl Cashin, Kalipso Chalkidou, David Evans, Eduardo González-Pier, Yan Guo, Jeanna Holtz et al. "Implementing pro-poor universal health coverage." *The Lancet Global Health* 4(1) (January 1, 2016): e14–e16. https://doi.org/10.1016/S2214-109X(15)00274-0.

Busse, Reinhard, Jacques Orvain, Marcial Velasco, Matthias Perleth, Michael Drummond, Felix Grtner, Torben Jørgensen, A. Rüther and C. Wild. "Best practice in undertaking and reporting health technology assessments: Working group 4 report." *International Journal of Technology Assessment in Health Care* 18(2) (April 2002): 361–422. https://doi.org/10.1017/S0266462302000284.

Calabresi, Guido and Philip Bobbit. *Tragic Choices.* New York: Norton, 1978.

Callahan, Daniel. "End-of-life care: A philosophical or management problem?." *Journal of Law, Medicine and Ethics* 39(2) (Summer 2011): 114–120. https://doi.org/10.1111%2Fj.1748-720X.2011.00581.x.

Canadian Agency for Drugs and Technologies in Health. "CADTH presentation on the common drug review to the house of commons standing committee on health." *Speaking notes for a presentation at the House of Commons Standing Committee on Health*, Ottawa (April 25, 2007). https://www.cadth.ca/media/media/Standing_Committee_CADTH_Sanders_FINAL_2007Apr25.pdf.

Cane, Peter. "Understanding judicial review and its impact." In: *Judicial Review and Bureaucratic Impact: International and Interdisciplinary Perspectives*, edited by Marc Hertogh and Simon Halliday, 15–42. Cambridge: Cambridge University Press, 2009. https://doi.org/10.1017/CBO9780511493782.002.

Capucho, Helaine Carneiro, Salomon Flávia Cristina Ribeiro, Vida Ávila Teixeira, Louly Priscila Gebrim, Santos Vania Cristina Canuto and Petramale Clarice Alegre. "Incorporation of technologies in health in Brazil: A new model for the Brazilian public health system (sistema único de Saúde - SUS)." *Boletim do instituto de saúde* 13(3) (July 2012): 215–222. http://periodicos.ses.sp.bvs.br/scielo.php?script=sci_arttext&pid=S1518-18122012000300004&lng=en.

Castro, Hector E. "Advancing HTA in Latin America: The policy process of setting up an HTA agency in Colombia." *Global Policy* 8(S2) (March 2017): 97–102. https://doi.org/10.1111/1758-5899.12333.

Catanheide, Izamara Damasceno, Erick Soares Lisboa and Luis Eugenio Portela Fernandes de Souza. "Characteristics of the judicialization of access to medicines in Brazil: A systematic review." *Physis: Revista de Saúde Coletiva* 26(4) (October 2016): 1335–1356. https://doi.org/10.1590/S0103-73312016000400014.

Chabbouh, Gabriela Pinheiro Lima. "O impacto da judicialização da saúde sobre o município de São Paulo: Orçamento e organização administrativa." Master's diss. Universidade Federal do ABC, 2019.

Chalkidou, Kalipso. "Comparative effectiveness review within the U.K.'s National Institute for Health and Clinical Excellence." *The Commonwealth Fund* 59 (July 2009): 1–12. https://www.commonwealthfund.org/publications/issue-briefs/2009/jul/comparative-effectiveness-review-within-uks-national-institute.

Chalkidou, Kalipso, Amanda Glassman, Robert Marten, Jeanette Vega, Yot Teerawattananon, Nattha Tritasavit, Martha Gyansa-Lutterodt et al.

"Priority-setting for achieving universal health coverage." *Bulletin of the World Health Organization* 94(6) (June 2016): 462–467. https://doi.org/10.2471/BLT.15.155721.

Chalkidou, Kalipso, Ryan Li, Anthony J. Culyer, Amanda Glassman, Karen J. Hofman and Yot Teerawattananon. "Health technology assessment: Global advocacy and local realities comment on 'priority setting for universal health coverage: We need evidence-informed deliberative processes, not just more evidence on cost-effectiveness'." *International Journal of Health Policy and Management* 6(4) (April 2017): 233–236. https://doi.org/10.15171/ijhpm.2016.118.

Chalkidou, Kalipso, Joanne Lord, Alastair Fischer and Peter Littlejohns. "Evidence-based decision making: When should we wait for more information?. " *Health Affairs* 27(6) (November/December 2008): 1642–1653. https://doi.org/10.1377/hlthaff.27.6.1642.

Chalkidou, Kalipso, Robert Marten, Derek Cutler, Tony Culyer, Richard Smith, Yot Teerawattananon, Francoise Cluzeau et al. "Health technology assessment in universal health coverage." *The Lancet* 382(9910) (December 21, 2013): e48–e49. https://doi.org/10.1016/S0140-6736(13)62559-3.

Chamova, Julia. *Mapping of HTA National Organisations, Programmes and Processes in EU and Norway.* Luxembourg: Publications Office of the European Union, 2017. https://doi.org/10.2875/5065.

Chapman, Audrey R. "Globalization, human rights, and the social determinants of health." *Bioethics* 23(2) (February 2009): 97–111. https://doi.org/10.1111/j.1467-8519.2008.00716.x.

Chapman, Audrey R. "The social determinants of health, health equity, and human rights." *Health and Human Rights Journal* 12(2) (December 15, 2010): 17–30. https://www.hhrjournal.org/2013/08/the-social-determinants-of-health-health-equity-and-human-rights/.

Chapman, Audrey R. "Assessing the universal health coverage target in the Sustainable Development Goals from a human rights perspective." *BMC International Health and Human Rights* 16 (December 15, 2016a). https://doi.org/10.1186/s12914-016-0106-y.

Chapman, Audrey R. "The contributions of human rights to universal health coverage." *Health and Human Rights Journal* 18(2) (December 5, 2016b): 1–6. http://www.ncbi.nlm.nih.gov/pmc/articles/pmc5395008/.

Chapman, Audrey R. *Global Health, Human Rights, and the Challenge of Neoliberal Policies.* Cambridge: Cambridge University Press, 2016c. https://doi.org/10.1017/CBO9781316104576.

Chapman, Audrey R., Lisa Forman and Everaldo Lamprea. "Evaluating essential health packages from a human rights perspective." *Journal of Human Rights* 16(2) (2017): 142–159. https://doi.org/10.1080/14754835.2015.1107828.

Charlton, Victoria. "Does NICE apply the rule of rescue in its approach to highly specialised technologies?" *Journal of Medical Ethics* (March 8, 2021). https://doi.org/10.1136/medethics-2020-106759.

Charlton, Victoria, Peter Littlejohns, Katharina Kieslich, Polly Mitchell, Benedict Rumbold, Albert Weale, James Wilson and Annette Rid. "Cost effective but unaffordable: An emerging challenge for health systems." *BMJ* 356(8098) (March 25, 2017): j1402. https://doi.org/10.1136/bmj.j1402.

Chi, Y.-Ling, Mark Blecher, Kalipso Chalkidou, Anthony Culyer, Karl Claxton, Ijeoma Edoka, Amanda Glassman et al. "What next after GDP-based cost-effectiveness thresholds?" *Gates Open Research* 4 (2020). https://doi.org/10.12688/gatesopenres.13201.1.

Chieffi, Ana Luiza and Rita de Cássia Barradas Barata. "'Judicialization' of public health policy for distribution of medicines." *Cadernos de saúde pública* 25(8) (August 2009): 1839–1849. https://doi.org/10.1590/S0102-311X2009000800020.

Chieffi, Ana Luiza and Rita de Cássia Barradas Barata. "Legal suits: Pharmaceutical industry strategies to introduce new drugs in the Brazilian public healthcare system." *Revista de saúde pública* 44(3) (June 2010): 421–429. https://doi.org/10.1590/S0034-89102010000300005.

Chieffi, Luiza Ana, Rita de Cassia Barradas Barata and Moisés Golbaum. "Legal access to medications: a threat to Brazil's public health system?" *BMC Health Services Research* 17 (July 19, 2017). https://doi.org/10.1186/s12913-017-2430-x.

Clark, Sarah and Albert Weale. "Social values in health priority setting: A conceptual framework." *Journal of Health Organization and Management* 26(3) (2012): 293–316. https://doi.org/10.1108/14777261211238954.

Clement, Fiona M., Anthony Harris, Jing Jing Li, Karen Yong, Karen M. Lee and Braden J. Manns. "Using effectiveness and cost-effectiveness to make drug coverage decisions: A comparison of Britain, Australia, and Canada." *JAMA* 302(13) (October 7, 2009): 1437–1443. https://doi.org/10.1001/jama.2009.1409.

Coast, Joanna. "Rationing within the NHS should be explicit – The case against." In: *Rationing: Talk and Action in Health Care*, edited by Bill New, 149–155. London: BMJ/King's Fund, 1997. https://archive.kingsfund.org.uk/concern/published_works/000018606?locale=en.

Cobos, Felipe Curcó. "The new Latin American constitutionalism: A critical review in the context of neo-constitutionalism." *Canadian Journal of Latin American and Caribbean Studies/Revue Canadienne des Études Latino-Américaines et Caraïbes* 43(2) (April 19, 2018): 212–230. https://doi.org/10.1080/08263663.2018.1456141.

Cochrane, Archie. *Effectiveness and Efficiency: Random Reflections on Health Services.* London: The Nuffield Provincial Hospitals Trust, 1971. https://www.nuffieldtrust.org.uk/research/effectiveness-and-efficiency-random-reflections-on-health-services.

Collum, Nicky, Diane Dawson, Annette Lankshear, Karin Lowson, James Mahon, Pauline Raynor, Trevor Sheldon et al. *The Evaluation of the Dissemination, Implementation and Impact of NICE Guidance: Final Report.* London: National Institute for Health and Care Excellence, 2004.

Comissão Nacional de Incorporação de Tecnologias no SUS. Insulinas análogas de ação prolongada para o tratamento de diabetes mellitus tipo *I.* In: *Relatório de recomendação 440.* Brasília: Comissão Nacional de Incorporação de Tecnologias no SUS, 2018a. http://conitec.gov.br/images/Relatorios/2019/Relatorio_Insulinas_Analogas_DM1.pdf.

Comissão Nacional de Incorporação de Tecnologias no SUS. Insulinas análogas de ação prolongada para o tratamento de diabetes mellitus tipo II. In: *Relatório de recomendação 434.* Brasília: Comissão Nacional de Incorporação de Tecnologias no SUS, 2018b. http://conitec.gov.br/images/Relatorios/2019/Relatorio_InsulinasAnalogas_AcaoProlongada_DM2.pdf.

Cookson, Richard, C. McCabe and A. Tsuchiya. "Public healthcare resource allocation and the rule of rescue." *Journal of Medical Ethics* 34(7) (June 30, 2008): 540–544. https://doi.org/10.1136/jme.2007.021790.

Cookson, Richard, Andrew J. Mirelman, Susan Griffin and Miqdad Asaria, Bryony Dawkins, Ole Frithjof Norheim, Stéphane Verguet and Anthony J. Culyer. "Using cost-effectiveness analysis to address health equity concerns." *Value in Health* 20(2) (February 2017): 206–212. https://doi.org/10.1016/j.jval.2016.11.027.

Cotlear, Daniel, Somil Nagpal, Owen Smith, Ajay Tandon and Rafael Cortez. *Going Universal: How 24 Developing Countries are Implementing Universal Health Coverage from the Bottom Up*. Washington, DC: World Bank, 2015. http://hdl.handle.net/10986/22011.

Coulter, A. "NICE and CHI: Reducing variations and raising standards." In: *Health Care UK*. London: King's Fund (1999/2000), 1999.

Craig, Paul. "The Common law, Reasons and administrative justice." *Cambridge Law Journal* 53(2) (July 1994): 282–302. https://doi.org/10.1017/S0008197300099050.

Craig, Paul. *Administrative Law*, 6th ed. London: Sweet & Maxwell U.K., 2008.

Crippen, Dan and Amber E. Barnato. "The ethical implications of health spending: Death and other expensive conditions." *Journal of Law, Medicine and Ethics* 39(2) (Summer 2011): 121–129. https://doi.org/10.1111/j.1748-720x.2011.00582.x.

Crisholm, John. "Viagra: A botched test case for rationing." *BMJ* 318(7179) (January 30, 1999): 273–274. https://doi.org/10.1136/bmj.318.7179.273.

Cubillos, Leonardo, Maria-Luisa Escobar, Sebastian Pavlovic and Roberto Iunes. "Universal health coverage and litigation in Latin America." *Journal of Health Organization and Management* 26(3) (June 15, 2012): 390–406. https://doi.org/10.1108/14777261211239034.

Daniels, Joe Parkin. "Colombian protest over inequalities in health care." *The Lancet* 397 (10293) (June 2021). https://doi.org/10.1016/S0140-6736(21)01436-7.

Daniels, Norman. *Just Health: Meeting Health Needs Fairly*. Cambridge: Cambridge University Press, 2007. https://doi.org/10.1017/CBO9780511809514.

Daniels, Norman, Sofia Charvel, Adriane H. Gelpi, Thalia Porteny and Julian Urrutia. "Role of the courts in the progressive realization of the right to health: Between the threat and the promise of judicialization in Mexico." *Health Systems and Reform* 1(3) (2015): 229–234. https://doi.org/10.1080/23288604.2014.1002705.

Daniels, Norman and James E. Sabin. *Setting Limits Fairly: Learning to Share Resources for Health*, 2nd ed. New York: Oxford University Press, 2008. https://doi.org/10.1093/acprof:oso/9780195149364.001.0001.

Davis, Kenneth Culp. *Discretionary Justice: A Preliminary Inquiry*. Urbana: University of Illinois Press, 1971.

Deaton, Angus and Nancy Cartwright. "Understanding and misunderstanding randomized controlled trials." *Social Science and Medicine* 210 (August 2018): 2–21. https://doi.org/10.1016/j.socscimed.2017.12.005.

Defensoría del pueblo de Colombia. *Informes "La tutela y el derecho a la salud, período 1999–2010*. Bogotá: Defensoría del Pueblo de Colombia, 2011.

Defensoría del pueblo de Colombia. *La tutela y el derecho a la salud –2010*. Bogotá: Defensoria del Pueblo de Colombia, 2011.

Defensoría del pueblo de Colombia. *La tutela y los derechos a la salud y a la seguridad social 2018*. Bogotá: Defensoría del Pueblo de Colombia, 2019.

Defensoría del pueblo de Colombia. *La tutela y los derechos a la salud y a la seguridad social 2019.* Bogotá: Defensoría del Pueblo de Colombia, 2020.

Department of Health. *The New NHS: Modern and Dependable.* London: Department of Health, 1997.

Department of Health. *A First Class Service: Quality in the New NHS.* London: Department of Health, 1998.

Department of Health. *Defining Guiding Principles for Processes Supporting Local Decision-Making about Medicines.* London: Department of Health, 2009a.

Department of Health. *Supporting Rational Local Decision-Making about Medicines (and Treatments): A Handbook of Practical Guidance.* London: Department of Health, 2009b.

Dewar, S. "Viagra: The political management of rationing." In *Health Care UK.* London: King's Fund (1999/2000), 1999.

Dilnot, Andrew. "The burden of triumph: Meeting health and social care needs." *The Lancet* 390(10103) (October 2017): 1630–1631. https://doi.org/10.1016/S0140-6736(17)31938-4.

Dittrich, Rebecca, Leonardo Cubillos, Lawrence Gostin, Kalipso Chalkidou and Ryan Li. "The international right to health: What does it mean in legal practice and how can it affect priority setting for universal health coverage?. " *Health Systems and Reform* 2(1) (2016): 23–31. https://doi.org/10.1080/23288604.2016.1124167.

Dixon, Rosalind. "Creating dialogue About socioeconomic rights: Strong-Form Versus Weak-Form judicial review revisited." *International Journal of Constitutional Law* 5(3) (July 2007): 391–418. https://doi.org/10.1093/icon/mom021.

Dmytraczenko, Tania and Gisele Almeida, eds. Toward universal health coverage and equity in Latin America and the Caribbean: Evidence from selected countries. In *Directions in Development – Human Development.* Washington, DC: World Bank Publications, 2015. http://hdl.handle.net/10986/22026.

Doyal, Len. "Rationing within the NHS should be explicit – The case For." In: *Rationing: Talk and Action in Health Care*, edited by Bill New, 139–146. London: BMJ/King's Fund, 1997. https://archive.kingsfund.org.uk/concern/published_works/000018606?locale=en.

Drummond, Michael F. "Health technology assessment and its interface with regulation, policy and management." In: *Health Technology Assessment and Health Today: A Multifaceted View and Their Unstable Crossroads*, edited by Jean E. del Llano-Señaris and Carlos Campillo-Artero, 3–14. Springer, 2015. https://doi.org/10.1007/978-3-319-15004-8.

Drummond, Michael F., J. Sandord Schwartz, Bengt Jönsson, Bryan R. Luce, Peter J. Neumann, Uwe Siebert and Sean D. Sullivan. "Key principles for the improved conduct of health technology assessments for resource allocation decisions." *International Journal of Technology Assessment in Health Care* 24(3) (July 2008): 244–258. https://doi.org/10.1017/S0266462308080343.

Edwards, Nigel, Helen Crump and Mark Dayan. "Rationing in the NHS." In: *Nuffield Trust Policy Briefing 2.* London: Nuffield Trust, 2015. https://www.nuffieldtrust.org.uk/resource/rationing-in-the-nhs.

Elliot, M. "Has the common law Duty to give reasons come of age yet?" *Public Law.* 1 (2011): 56–74.

Elshaug, Adam G., Meredith B. Rosenthal, John N. Lavis, Shannon Brownlee, Harald Schmidt, Somil Nagpal, Peter Littlejohns, et al. "Levers for addressing medical underuse and overuse: achieving high-value health care." *The Lancet* 390(10090) (July 2017): 191–202. https://doi.org/10.1016/s0140-6736(16)32586-7.

Entwistle, V., I. Watt, R. Bradbury and L. Pehl. "The media and the message: How did the media cover the child B Case." In: *Sense and Sensibility in Health Care*, edited by Marshall Marinker, 87–171. London: BMJ, 1996.

Ettelt, Stefanie. "Access to treatment and the constitutional right to health in Germany: A triumph of hope over evidence?. " *Health Economics, Policy and Law* 15(1) (January 2020): 30–42. https://doi.org/10.1017/S1744133118000282.

European Commission. *Inception impact assessment on strengthening of the EU cooperation on health technology assessment (HTA)*. European Commission, 2016. http://ec.europa.eu/smart-regulation/roadmaps/docs/2016_sante_144_health_technology_assessments_en.pdf.

European Commission. "Health systems." In: *European Semester: Thematic Factsheet*. European Commission, 2017. https://ec.europa.eu/info/sites/default/files/file_import/european-semester_thematic-factsheet_health-systems_en_0.pdf.

Exter, Andre den and Martin Buijsen. *Hard Choices and Unavoidable Trade-Offs*, edited by Rationing Health Care. Antwerp: Maklu, 2012.

Ferraz, Octavio Luiz Motta. "The right to health in the courts of Brazil: Worsening health inequities?. " *Health and Human Rights Journal* 11(2) (December 2009): 33–45. https://www.hhrjournal.org/2013/08/the-right-to-health-in-the-courts-of-brazil-worsening-health-inequities/.

Ferraz, Octavio Luiz Motta. "Harming the poor Through social rights litigation: Lessons from Brazil." *Texas Law Review* 89(7) (June 2011): 1643–1668. https://texaslawreview.org/wp-content/uploads/2015/08/Ferraz-89-TLR-1643.pdf.

Ferraz, Octávio Luiz Motta. *Health as a Human Right: The Politics and Judicialization of Health in Brazil*. Cambridge: Cambridge University Press, 2020. https://doi.org/10.1017/9781108678605.

Ferraz, Octavio Luiz Motta and Daniel Wei Liang Wang. "As duas Portas do SUS." *Folha de São Paulo*. https://www1.folha.uol.com.br/opiniao/2014/06/1472761-octavio-ferraz-e-daniel-wang-as-duas-portas-do-sus.shtml A3, June 19, 2014.

Ferreira, Camila Duran, Ana Carolina Carlos de Oliveira, Ana Mara França Machado, André Vereta Nahoum, Brisa Lopes de Mello Ferrão, Evorah Lusci Costa Cardoso et al. "O Judiciário e as políticas públicas de saúde no Brasil: o caso AIDS." In: *40 Anos: Monografias premiadas*, edited by Prêmio Ipea. Brasília: Ipea, 2004.

Figueiredo, Tatiana Aragão. "Analysis of drugs dispensed by court order in the county of Rio de Janeiro: The application of scientific evidence in decision-making process." Master's diss., Sergio Arouca National School of Public Health, 2010. https://www.arca.fiocruz.br/handle/icict/2508.

Fiss, Owen M. "The social and political foundations of adjudication." *Law and Human Behavior* 6(2) (1983): 121–128. https://doi.org/10.1007/BF01044858.

Flood, Colleen M. "Just medicare: The role of Canadian courts in determining health care rights and access." *Journal of Law, Medicine and Ethics* 33(4) (Winter 2005): 669–680. https://doi.org/10.1111/j.1748-720X.2005.tb00535.x.

Flood, Colleen M. and Insiya Essajee. "Setting limits on health care: Challenges in and out of the courtroom in Canada and down-under." In: *Rationing Health Care: Hard Choices and Unavoidable Trade-Offs*, edited by Andre den Exter and Martin Buijsen, 171–196. Antwerp: Maklu, 2012.

Flood, Colleen M. and Aeyal Gross, eds. *The Right to Health at the Public/Private Divide: A Global Comparative Study.* New York: Cambridge University Press, 2014. https://doi.org/10.1017/CBO9781139814768.

Ford, Amy. "The concept of exceptionality: A legal farce?. " *Medical Law Review* 20(3) (Summer 2012): 304–336. https://doi.org/10.1093/medlaw/fws002.

Forman, Lisa, Claudia Beiersmann, Claire E. Brolan, Martin Mckee, Rachel Hammonds and Gorik Ooms. "What do core obligations under the right to health bring to universal health coverage?. " *Health and Human Rights Journal* 18(2) (December 5, 2016): 23–34. https://www.hhrjournal.org/2016/12/what-do-core-obligations-under-the-right-to-health-bring-to-universal-health-coverage/.

Forman, Lisa, Luljeta Caraoshi, Audrey R. Chapman and Everaldo Lamprea. "Conceptualising minimum core obligations under the right to health: How should we define and implement the 'morality of the depths'. " *The International Journal of Human Rights* 20(4) (2016): 531–548. https://doi.org/10.1080/13642987.2015.1128137.

Fried, Susana T., Atif Khurshid, Dudley Tarlton, Douglas Webb, Sonia Gloss, Claudia Paz and Tamara Stanley. "Universal health coverage: Necessary but not sufficient." *Reproductive Health Matters* 21(42) (2013): 50–60. https://doi.org/10.1016/s0968-8080(13)42739-8.

Fuller, Lon L. and K. I. Winston. "The forms and limits of adjudication." *Harvard Law Review* 92(2) (December 1978): 353–409. https://doi.org/10.2307/1340368.

Gallanter, Marc. "Why the 'haves' come out ahead: Speculations on the limits of legal change." *Law and Society Review* 9(1) (Autumn 1974): 95–160. https://doi.org/10.2307/3053023.

Gardbaum, Stephen. "The new commonwealth model of constitutionalism." In: *Theory into Practice.* Cambridge: Cambridge University Press, 2013. https://doi.org/10.1017/CBO9780511920806.

Gargarella, Roberto. "Dialogic justice in the enforcement of social rights: Some initial arguments." In: *Litigating Health Rights: Can Courts Bring More Justice to Health?*, edited by Alicia Yamin and Siri Gloppen, 232–245. Cambridge, MA: Harvard University Press, 2011.

Gaviria, Alejandro. "Strengthening Governments' capacity to discern value: The need to address technological pressure on health expenditure." In: *Breve 13.* Washington, DC: Inter-American Development Bank, 2016.

GBD 2019 Universal Health Coverage Collaborators. "Measuring universal health coverage based on an index of effective coverage of health services in 204 countries and territories, 1990–2019: a systematic analysis for the Global Burden of Disease Study 2019." *The Lancet* 396(10258) (October 17, 2020): 1250–1284. https://doi.org/10.1016/S0140-6736(20)30750-9.

Ghebreyesus, Tedros Adhanom. "All roads lead to universal health coverage." *The Lancet Global Health* 5(9) (September 1, 2017): e839–e840. https://doi.org/10.1016/S2214-109X(17)30295-4.

Giedion, Ursula, Eduardo Andrés Alfonso and Yadira Díaz. *The Impact of Universal Coverage Schemes in the Developing World: A Review of the Existing Evidence.* UNICO Studies Series 25. Washington, DC: The World Bank, 2013. http://hdl.handle.net/10986/13302.

Giedion, Ursula, Ricardo Bitrán and Ignez Tristao, eds. *Health Benefit Plans in Latin America: A Regional Comparison.* Washington, DC: Inter-American Development

Bank – Social Protection and Health Division, 2014. https://publications.iadb.org/en/health-benefit-plans-latin-america-regional-comparison.

Giedion, Úrsula, Marcela Distrutti, Ana Lucía Muñoz, Diana M. Pinto and Ana M. Díaz. *La priorización en salud paso a paso: Cómo articulan sus procesos México, Brasil y Colombia*. Washington, DC: Inter-American Development Bank, 2018. http://doi.org/10.18235/0001092.

Giedion, Ursula and Pamela Góngora. "Para decir 'SÍ' a la salud, Colombia debe aprender a decir 'NO'." *IADB Blog*, November 5, 2018. https://blogs.iadb.org/salud/es/priorizar-el-gasto-en-salud/.

Giedion, Ursula, Ana Lucía Muñoz and Adriana Ávila. *Serie de notas técnicas sobre procesos de priorización en salud: Nota 1: Introducción*. Nota técnica 837. Washington, DC: Inter-American Development Bank, 2015. https://publications.iadb.org/en/publication/15422/serie-de-notas-tecnicas-sobre-procesos-de-priorizacion-en-salud-nota-1.

Giedion, Ursula, Giota Panopoulou and Sandra Gómez-Fraga. *Diseño y ajuste de los planes explícitos de beneficios: El caso de Colombia y México*. Santiago, Chile: United Nations Economic Commission for Latin America and the Caribbean, Swedish International Development Cooperation Agency, 2009. https://www.cepal.org/es/publicaciones/5201-diseno-ajuste-planes-explicitos-beneficios-caso-colombia-mexico.

Giedion, Ursula and Manuela Villar Uribe. "Colombia's universal health insurance system." *Health Affairs* 28(3) (May/June 2009): 853–863. https://doi.org/10.1377/hlthaff.28.3.853.

Glassman, Amanda and Kalipso Chalkidou. *Priority-Setting in Health Building Institutions for Smarter Public Spending*. Washington, DC: Center for Global Development, 2012. https://www.cgdev.org/publication/priority-setting-health-building-institutions-smarter-public-spending.

Glassman, Amanda L., Maria-Luisa Escobar, Antonio Giuffrida and Ursula Giedion, eds. *From Few to Many: Ten Years of Health Insurance Expansion in Colombia*. New York/Washington, DC: Inter-American Development Bank/Brookings Institution, 2009. https://publications.iadb.org/en/few-many-ten-years-health-insurance-expansion-colombia.

Glassman, Amanda, Ursula Giedion, Yuna Sakuma and Peter C. Smith. "Defining a health benefits package: What are the necessary processes?. " *Health Systems and Reform* 2(1) (2016): 39–50. https://doi.org/10.1080/23288604.2016.1124171.

Glassman, Amanda, Ursula Giedion and Peter C. Smith. *What's in, What's Out: Designing Benefits for Universal Health Coverage*. Center for Global Development, 2017. https://www.cgdev.org/publication/whats-in-whats-out-designing-benefits-universal-health-coverage.

Global Burden of Disease Health Financing Collaborator Network. "Past, present, and future of global health financing: A review of development assistance, government, out-of-pocket, and other private spending on health for 195 countries, 1995–2050." *The Lancet* 393(10187) (June 1, 2019): 2233–2260. https://doi.org/10.1016/S0140-6736(19)30841-4.

Goldacre, Ben. *Bad Pharma: How Drug Companies Mislead Doctors and Harm Patients*. Farrar, Straus and Giroux, 2012.

Gomes, Vanessa Santana and Tânia Alves Amador. "Studies published in indexed journals on lawsuits for medicines in Brazil: A systematic review." *Cadernos de saúde pública* 31(3) (March 2015): 451–462. https://doi.org/10.1590/0102-311X00219113.

González, Ana C. and Juanita Durán. "Impact of court rulings on health care coverage: The case of HIV/AIDS in Colombia." *MEDICC Review* 13(3) (July 2011): 54–57. https://doi.org/10.37757/MR2011V13.N3.13.

González, Claudia Patricia Vaca. "El plan de beneficios de colombia ¿qué lecciones nos deja?" *Presentation, International Development Bank/Criteria*, April 2015. https://publications.iadb.org/publications/spanish/document/Breve-8-El-plan-de-beneficios-de-Colombia-%C2%BFQu%C3%A9-lecciones-nos-deja.pdf.

Gostin, Lawrence O., Benjamin M. Meier, Rebekah Thomas, Veronica Magar and Tedros Adhanom Ghebreyesus. "70 years of human rights in global health: Drawing on a contentious past to secure a hopeful future." *The Lancet* 392(10165) (December 22, 2018): 2731–2735. https://doi.org/10.1016/S0140-6736(18)32997-0.

Gostin, Lawrence O., John T. Monahan, Jenny Kaldor, Mary DeBartolo, Eric A. Friedman, Katie Gottschalk, Susan C. Kim et al. "The legal determinants of health: Harnessing the power of law for global health and sustainable development." *The Lancet* 393(10183) (May 4, 2019): 1857–1910. https://doi.org/10.1016/S0140-6736(19)30233-8.

Government Legal Department. *The Judge Over Your Shoulder*, 5th ed. London: Government Legal Department, 2018.

Grinover, Ada Pellegrini, Kazuo Watanabe, Ligia Paula Pires Pinto Sica, Lucélia de Sena Alves, Maria Tereza Sadek, Natalia Langenegger and Vivian Maria Pereira Ferreira. *Avaliação da prestação jurisdicional coletiva e individual a partir da judicialização da saúde.* São Paulo: CEBEPEJ/DIREITOGV, 2014. http://hdl.handle.net/10438/18674.

Grupo de Economia de Salud (G. E. S.) "Transición en el Sistema de Salud Colombiano." *Observatorio de Seguridad Social* 15(30) (June, 2015). http://hdl.handle.net/10495/3622.

Gruskin, Sofia, Edward J. Mills and Daniel Tarantola. "History, principles, and practice of health and human rights." *The Lancet* 370(9585) (August 4, 2007): 449–455. https://doi.org/10.1016/S0140-6736(07)61200-8.

Guyatt, Gordon, Andrew D. Oxman, Elie A. Akl, Regina Kunz, Gunn Vist, Jan Brozek, Susan Norris et al. "GRADE guidelines: 1. Introduction—GRADE evidence profiles and summary of findings tables: 1. Introduction - GRADE evidence profiles and summary of findings tables." *Journal of Clinical Epidemiology* 64(4) (April 2011): 383–394. https://doi.org/10.1016/j.jclinepi.2010.04.026.

Guyatt, Gordon, Gunn Vist, Yngve Falck-Ytter, Regina Kunz, Nicola Magrini and Holger Schunemann. "An emerging consensus on grading recommendations?. " *BMJ Evidence-Based Medicine* 11(1) (February 2006): 2–4. http://doi.org/10.1136/ebm.11.1.2-a.

Ham, Chris. "Tragic choices in health care: Lessons from the child B Case." In: *The Global Challenge of Health Care Rationing*, edited by Angela Coulter and Chris Ham, 107–116. Buckingham: Open University Press, 2000.

Ham, Chris and Shirley McIver. *Contested Decisions: Priority Setting in the NHS.* London: King's Fund, 2000. https://archive.kingsfund.org.uk/concern/published_works/000024675.

Ham, Chris and Susan Pickard. *Tragic choices in health care: The case of child B.* London. King's Fund, 1998. https://archive.kingsfund.org.uk/concern/published_works/000019505.

Harlow, Carol and Richard Rawlings. *Law and Administration*, 3rd ed. Cambridge: Cambridge University Press, 2009. https://doi.org/10.1017/CBO9780511809941.

Harris, Gardiner. "The British balance benefit vs. cost of latest drugs." *New York Times*, December 2, 2018.

Hawkins, Benjamin and Arturo Alvarez-Rosete. "Judicialization and health policy in Colombia: The implications for evidence-informed policymaking." *Policy Studies Journal* 47(4) (November 2019): 953–977. https://doi.org/10.1111/psj.12230.

Healy, Paul and Meir P. Pugatch. *Theory versus Practice: Discussing the Governance of Health Technology Assessment Systems.* London: Stockholm Network, 2009.

Herring, Jonathan. *Medical Law and Ethics*, 6th ed. Oxford: Oxford University Press, 2008.

Hertogh, Marc and Simon Halliday, eds. *Judicial Review and Bureaucratic Impact: International and Interdisciplinary Perspectives.* Cambridge: Cambridge University Press, 2004. https://doi.org/10.1017/CBO9780511493782.

Higgins, Julian, James Thomas, Jacqueline Chandler, Miranda Cumpston, Tianjing Li, Matthew Page and Vivian Welch, eds. *Cochrane Handbook for Systematic Reviews of Interventions version 6.2. (updated February 2021).* Chichester, UK: Cochrane, 2021. www.training.cochrane.org/handbook.

Hoffman, Florian F. and Fernando R. N. M. Bentes. "Accountability and social and economic rights in Brazil." In: *Courting Social Justice: Judicial Enforcement of Social and Economic Rights in the Developing World*, edited by Varun Gauri and Daniel M. Brinks, 100–145, New York: Cambridge University Press, 2010. https://doi.org/10.1017/CBO9780511511240.005.

Honigsbaum, Frank, Stefan Holmström and Johan Calltorp. *Making Choices for Health Care.* London: CRC Press, 1997. https://doi.org/10.1201/9781315384849.

Horowitz, Donald L. "The judiciary: Umpire or empire?" *Law and Human Behavior* 6(2) (1982): 129–143. https://doi.org/10.1007/BF01044859.

Horton, Richard. "Offline: UHC – One promise and two misunderstandings." *The Lancet* 391(10128) (April 7, 2018): 1342. https://doi.org/10.1016/S0140-6736(18)30847-X. https://www.minsalud.gov.co/proteccionsocial/Financiamiento/Paginas/matriz-continuidad.aspx.

Hunt, Murray. "Sovereign's blight: Why contemporary public law needs the concept of 'due deference'. " In: *Public Law in a Multi-Layered Constitution*, edited by Nicholas Bamforth and Peter Leyland, 337–370. Oxford: Hart, 2003. http://doi.org/10.5040/9781472559494.

Institution of Education and Research and Insper. "Judicialização da Saúde no Brasil: Perfil da demanda, causas e propostas de solução." In: *Justiça pesquisa – Relatório analítico propositivo.* Brasília: National Council of Justice, 2019. http://cnsaude.org.br/publicacoes/judicializacao-da-saude-perfil-das-demandas-causas-e-propostas-de-solucao-insper/.

Instituto de Evaluación Tecnológica em Salud. *Manual para la elaboración de evaluaciones económicas en salud.* Bogotá: Instituto de Evaluación Tecnológica em Salud, 2014. http://doi.org/10.13140/2.1.4034.3049.

Interamerican Development Bank and the Department of Health of Costa Rica. *Apoyo a la Institucionalización de la Evaluación de Tecnologías en Salud en Costa Rica – Documento de Cooperación Técnica, CR-T1129.* Washington, DC/San José, Costa Rica: Interamerican Development Bank and the Department of Health of Costa

Rica, 2015. https://www.iadb.org/projects/document/EZSHARE-931821539-14.

Iyengar, Swathi, Kiu Tay-Teo, Sabine Vogler, Peter Beyer, Stefan Wiktor, Kees de Joncheere and Suzanne Hill. "Prices, costs, and affordability of new medicines for hepatitis C in 30 countries: An economic analysis." *PLOS Medicine* 13(5) (May 2016): e1002032. https://doi.org/10.1371/journal.pmed.1002032.

Izquierdo, Alejandro, Carola Pessino and Guillermo Vuletin, eds. *Better Spending for Better Lives: How Latin America and the Caribbean Can Do More with Less.* Washinton. DC: Interamerican Development Bank, 2018. https://flagships.iadb.org/es/DIA2018/Mejor-Gasto-para-Mejores-Vidas.

Jadad, Alejandro R., Andrew Moore, Dawn Carroll, Crispin Jenkinson, John M. Reynolds, David J. Gavaghan and Henry J. McQuay. "Assessing the quality of reports of randomized clinical trials: Is blinding necessary?. " *Controlled Clinical Trials* 17(1) (February 1996): 1–12. https://doi.org/10.1016/0197-2456(95)00134-4.

James, R. and D. Longley. "Judicial Review and Tragic Choices: Ex parte B." *Public Law* (Autumn 1995): 367–373.

Jamison, Dean T., Ala Alwan, Charles N. Mock, Rachel Nugent, David Watkins, Olusoji Adeyi, Shuchi Anand et al. "Universal health coverage and intersectoral action for health: Key messages from *Disease Control Priorities*, 3rd edition." *The Lancet* 391(10125) (March 17, 2018): 1108–1120. https://doi.org/10.1016/S0140-6736(17)32906-9.

Jamison, Dean T., Lawrence H. Summers, George Alleyne, Kenneth J. Arrow, Seth Berkley, Agnes Binagwaho, Flavia Bustreo et al. "Global health 2035: A world converging within a generation. Global health." *The Lancet* 382(9908) (December 7, 2013): 1898–1955. https://doi.org/10.1016/S0140-6736(13)62105-4.

Kapiszewski, Diana and Matthew M. Taylor. "Compliance: Conceptualizing, measuring, and explaining adherence to judicial rulings." *Law and Social Inquiry* 38(4) (Fall 2013): 803–835. https://doi.org/10.1111/j.1747-4469.2012.01320.x.

Kenyon, Kristi Heather, Lisa Forman and Claire E. Brolan. "Deepening the relationship between human rights and the social determinants of health: A focus on indivisibility and power." *Health and Human Rights* 20(2) (December 2018): 1–10. https://www.hhrjournal.org/2018/12/editorial-deepening-the-relationship-between-human-rights-and-the-social-determinants-of-health-a-focus-on-indivisibility-and-power/.

Kesselring, Felix. "First fundamental decision of the Federal Supreme Court of Switzerland on cost-effectiveness in the area of human healthcare." *European Journal of Risk Regulation* 2(3) (September 2011): 442–446. https://doi.org/10.1017/S1867299X00001483.

Kieslich, Katharina, Jesse B. Bump, Ole Frithjof Norheim, Sripen Tantivess and Peter Littlejohns. "Accounting for technical, ethical, and political factors in priority setting." *Health Systems and Reform* 2(1) (2016): 51–60. https://doi.org/10.1080/23288604.2016.1124169.

Kieslich, Katharina and Peter Littlejohns. "Does accountability for reasonableness work? A protocol for a mixed methods study using an audit tool to evaluate the decision-making of clinical commissioning groups in England." *BMJ Open* 5(7) (July 10, 2015): e007908. https://doi.org/10.1136/bmjopen-2015-007908.

King, Jeff. "The justiciability of resource allocation." *Modern Law Review* 70(2) (2007): 197–224. https://doi.org/10.1111/j.1468-2230.2007.00634.x.

King, Jeff. *Judging Social Rights*. Cambridge: Cambridge University Press, 9, "Flexibility." See esp. chap, 2012. https://doi.org/10.1017/CBO9781139051750.

Klein, Rudolf. "Defining a package of healthcare services the NHS is responsible for – The case against." In: *Rationing: Talk and Action in Health Care*, edited by Bill New, 85–92. London: BMJ/King's Fund, 1997. https://archive.kingsfund.org.uk/concern/published_works/000018606?locale=en.

Klein, Rudolf. "Has the NHS a future?" In: *Health Care UK*. London: King's Fund (1999/2000): 1999.

Klein, Rudolf. *The New Politics of the NHS: From Creation to Reinvention*. Abingdon, UK: Radcliffe, 2006. https://doi.org/10.1201/9780429088964.

Klein, Rudolf, Patricia Day and Sharon Redmayne. *Managing Scarcity*. Buckingham: Open University Press, 1996.

Klein, Rudolf and Jo Maybin. *Thinking About Rationing*. London: The King's Fund, 2012. https://www.kingsfund.org.uk/publications/thinking-about-rationing.

Klein, Rudolf and Heidrun Sturm. Viagra: A successful story for rationing? *Health Affairs* 21(6) (November/December 2002), 177–187.

Kneeshaw, Jack. "What does the public think about rationing." In: *Rationing: Talk and Action in Health Care*, edited by Bill New, 58–78. London: BMJ/King's Fund, 1997. https://archive.kingsfund.org.uk/concern/published_works/000018606?locale=en.

Krajewska, Atina. "Access to fertility treatment: A case of incidental discrimination?" *Medical Law Review* 23(4) (Autumn 2015): 620–645. https://doi.org/10.1093/medlaw/fwv031.

Kristensen, Finn Børlum and Helga Sigmund, eds. *Health Technology Assessment Handbook*. Copenhagen: Danish Centre for Health Technology Assessment, National Board of Health, 2007. https://vortal.htai.org/index.php?q=node/1205.

La República. "Valor de los Recobros no PBS en 2017." https://imgcdn.larepublica.co/i/1200/2018/06/22223303/ECO_COSTODELNOPOS_PG_FDS.jpg, 2018.

La República. "El déficit de la salud se financiará con deuda pública: Juan Pablo Uribe." https://www.larepublica.co/economia/el-deficit-de-la-salud-se-financiara-con-deuda-publica-juan-pablo-uribe-2827267, February 13, 2019.

Lamprea, Everaldo. "Colombia's right to health litigation in a context of health care reform." In: *The Right to Health at a Public/Private Divide: A Global Comparative Study*, edited by Colleen M. Flood and Aeyal Gross, 131–158. Cambridge: Cambridge University Press, 2014, https://doi.org/10.1017/CBO9781139814768.008.

Lamprea, Everaldo. *Derechos en la práctica: Jueces, litigantes y operadores de salud en Colombia (1991–2014)*. Bogotá: Universidad de los Andes, 2015. https://www.jstor.org/stable/10.7440/j.ctt1bd6k82.

Lamprea, Everaldo. "The judicialization of health care: A global south perspective." *Annual Review of Law and Social Science* 13(1) (October 2017): 431–449. https://doi.org/10.1146/annurev-lawsocsci-110316-113303.

Lamprea, Everaldo and Johnattan García. "Closing the gap Between formal and material health care coverage in Colombia." *Health and Human Rights Journal*

18(2) (December 2016). https://www.hhrjournal.org/2016/12/closing-the-gap-between-formal-and-material-health-care-coverage-in-colombia/.

Landau, David. "Political institutions and judicial role in comparative constitutional law." *Harvard International Law Journal* 51(2) (Summer 2010): 319–378. https://ir.law.fsu.edu/articles/558.

Landau, David. "The reality of social rights enforcement." *Harvard International Law Journal* 53(1) (Winter 2012): 189–248. https://harvardilj.org/2012/01/issue_53-1_landau/.

Landwehr, Claudia and Katharina Bohm. "Delegation and institutional design in health-care rationing." *Governance: an International Journal of Policy, Administration, and Institutions* 24(4) (October 2011): 665–688. https://doi.org/10.1111/j.1468-0491.2011.01542.x.

Laws, John. "Is the High Court the Guardian of fundamental constitutional rights?. " *Commonwealth Law Bulletin* 18(4) (1992): 1385–1396. https://doi.org/10.1080/03050718.1992.9986233.

Laxminarayan, Ramanan, Jeffrey Chow and Sonbol A. Shahid-Salles. "Intervention cost-effectiveness: Overview of main messages." In: *Disease Control Priorities in Developing Countries*, 2nd ed., edited by Dean T. Jamison, Joel G. Breman, Anthony R. Measham, George Alleyne, Mariam Claeson, David B. Evans, Prabhat Jha, Anne Mills and Philip Musgrove, 35–86. Washington, DC: World Bank, 2006. http://hdl.handle.net/10986/7242.

Leite, Silvana Nair, Sônia Maria Polidório Pereira, Patrícia da Silva, José Miguel do Nascimento Junior, Benedito Carlos Cordeiro and Ana Paula Veber. "Legal actions and administrative demands related to the guarantee of the right to drugs access in the city of Florianópolis-SC." *Revista de direito sanitário* 10(2) (2009). https://doi.org/10.11606/issn.2316-9044.v10i2p13-28.

Lenaghan, Jo. "Central government should have a greater role in rationing decisions – The case For." In: *Rationing: Talk and Action in Health Care. BMJ*, edited by Bill New, 139–146. London: King's Fund, 1997. https://archive.kingsfund.org.uk/concern/published_works/000018606?locale=en.

Lester, Anthony. "Human rights and the British constitution." In: *The Changing Constitution*, 7th ed., edited by Jeffrey Jowell and Dawn Oliver, 70–101. Oxford: Oxford University Press, 2011.

Leyland, Peter. *The Constitution of the United Kingdom: A Contextual Analysis*, 2nd ed. Oxford: Hart, 7, 2012. See esp. chap.

Lock, David. *Local Decision Making Judicial Script: What It Is; What It Is Not; When It Is Used and How It Works.* London: Department of Health, 2009.

Locock, Louise. "The changing nature of rationing in the UK National Health System." *Public Administration* 78(1) (Spring 2000): 91–109. https://doi.org/10.1111/1467-9299.00194.

Lopes, Luciane Cruz, Silvio Barberato-Filho, Augusto Chad Costa and Claudia Garcia Serpa Osorio-de-Castro. "Rational use of anticancer drugs and patient lawsuits in the state of São Paulo, Southeastern Brazil." *Revista de saúde pública* 44(4) (August 2010): 620–628. https://doi.org/10.1590/S0034-89102010000400005.

Lopes, Luciana de Melo Nunes, Tiago Lopes Coelho, Semíramis Domingues Diniz and Eli Iola Gurgel de Andrade. "Comprehensiveness and universality of the pharmaceutical assistance in times of judicialization of health care." *Saúde e Sociedade* 28(2) (2019): 124–131. https://doi.org/10.1590/S0104-12902019180642.

Lougarre, Claire. "Using the right to health to promote universal health coverage: A better tool for protecting non-nationals' access to affordable health care?. " *Health and Human Rights Journal* 18(2) (December 2016): 35–47. https://www.hhrjournal.org/2016/12/using-the-right-to-health-to-promote-universal-health-coverage-a-better-tool-for-protecting-non-nationals-access-to-affordable-health-care/.

Lubbe, Weyma. "Social value maximization and the multiple goals assumption: Is priority setting a maximizing task at all?" In: *Prioritization in Medicine: An International Dialogue*, edited by Eckhard Nagel and Michael Lauerer, 57–66. Heidelberg: Springer, 2015. https://doi.org/10.1007/978-3-319-21112-1.

de Macedo, Eloisa Israel, Luciane Cruz Lopes and Silvio Barberato-Filho. "A technical analysis of medicines request-related decision-making in Brazilian courts." *Revista de saúde pública* 45(4) (August 2011). https://doi.org/10.1590/S0034-89102011005000044.

Machado, Marina Amaral de Ávila, Francisco de Assis Acurcio, Cristina Mariano Ruas Brandão, Daniel Resende Faleiros, Augusto Afonso Guerra Jr, Mariângela Leal Cherchiglia and Eli Iola Gurgel Andrade. "Judicialization of access to medicines in Minas Gerais state, South eastern Brazil." *Revista de saúde pública* 45(3) (June 2011): 590–598. https://doi.org/10.1590/S0034-89102011005000015.

Mandeville, Kate L., Rosie Barker, Alice Packham, Charlotte Sowerby, Kielan Yarrow and Hannah Patrick. "Financial interests of patient organisations contributing to technology assessment at England's National Institute for Health and Care Excellence: Policy review." *BMJ* 364 (January 2019): k5300. https://doi.org/10.1136/bmj.k5300.

Mann, Jonathan M., Lawrence Gostin Sofia Gruskin, Troyen Brennan, Zita Lazzarini, Harvey V. Fineberg and H. V. Fineberg. "Health and human rights." *Health and Human Rights Journal* 1(1) (Fall 1994): 6–23. https://doi.org/10.2307/4065260.

Mantouvalou, Virginia. "In support of legislation." In: *Debating Social Rights*, edited by Conor Gearty and Virginia Mantouvalou, 85–171. Oxford: Hart, 2011.

Marques, Silvia Badim and Sueli Gandolfi Dallari. "Safeguarding of the social right to pharmaceutical assistance in the state of São Paulo, Brazil." *Revista de saúde pública* 41(1) (February 2007): 101–107. https://doi.org/10.1590/S0034-89102007000100014.

Mashaw, Jerry L. "Bureaucracy, democracy, and judicial review." In: *The Oxford Handbook of American Bureaucracy*, edited by Robert F. Durant, 569–589. Oxford: Oxford University Press, 2010. https://doi.org/10.1093/oxfordhb/9780199238958.003.0024.

Masters, Rebecca, Elspeth Anwar, Brendan Collins, Richard Cookson and Simon Capewell. "Return on investment of public health interventions: A systematic review." *Journal of Epidemiology and Community Health* 71(8) (August 2017): 827–834. http://doi.org/10.1136/jech-2016-208141.

Mathes, Tim, Esther Jacobs, Jana-Carina Morfeld and Dawid Pieper. "Methods of international health technology assessment agencies for economic evaluations – A comparative analysis." *BMC Health Services Research* 13 (September 30, 2013). https://doi.org/10.1186/1472-6963-13-371.

McIver, Shirley and Chris Ham. "Five cases, four actors and a moral: Lessons from studies of contested decisions." *Health Expectations* 3(2) (June 2000): 114–124. https://doi.org/10.1046/j.1369-6513.2000.00089.x.

Medeiros, Marcelo, Debora Diniz and Ida Vanessa Doederlein Schwartz. "The Thesis of Judicialization of Health Care by the Elites: Medication for Mucopolysaccharidosis." *Ciência & Saúde Coletiva* 18(4) (April 2013): 1089–1098. https://doi.org/10.1590/S1413-81232013000400022.

Meier, Benjamin Mason, Oscar A. Cabrera, Ana Ayala and Lawrence O. Gostin. "Bridging international law and rights-based litigation: Mapping health-related rights through the development of the Global Health and Human Rights Database." *Health and Human Rights Journal* 14(1) (June 2012): 1–16. https://scholarship.law.georgetown.edu/facpub/935/.

Meier, Benjamin Mason, Adriane Gelpi, Matthew M. Kavanagh, Lisa Forman and Joseph J. Amon. "Employing human rights frameworks to realize access to an HIV cure." *Journal of the International AIDS Society* 18(1) (November 13, 2015). https://doi.org/10.7448/IAS.18.1.20305.

Mejía, Aurelio and Ana Lucía Muñoz. "Institutos de evaluación de tecnologias sanitarias: Recomendaciones para su estrucutración a partir del caso Colombia." In: *Serie de notas técnicas sobre procesos de priorización en salud – Nota 5. Nota técnica IDB-TN-1253.* Washington, DC: Interamerican Development Bank, 2017.

Mendes, Gilmar. "Opening of the public hearing n. 4 at the Supreme Federal Court. " *Supreme Federal Court*, March 5, 2009. www.stf.jus.br/arquivo/cms/processoAudienciaPublicaSaude/anexo/Abertura_da_Audiencia_Publica__MGM.pdf.

Messeder, Ana Márcia, Claudia Garcia Serpa Osorio-de-Castro and Vera Lucia Luiza. "Can court injunctions guarantee access to medicines in the public sector? The experience in the State of Rio de Janeiro, Brazil." *Cadernos de saúde pública* 21(2) (April 2005): 525–534. https://doi.org/10.1590/S0102-311X2005000200019.

Ministério da Saúde. *Avaliação de tecnologias em saúde: Seleção de estudos apoiados pelo Decit.* Brasília: Ministério da Saúde, 2011. http://livroaberto.ibict.br/handle/1/494.

Ministério da Saúde. *Insulinas Análogas de Longa Duração – Diabetes Mellitus tipo II. Relatório de recomendação da Comissão Nacional de Incorporação de Tecnologias No SUS – CONITEC –103.* Brasília: Ministério da Saúde, 2014. http://conitec.gov.br/images/Insulinastipo2-103-FINAL.pdf.

Ministerio de Salud y Protección Social. *Cifras financieras del Sector Salud, Gasto en salud de Colombia 2004–2011.* Boletín Bimestral No. 2 (January–February, 2014). https://www.minsalud.gov.co/sites/rid/Lists/BibliotecaDigital/RIDE/VP/FS/Cifras%20financieras%20del%20Sector%20Salud%20-%20Bolet%C3%ADn%20No%202.pdf.

Ministerio de Salud y Protección Social. *Cifras financieras del sector salud.* Boletín Bimestral No. 11 (July–August, 2015). https://www.minsalud.gov.co/sites/rid/Lists/BibliotecaDigital/RIDE/VP/FS/cifras-financieras-del-sector-salud%20-boletin-numero-11.pdf.

Ministerio de Salud y Protección Social. "Cifras Financieras del Sector Salud, Fuentes y usos de los recursos del Sistema General de Seguridad Social en Salud (SGSSS)." In: *Actualización 2016. Boletín bimestral* Vol. 13, 2016a. https://www.minsalud.gov.co/sites/rid/Lists/BibliotecaDigital/RIDE/VP/FS/boletin-flujo-de-recursos-2012-2016-no-13.pdf.

Ministerio de Salud y Protección Social. *Seguimiento A recobros no pos régimen contributivo – Resultados 2014 y 2015.* Bogotá: Ministerio de Salud y Proteccíon Social, 2016b. https://www.minsalud.gov.co/sites/rid/Lists/BibliotecaDigital/RIDE/DE/PES/Seguimiento-a-recobros-no-pos.pdf.

Ministerio de Salud y Protección Social. *Estructura del Gasto en Salud Pública en Colombia*. Papeles en salud 17. Bogotá: Ministerio de Salud y Proteccíon social, 2018a.

Ministerio de Salud y Protección Social. *Informe al Congreso de la República, Cuatrienio 2014–2018, 2017–2018*. Bogotá: Ministerio de Salud y Protección Social, 2018b. https://www.minsalud.gov.co/sites/rid/Lists/BibliotecaDigital/RIDE/DE/PES/Informe-congreso-2014-2018-2017-2018.pdf.

Ministerio de Salud y Protección Social. *Cifras de aseguramiento en salud*. Bogotá: Ministerio de Salud y Protección Social, 2020a. https://www.minsalud.gov.co/proteccionsocial/Paginas/cifras-aseguramiento-salud.aspx.

Ministerio de Salud y Protección Social. *Comportamiento del aseguramiento*. Bogotá: Ministerio de Salud y Protección Social, 2020b. https://www.minsalud.gov.co/sites/rid/Lists/BibliotecaDigital/RIDE/VP/DOA/serie-departamental-afiliados-contributivo-2005-2016.zip.

Ministerio de Salud y Protección Social. *Matriz de continuidad*. Bogotá: Ministerio de Salud y Protección Social, 2020c.

Moes, Floortje, Eddy Houwaart, Diana Delnoij and Klasien Horstman. "Contested evidence: A Dutch reimbursement decision taken to court." *Health Economics, Policy and Law* 12(3) (July 2017): 325–344. https://doi.org/10.1017/S1744133116000281.

Mœstad, Ottar, Lise Rakner and Octavio L. Motta Ferraz. "Assessing the impact of health rights litigation: A comparative analysis of Argentina, Brazil, Colombia, Costa Rica, India, and South Africa." In: *Litigating Health Rights: Can Courts Bring More Justice to Health?*, edited by Alicia Yamin and Siri Gloppen, 273–303. Cambridge, MA: Harvard University Press, 2011.

Moher, D., D. J. Cook, A. R. Jadad, P. Tugwell, M. Moher, A. Jones, B. Pham and T. P. Klassen. "Assessing the quality of reports of randomised trials: Implications for the conduct of meta-analyses." *Health Technology Assessment* 3(12) (1999): i–iv, 1–98. https://doi.org/10.3310/hta3120.

Montenegro Torres, Fernando and Oscar Bernal Acevedo. *Colombia Case Study: The Subsidized Regime of Colombia's National Health Insurance System*. UNICO Studies Series 15. Washington, DC: The World Bank, 2013. http://hdl.handle.net/10986/13285.

Montgomery, Jonathan. "Law and the demoralization of medicine." *Legal Studies* 26(2) (2006): 185–210. http://doi.org/10.1111/j.1748-121X.2006.00004.x.

Moon, James C., Andrew S. Flett, Brian B. Godman, Anthony M. Grosso and Anthony S. Wierzbicki. "Getting better value from the NHS drug budget." *BMJ* 341 (December 17, 2010). https://doi.org/10.1136/bmj.c6449.

Moreno, Jaime Ramírez. "The healthcare social emergency: from regulatory contingencies to citizen disappointment." *Revista gerencia y politicas de salud S* 9(18) (February–June, 2010): 124–143. https://revistas.javeriana.edu.co/index.php/gerepolsal/article/view/2653.

Moreno-Serra, Rodrigo and Peter C. Smith. "Does progress towards universal health coverage improve population health?. " *The Lancet* 380(9845) (September 8, 2012): 917–923. https://doi.org/10.1016/s0140-6736(12)61039-3.

Morgan, Steven G., Kenneth L. Bassett, James M. Wright, Robert G. Evans, Morris L. Barer, Patricia A. Caetano and Charlyn D. Black. "'Breakthrough' drugs and growth in expenditure on prescription drugs in Canada." *BMJ* 331(7520) (October 2005): 815–816. https://doi.org/10.1136/bmj.38582.703866.ae.

Morozowski, Ana Carolina and Daniel Wang. "Soliris: A esperança na corda bamba de sombrinha." *Direito em Comprimidos* (September 20, 2020). https://direitoemcomprimidos.com.br/soliris/.

Mossialos, Elias and Martin McKee. "Rationing treatment on the NHS – Still a political issue." *Journal of the Royal Society of Medicine* 96(8) (2003): 372–373. https://doi.org/10.1177%2F014107680309600802.

Mullen, Penelope and Peter Spurgeon. *Priority Setting and the Public*. Boca Raton, FL: Radcliffe, 1999.

Muller, Sérgio Swain. "Judicialização da saúde." In *PowerPoint presentation Seminário sobre Gestão e Saúde, Insper/CONASS*. https://slideplayer.com.br/slide/17057062/.

Musgrove, Philip and Julia Fox-Rushby. "Economic analysis for priority setting." In: *Disease Control Priorities in Developing Countries*, 2nd ed., edited by Dean T. Jamison, Joel G. Breman, Anthony R. Measham, George Alleyne, Mariam Claeson, David B. Evans, Prabhat Jha, Anne Mills and Philip Musgrove, 271–285. Washington, DC: World Bank, 2006. http://hdl.handle.net/10986/7242.

Naci, Huseyin, Alexander Carter and Elias Mossialos. "Why the drug development pipeline is not delivering better medicines." *BMJ* 351 (October 2015): h5542. https://doi.org/10.1136/bmj.h5542.

Naffah Filho, Michel, Ana Luiza Chieffi and Maria Cecília M. M. A. Correa. "S-codes: A new system of information on lawsuits of the state Department of Health of São Paulo." *Boletim epidemiológico paulista* 7(84) (2010): 18–30. http://periodicos.ses.sp.bvs.br/scielo.php?script=sci_arttext&pid=S1806-42722010001200003&lng=en&nrm=iso.

National Council of Justice. *Relatórios de cumprimento da Resolução CNJ n. 107*. Brasília: National Council of Justice, 2015. https://www.cnj.jus.br/wp-content/uploads/2015/03/demandasnostribunais.forumSaude.pdf.

National Council of Justice. *Justiça em números*. Brasília: National Council of Justice, 2017, 2018, 2019, 2020. https://www.cnj.jus.br/pesquisas-judiciarias/justica-em-numeros/.

National Health Service. *Directions to Primary Care Trusts and NHS Trusts Concerning Decisions About Drugs and Other Treatments*. London: National Health Service, 2009.

National Institute for Clinical Excellence. *Social Value Judgements: Principles for the Development of NICE Guidance*, 2nd ed. London: National Institute for Health and Clinical Excellence, 2008. https://www.ncbi.nlm.nih.gov/books/NBK395865/.

National Institute for Health and Care Excellence. *The Patient's Progress towards a Better Service*. London: NHS Executive's Value for Money Unit, 1994.

National Institute for Health and Care Excellence. *Guide to the Methods of Technology Appraisal 2013*. National Institute for Health and Care Excellence, 20–23, 2013. https://www.nice.org.uk/process/pmg9/chapter/evidence. See esp. "Evidence".

National Institute for Health and Care Excellence. *Our Charter* Vols. 2–3. https://www.nice.org.uk/about/who-we-are/our-charter.

National Institute for Health and Care Excellence. "The Principles that guide the development of NICE guidance and standards." *Our Principles*. https://www.nice.org.uk/about/who-we-are/our-principles.

Naundorf, Bruno, Patrícia de Carli and Bárbara Goulart. "O Estado do Rio Grande do Sul e os Impactos da Judicialização da Saúde na Gestão Pública." In: *Dilemas do fenômeno da Judicialização da saúde* Vol. 2 of *Coletânea Direito e Saúde*, edited by Alethele de Oliveira Santos and Luciana Tolêdo Lopes, 208–217. Brasília: CONASS, 2018. https://www.conasems.org.br/orientacao_ao_gestor/coletanea-direito-a-saude-volume-2-dilemas-do-fenomeno-da-judicializacao/.

Neto, Campos, Orozimbo Henrique, Luiz Alberto de Oliveira Gonçalves and Eli Iola Gurgel Andrade. "Estratégias do poder econômico interferindo no fenômeno da judicialização da saúde." In: *Dilemas do fenômeno da Judicialização da saúde* Vol. 2 of *Coletânea Direito e Saúde*, edited by Alethele de Oliveira Santos and Luciana Tolêdo Lopes, 62–75. Brasília: CONASS, 2018. https://www.conasems.org.br/orientacao_ao_gestor/coletanea-direito-a-saude-volume-2-dilemas-do-fenomeno-da-judicializacao/.

New, Bill. "Introduction." In: *Rationing: Talk and Action in Health Care. BMJ*, edited by Bill New. London: King's Fund, 3–7, 1997. https://archive.kingsfund.org.uk/concern/published_works/000018606?locale=en.

New, Bill and Julian Le Grand. *Rationing in the NHS: Principles and Pragmatism.* London: King's Fund, 1996. https://archive.kingsfund.org.uk/concern/published_works/000016065?locale=en.

Newdick, Christopher. *Who Should We Treat: Rights, Rationing, and Resources in the NHS.* Oxford: Oxford University Press, 2005. https://doi.org/10.1093/acprof:oso/9780199264186.001.0001.

Newdick, Christopher. *Priority Setting: Legal Considerations.* London: NHS Confederation, 2008.

Newdick, Christopher. "Rebalancing the rationing debate: Tackling the tensions Between individual and community rights." In: *Prioritization in Medicine: An International Dialogue*, edited by Eckhard Nagel and Michael Lauerer, 123–140. Heidelberg: Springer, 2015.

NHS Confederation. *Priority Setting: Managing Individual Funding Requests.* London: NHS Confederation, 2008.

Nicholls, Stuart G., Ainsley J. Newson and Richard E. Ashcroft. "The need for ethics as well as evidence in evidence-based medicine." *Journal of Clinical Epidemiology* 77 (September 1, 2016): 7–10. https://doi.org/10.1016/j.jclinepi.2016.05.006.

Nishtar, Sania, Sauli Niinistö, Maithripala Sirisena, T. Vázquez, V. Skvortsova, A. Rubinstein, F. G. Mogae et al. "Time to deliver: report of the WHO Independent High-Level Commission on NCDs." *The Lancet* 392(10143) (July 21, 2018): 245–252. https://doi.org/10.1016/S0140-6736(18)31258-3.

Nissen, Aleydis. "A right to access to emergency health care: The European Court of Human Rights pushes the envelope." *Medical Law Review* 26(4) (Autumn 2018): 693–702. https://doi.org/10.1093/medlaw/fwx059.

Nolan, Aoife. *Children's Socio-Economic Rights, Democracy and the Courts.* Oxford: Hart, 2011.

Nolan, Aoife, Bruce Porter and Malcolm Langford. *The Justiciability of Social and Economic Rights: An Updated Appraisal.* CHRGJ Working Paper 15. Center for Human Rights and Global Justice, 2007.

Norheim, Ole F. "Disease control priorities third edition is published: A theory of change is needed for translating evidence to health policy." *International Journal of Health Policy and Managment* 7(9) (2018): 771–777. https://doi.org/10.15171/ijhpm.2018.60.

Norheim, Ole F., Rob Baltussen, Mira Johri, Dan Chisholm, Erik Nord, Dan W. Brock, Per Carlsson et al. "Guidance on priority setting in health care (GPS-Health): The inclusion of equity criteria not captured by cost-effectiveness analysis." *Cost Effectiveness and Resource Allocation: C/E* 12 (August 2014). https://doi.org/10.1186/1478-7547-12-18.

Norheim, Ole F. and Siri Gloppen. "Litigating for medicines: How can we assess impact on health outcomes." In: *Litigating Health Rights: Can Courts Bring More Justice to Health?*, edited by Alicia Yamin and Siri Gloppen, 304–332. Cambridge, MA: Harvard University Press, 2011.

O'Donnell, C. John, Sissi V. Pham, Chris L. Pashos, David W. Miller and Marilyn Dix Smith. "Health technology assessment: Lessons learned from around the world – An overview." *Value Health* 12(S2) (June 2009): S1–S5. https://doi.org/10.1111/j.1524-4733.2009.00550.x.

Ochalek, Jessica, James Lomas and Karl Claxton. "Estimating health opportunity costs in low-income and middle-income countries: A novel approach and evidence from cross-country data." *BMJ Global Health* 3(6) (November 2018): e000964. https://doi.org/10.1136/bmjgh-2018-000964.

O'Connell, Thomas, Kumanan Rasanathan and Mickey Chopra. "What does universal health coverage mean?" *The Lancet* 383(9913) (January 18, 2014): 277–279. https://doi.org/10.1016/s0140-6736(13)60955-1.

Okunade, Albert A. and Vasudeva N. R. Murthy. "Technology as a 'major driver' of health care costs: A Cointegration analysis of the Newhouse conjecture." *Journal of Health Economics* 21(1) (January 2002): 147–159. https://doi.org/10.1016/s0167-6296(01)00122-9.

Ooms, Gorik, Claire Brolan, Natalie Eggermont, Asbjørn Eide, Walter Flores, Lisa Forman, Eric A. Friedman et al. "Universal health coverage anchored in the right to health." *Bulletin of the World Health Organization* 91(1) (January 2013): 2–2A. https://doi.org/10.2471/blt.12.115808.

Ooms, Gorik, Laila A. Latif, Attiya Waris, Claire E. Brolan, Rachel Hammonds, Eric A. Friedman, Moses Mulumba and Lisa Forman. "Is universal health coverage the practical expression of the right to health care?. " *BMC International Health and Human Rights* 14 (2014). https://doi.org/10.1186%2F1472-698X-14-3.

Organization for Economic Co-operation and Development. *Fiscal Sustainability of Health Systems: Bridging Health and Finance Perspectives*. Paris: OECD Publishing, 2015. https://doi.org/10.1787/9789264233386-en.

Orr, Shepley and Jonathan Wolff. "Reconciling cost-effectiveness with the rule of rescue: The institutional division of moral labour." *Theory and Decision* 78(4) (2015): 525–538. https://doi.org/10.1007/s11238-014-9434-3.

Ottersen, Trygve, Ole F. Norheim, Bona M. Chitah, Richard Cookson, Norman Daniels, Frehiwot B. Defaye et al. *Making Fair Choices on the Path to Universal Health Coverage – Final Report of the WHO Consultative Group on Equity and Universal Health Coverage*. Geneva: World Health Organization, 2014. https://apps.who.int/iris/handle/10665/112671.

Palmer, Ellie. *Judicial Review, Socio-Economic Rights and the Human Rights Act*. Oxford: Hart, 2007.

Parkhurst, Justin. *The Politics of Evidence: from Evidence-Based Policy to the Good Governance of Evidence*. Abingdon, Oxon: Routledge, 2017. http://doi.org/10.4324/9781315675008.

Parkhurst, Justin and Sudeepa Abeysinghe. "What constitutes 'good' evidence for public health and social policy-making? From hierarchies to appropriateness." *Social Epistemology* 30(5–6) (2016): 665–679. https://doi.org/10.1080/02691728.2016.1172365.

Parkin, Alan. "Allocating health care resources in an imperfect world." *Modern Law Review* 58(6) (1995): 867–677. https://doi.org/10.1111/j.1468-2230.1995.tb02057.x.

Parmar, Sharanjeet and Namita Wahi. "India: Citizens, courts and the right to health: Between promise and progress?. " In: *Litigating Health Rights: Can Courts Bring More Justice to Health?*, edited by Alicia Yamin and Siri Gloppen, 155–189. Cambridge, MA: Harvard University Press, 2011.

Pepe, Vera Lúcia Edais, Miriam Ventura, João Maurício Brambati Sant'ana, Tatiana Aragão Figueiredo, Vanessa dos Reis de Souza, Luciana Simas and Claudia Garcia Serpa Osorio-de-Castro. "Characterization of Lawsuits for the Supply of 'essential' Medicines in the State of Rio de Janeiro, Brazil." *Cadernos de saúde pública* 26(3) (March 2010): 461–471. https://doi.org/10.1590/S0102-311X2010000300004.

Pereira, Januária Ramos, Rosana Isabel dos Santos, José Miguel do Nascimento Junior and Eloir Paulo Schenkel. "Situation of Lawsuits Concerning the Access to Medical Products by the Health Department of Santa Catarina State, Brazil, during the years 2003 and 2004." *Ciência and Saúde Coletiva* 15(S3) (November 2010): 3551–3560. https://doi.org/10.1590/S1413-81232010000900030.

Pharmaceutical Benefits Advisory Committee Guidelines. "Section 5.4 Basis for any claim for the 'rule of rescue'." *Submission Structure for Submissions Requiring Evaluation.* https://pbac.pbs.gov.au/section-5/5-4-basis-for-any-claim-for-the-rule-of-rescue.html.

Pichon-Riviere, Andres, Natalie Soto, Federico Augustovski and Laura Sampietro-Colom. "Stakeholder involvement in the health technology assessment process in Latin America." *International Journal of Technology Assessment in Health Care* 34(3) (2018): 248–253. https://doi.org/10.1017/s0266462318000302.

Pickard, Susan and Rod Sheaff. "Primary care groups and NHS rationing: Implications of the child B Case." *Health Care Analysis* 7(1) (1999): 37–56. https://doi.org/10.1023/a:1009412406958.

Pillay, Anashri. "Economic and social rights adjudication: Developing principles of judicial restraint in South Africa and the United Kingdom." *Public Law* (2013): 599–617.

Pillay, Anashri. "Revisiting the Indian experience of economic and social rights adjudication: The need for principled approach to judicial activism and restraint." *International and Comparative Law Quarterly* 63(2) (April 2014): 385–408. http://doi.org/10.1017/S0020589314000074.

Piovesan, Flavia. "Brazil: Impact and challenges of social rights in the courts." In: *Social Rights Jurisprudence: Emerging Trends in International and Comparative Law*, edited by Malcolm Langford, 182–191. Cambridge: Cambridge University Press, 2009. https://doi.org/10.1017/CBO9780511815485.011.

Platt, Lucinda, Maurice Sunkin and Kerman Calvo. "Judicial review litigation as an incentive to change in local authority public services in England and Wales." *Journal of Public Administration Research and Theory* 20(S2) (July 2010): i243–i260. https://doi.org/10.1093/jopart/muq027.

Pontarolli, Deise, Paula Rossignoli and Cláudia Moretoni. "Panorama da judicialização de medicamentos na secretaria estadual de saúde do Paraná." In:

Dilemas do fenômeno da Judicialização da saúde Vol. 2 of *Coletânea Direito e Saúde*, edited by Alethele de Oliveira Santos and Luciana Tolêdo Lopes, 174–187. Brasília: CONASS, 2018. https://www.conasems.org.br/orientacao_ao_gestor/coletanea-direito-a-saude-volume-2-dilemas-do-fenomeno-da-judicializacao/.

Poole, Thomas. "Legitimacy, rights and judicial review." *Oxford Journal of Legal Studies* 25(4) (Winter 2005): 697–725. https://doi.org/10.1093/ojls/gqi034.

Poole, Thomas. "Tilting at windmills? Truth and illusion in 'the political constitution'." *Modern Law Review* 70(2) (March 2007): 250–277. https://doi.org/10.1111/j.1468-2230.2007.00636.x.

Prachniak-Rincón, Corey and Jimena Villar de Onís. "HIV and the right to health in Colombia." *Health and Human Rights Journal* 18(2) (December 2016): 157–169. https://www.hhrjournal.org/2016/10/hiv-and-the-right-to-health-in-colombia/.

Prada, Sergio I., Victoria E. Soto, Tatiana S. Andía, Claudia P. Vaca, Álvaro A. Morales, Sergio R. Márquez and Alejandro Gaviria. "Higher pharmaceutical public expenditure after direct price control: Improved access or induced demand? The Colombian case." *Cost Effectiveness and Resource Allocation: C/E* 16 (2018). https://doi.org/10.1186/s12962-018-0092-0.

Price, David. "Lessons for health care rationing from the case of child B." *BMJ* 132(7024) (1996). https://doi.org/10.1136/bmj.312.7024.167.

Puras, Dainius. "Universal health coverage: A return to Alma-Ata and Ottawa." *Health and Human Rights Journal* 18(2) (December 2016): 7–10. https://www.hhrjournal.org/2016/12/foreword-universal-health-coverage-a-return-to-alma-ata-and-ottawa/.

Rawlins, Michael D. "De Testimonio: On the evidence for decisions about the use of therapeutic interventions." *The Lancet* 372(9656) (December 2008): 2152–2161. https://doi.org/10.1016/s0140-6736(08)61930-3.

Rawlins, Michael D. "Playing fair on treatments." *Health Service Journal* (26 July 2012). https://www.hsj.co.uk/comment/michael-rawlins-playing-fair-on-treatments/5047276.article/.

Rawlins, Michael D. "Evidence, values, and decision making." *International Journal of Technology Assessment in Health Care* 30(2) (April 2014): 233–238. https://doi.org/10.1017/s0266462314000154.

Restrepo-Zea, Jairo Humberto, Lina Patricia Casas-Bustamante and Juan José Espinal-Piedrahita. "Universal coverage and effective access to health care: What has happened in Colombia ten years after Sentence T-760?" *Revista de salud pública* 20(6) (2018): 670–676. https://doi.org/10.15446/rsap.v20n6.78585.

Richardson, Genevra. "The Duty to Give Reasons: Potential and practice." *Public Law* (Autumn 1986): 437–469.

Richardson, Genevra. "Impact studies in the United Kingdom." In: *Judicial Review and Bureaucratic Impact: International and Interdisciplinary Perspectives*, edited by Marc Hertogh and Simon Halliday, 103–108. Cambridge: Cambridge University Press, 2009. https://doi.org/10.1017/CBO9780511493782.005.

Roberts, Marc J., William C. Hsiao and Michael R. Reich. "Disaggregating the universal coverage cube: Putting equity in the picture." *Health Systems and Reform* 1(1) (2015): 22–27. https://doi.org/10.1080/23288604.2014.995981.

Robinson, Suzanne, Helen Dickinson, Iestyn Williams, Tim Freeman, Benedict Rumbold and Katie Spence. *Setting Priorities in Health: A Study of English*

Primary Trusts. London: Nuffield Trust, 2011. https://www.nuffieldtrust.org.uk/research/setting-priorities-in-health-the-challenge-of-clinical-commissioning.

Rodríguez-Garavito, César. "Beyond the courtroom: The impact of judicial activism on socioeconomic rights in Latin America." *Texas Law Review* 89 (2011): 1669–1698.

Rodríguez-Garavito, César. "Constructing and contesting the global intellectual property legal field: The struggle over patent rights and access to medicines in Colombia." In: *Balancing Wealth and Health*, edited by Rochelle Dreyfuss and César Rodríguez-Garavito, 169–194. Oxford: Oxford University Press, 2014.

Rodríguez-Garavito, César. "La judicialización de la salud: Síntomas, diagnóstico y prescripciones." In: *La Salud en Colombia: Logros, retos y recomendaciones*, edited by Óscar Bernal and Catalina Gutiérrez, 507–560. Bogotá: Universidad de Los Andes, 2012.

Rosanvallon, Pierre. *La Legitimité démocratique*. Paris: Seuil, 2008.

Rumbold, Benedict E. and James Wilson. "Reasonable disagreement and the generally unacceptable: A philosophical analysis of Making Fair Choices." *Health Economics, Policy and Law* 11(1) (January 2016): 91–96. https://doi.org/10.1017/s1744133114000577.

Rumbold, Benedict, Albert Weale, Annette Rid, James Wilson and Peter Littlejohns. "Public reasoning and health-care priority setting: The case of NICE." *Kennedy Institute of Ethics Journal* 27(1) (March 2017): 107–134. https://doi.org/10.1353/ken.2017.0005.

Rumbold, Benedict, Rachel Baker, Octavio Ferraz, Sarah Hawkes, Carleigh Krubiner, Peter Littlejohns, Ole F. Norheim et al. "Universal health coverage, priority setting, and the human right to health." *The Lancet* 390(10095) (August 12, 2017): 712–714. https://doi.org/10.1016/s0140-6736(17)30931-5.

Sabel, Charles F. and William H. Simon. "Destabilization rights: How public law litigation succeeds." *Harvard Law Review* 117(4) (2004): 1017–1101. https://doi.org/10.2307/4093364.

Sabik, Lindsay M. and Reidar K. Lie. "Priority-setting in health care: Lessons from the experiences of eight countries." *International Journal for Equity in Health* 7 (2008). https://doi.org/10.1186/1475-9276-7-4.

Sackett, David L., William M. C. Rosenberg, J. A. Muir Gray, R. Brian Haynes and W. Scott Richardson. "Evidence based medicine: What it is and what it isn't: It's About integrating individual clinical expertise and the best external evidence." *BMJ* 312(7023) (January 13, 1996): 71–72. https://doi.org/10.1136/bmj.312.7023.71.

Sakae, Diana. "Otimização de recursos: Judicial versus política pública." In: *PowerPoint Presentation*. State of Santa Catarina Department of Health, 2020.

Sant'Anna, João Maurício Brambati. "Essentiality and Pharmaceutical Care: An Exploratory Study of Individual Legal Demands for Access to Medicines in the State of Rio de Janeiro." Master's diss., Sergio Arouca National School of Public Health, 2009. https://www.arca.fiocruz.br/handle/icict/2449.

Santos, Pedro Felipe de Oliveira. "Beyond minimalism and usurpation: Designing judicial review to control the mis-enforcement of socio-economic rights." *Washington University Global Studies Law Review* 18(3) (2019). https://doi.org/10.1186/s40985-017-0056-5.

Sarlet, Ingo Wolfgang and Mariana Filchtiner Figueiredo. "Reserva do possível, mínimo existencial e direito à saúde: Algumas aproximações." In: *Direitos*

Fundamentais: Orçamento e reserva do possível, edited by Ingo Wolfgang Sarlet and Luciano Benetti Timm, 11–53. Porto Alegre: Livraria do Advogado, 2008.

Schwettmann, Lars. "Let's talk About health economic evaluation: Relevant contextual factors for the German 'Sonderweg'." In: *Prioritization in Medicine: An International Dialogue*, edited by Eckhard Nagel and Michael Lauerer, 273–281. Heidelberg: Springer, 2015. https://doi.org/10.1007/978-3-319-21112-1.

Segatto, Cristiane. "O paciente de R$800 mil." *Época* (March 26, 2012).

Semana. "Pacientes multimillonarios." *Semana* (November 11, 2014). https://www.semana.com/nacion/articulo/las-criticas-del-ministro-gaviria-al-sistema-de-salud/407662-3.

Shapiro, Martin. "The giving reasons requirement." *University of Chicago Legal Forum* (1992): 179–220. https://chicagounbound.uchicago.edu/uclf/vol1992/iss1/8.

Sheldon, Trevor A. and Alan Maynard. *Rationing in Action*. London: BMJ, 1993.

Short, Jodi L. "The political turn in American administrative law: Power, rationality and Reasons." *Duke Law Journal* 61(8) (2012): 1811–1881. https://scholarship.law.duke.edu/dlj/vol61/iss8/4.

da Silva, Luiza Pinheiro Alves. *Orçamento Temático De Acesso A Medicamentos: Análise De 10 Anos De Recursos Federais Destinados À Assistência Farmacêutica – Avaliação das execuções financeiras do Ministério da Saúde Com medicamentos de 2008 a 2018*. Brasília: Inesc, 2019. http://cebes.org.br/site/wp-content/uploads/2020/08/OTMED-2018_miolo.pdf.

da Silva, Virgílio Afonso and Fernanda Vargas Terrazas. "Claiming the right to health in brazilian courts: The exclusion of the already excluded." *Law and Social Inquiry* 36(4) (Fall 2011): 825–853. https://doi.org/10.1111/j.1747-4469.2011.01252.x.

Smith, Richard. "NICE: A panacea for the NHS?. " *BMJ* 318(7187) (1999): 823–824. https://doi.org/10.1136/bmj.318.7187.823.

Sorenson, Corinna, Michael Drummond and Panos Kanavos. *Ensuring Value for Money in Health Care: The Role of Health Technology Assessment in the European Union*. Observatory Studies Series 11. Copenhagen: European Observatory on Health Systems and Policies, 2008. https://apps.who.int/iris/handle/10665/107886.

Sorenson, Corinna, Michael Drummond and Beena Bhuiyan Khan. "Medical technology as a key driver of rising health expenditure: Disentangling the relationship." *ClinicoEconomics and Outcomes Research* 5 (2013): 223–234. https://doi.org/10.2147/ceor.s39634.

Sourdís, Catalina Gutiérrez, Olga Lucía Acosta Navarro and Eduardo Andrés Alfonso Sierra. "Financiación de la Seguridad Social en Salud: Fuentes de recursos y su administración." In: *La Salud en Colombia: Logros, retos y recomendaciones*, edited by Óscar Bernal and Catalina Gutiérrez, 81–182. Bogotá: Universidad de Los Andes, 2012. http://www.jstor.org/stable/10.7440/j.cttlb3t87j.14.

Sourdís, Catalina Gutiérrez and Julián Urrutia Ripoll. "Hacia un sistema de priorización en salud para Colombia." In: *La Salud en Colombia: Logros, retos y recomendaciones*, edited by Óscar Bernal and Catalina Gutiérrez, 401–474. Bogotá: Universidad de Los Andes, 2012. http://www.jstor.org/stable/10.7440/j.cttlb3t87j.14.

Souza, Kleize Araújo de Oliveira, Luis Eugênio Portela Fernandes de Souza and Erick Soares Lisboa. "Legal actions and incorporation of medicines into SUS: The performance of Conitec." *Saúde em Debate* 42(119) (October/December 2018): 837–848. https://doi.org/10.1590/0103-1104201811904.

Spiers, John. "The realities of health care rationing in the NHS." In: *The Realities of Rationing: 'Priority Setting' in the NHS*. London: Institute of Economic Affairs Health & Welfare Unit, 1999.

Sreenivasan, Gopal. "Why justice requires rationing in health care." In: *Medicine and Social Justice: Essays on the Distribution of Health Care*, edited by Rosamond Rhodes, Margaret P. Battin and Anita Silvers, 143–153. New York: Oxford University Press, 2012. https://doi.org/10.1093/acprof:osobl/9780199744206.003.0013.

Stevens, Andrew and Ruairidh Milne. "Health technology assessment in England and Wales." *International Journal of Technology Assessment in Health Care* 20(1) (Winter 2004): 11–24. https://doi.org/10.1017/s0266462304000741.

Stewart, Cameron. "Tragic choices and the role of administrative law." *BMJ* 321(7253) (2000): 105–107. https://doi.org/10.1136%2Fbmj.321.7253.105.

Sunkin, Maurice. "The United Kingdom." In: *The Global Expansion of Judicial Power*, edited by C. Neal Tate and Torbjörn Vallinder, 67–78. New York: NYU Press, 1995.

Sunkin, Maurice. "Conceptual issues in researching the impact of judicial review on government bureaucracies." In: *Judicial Review and Bureaucratic Impact: International and Interdisciplinary Perspectives*, edited by Marc Hertogh and Simon Halliday, 43–75. Cambridge: Cambridge University Press, 2009. https://doi.org/10.1017/CBO9780511493782.003.

Sunkin, Maurice. "Impact of public law litigation." In: *The Cambridge Companion to Public Law*, edited Mark Elliot and David Feldman, 236–255. Cambridge: Cambridge University Press, 2015. https://doi.org/10.1017/CCO9781139342551.013.

Sunkin, Maurice and Kathryn Pick. "The changing impact of judicial review: The Independent Review Service of the Social Fund." *Public Law* (Winter 2001): 736–762.

Sunkin, Maurice and Genevra Richardson. "Judicial review: Questions of impact." *Public Law* (1999): 79–103.

Syrett, Keith. "A technocratic fix to the 'legitimacy problem'? The Blair government and health care rationing in the United Kingdom." *Journal of Health Politics, Policy and Law* 28(4) (August 2003): 715–746. https://doi.org/10.1215/03616878-28-4-715.

Syrett, Keith. "Impotence or importance? Judicial review in an era of explicit NHS rationing." *Modern Law Review* 67(2) (March 2004): 289–304. https://doi.org/10.1111/j.1468-2230.2004.00487.x.

Syrett, Keith. *Law, Legitimacy and the Rationing of Health Care: A Contextual and Comparative Perspective*. New York: Cambridge University Press, 6. https://doi.org/10.1017/CBO9780511495380. See esp. chap, 2007, "Rationing in the Courts: England".

Syrett, Keith. "Health technology appraisal and the courts: Accountability for reasonableness and the judicial model of procedural justice." *Health Economics, Policy and Law* 6(4) (September 2011a): 469–488. https://doi.org/10.1017/S1744133110000228.

Syrett, Keith. "The English National Health Service and the 'transparency turn' in regulation of healthcare rationing." *Amsterdam Law Forum* 3(1) (2011b): 101–114. http://doi.org/10.37974/ALF.167.

Tantivess, Sripen, Kalipso Chalkidou, Nattha Tritasavit and Yot Teerawattananon. "Health Technology Assessment capacity development in low- and middle-income countries: Experiences from the international units of HITAP and NICE." *F1000Research* 6(2119) (December 11, 2017). https://doi.org/10.12688/f1000research.13180.1.

Tantivess, Sripen and Viroj Tangcharoensathien. "Coverage decisions and the court: A public health perspective on glucosamine reimbursement in Thailand." *Health Systems and Reform* 2(2) (2016): 106–111. https://doi.org/10.1080/23288604.2016.1128514.

Tasioulas, John. *Minimum Core Obligations: Human Rights in the Here and Now*. Research Paper. Washington, DC: The World Bank, October 2017. http://hdl.handle.net/10986/29144.

Tasioulas, John and Effy Vayena. "Getting human rights right in global health policy." *The Lancet* 385(9978) (April 2015): e42–e44. https://doi.org/10.1016/s0140-6736(14)61418-5.

Thatcher, Mark. *Governance Structures and Health Technology Assessment Agencies: A Comparative Approach*. LSE Research project 4869. London: Department of Government, London School of Economics and Political Science, 2010. http://eprints.lse.ac.uk/id/eprint/29471.

Thokala, Praveen and Alejandra Duenas. "Multiple criteria decision analysis for health technology assessment." *Value in Health* 15(8) (December 2012): 1172–1181. https://doi.org/10.1016/j.jval.2012.06.015.

El Tiempo, Redación. "'Magistrados no entendieron Ley Estatutaria que aprobaron': Minsalud." *El Tiempo*, November 5, 2014. https://www.eltiempo.com/archivo/documento/CMS-14793359.

Towse, Adrian and Martin Buxton. Three challenges to achieving better analysis for better decisions: Generalisability, complexity and thresholds. *Notes on a Conference in Honour of Bernie O'Brien. OHE Briefing 42*. London: Office of Health Economics, October, 2006. https://www.ohe.org/publications/three-challenges-achieving-better-analysis-better-decisions-generalisability-complexity.

Travassos, Denise Vieira, Raquel Conceição Ferreira, Andréa Maria Duarte Vargas, Rosa Núbia Vieira de Moura, Elza Maria Conceição, Dde F. Marques and Efigênia Ferreira Ferreira. "The judicialization of health care: a case study of three state courts in Brazil." *Ciência & saúde coletiva* 18(11) (November 2013): 3419–3429. https://doi.org/10.1590/S1413-81232013001100031.

Turriago, Leonardo Cubillos, Roberto Iunes, Janet Bonilla Torres, Diego Bolívar, Jorge Luis Silva, Sandra Liliana Osses Rivera and Adriana Pulido Álvarez. *Estudio exploratorio sobre mecanismos de asistencia técnica en asuntos de salud y tutela en Colombia: grupos focales com jueces municipales y jueces de circuito de las ciudades de Bogotá, Medellín y Barranquilla*. Papeles em Salud 9. World Bank/Ministerio de Salud y Protección Social, 2017. https://bit.ly/2vfxa5f.

Tushnet, Mark. *Weak Courts, Strong Rights: Judicial Review and Social Welfare Rights in Comparative Constitutional Law*. Princeton, NJ: Princeton University Press, 2008.

"Understanding observational studies." *Drug and Therapeutics Bulletin* 54(9) (September 2016): 105–108. https://doi.org/10.1136/dtb.2016.9.0426.

da União, Advocacia-Geral. *Intervenção Judicial na Saúde Pública: Panorama no âmbito da Justiça Federal e Apontamentos na seara das Justiças Estaduais*. Brasília:

Advocacia-geral da união, 2012. http://portalarquivos.saude.gov.br/images/pdf/2014/maio/29/Panorama-da-judicializa----o---2012---modificado-em-junho-de-2013.pdf.

da União, Advocacia Geral. "Judicialização da saúde no âmbito da união em números: Recursos extraordinários 566471 e 657718." In *Power Point Presentation*. Brasília (May 2017). https://www.gov.br/saude/pt-br/composicao/consultoria-juridica-conjur/biblioteca-eletronica/apresentacoes/judicializacao-da-saude-no-ambito-da-unio-em-numeros-recursos-extraordinrios-566471-e-657718.pdf/view.

United Nations. *Sustainable Development Goals Report 2018*. New York: United Nations, 2018.

Uprimny, Rodrigo. "The recent transformation of constitutional law in Latin America: Trends and challenges." *Texas Law Review* 89(7) (June 2011): 1587–1609.

Uprimny, Rodrigo and Juanita Durán. Equidad y protección judicial del derecho a la salud en Colombia. *Serie Políticas Sociales* Vol. 197. Bogotá: ECLAC/GIZ, 2014. https://www.cepal.org/es/publicaciones/36758-equidad-proteccion-judicial-derecho-la-salud-colombia.

de Vasconcelos, Natalia Pires. "Writ of Mandamus or Ministry of Health? Managers, Prosecutors and Institutional Responses to Judicialization." PhD thesis. University of São Paulo, 2018. https://doi.org/10.11606/T.2.2018.tde-30102020-141923.

Ventura, Miriam, Luciana Simas, Vera Lúcia Edais Pepe and Fermin Roland Schramm. "Judicialization of the right to health, access to justice and the effectiveness of the right to health." *Physis: Revista de Saúde Coletiva* 20(1) (2010): 77–100. https://doi.org/10.1590/S0103-73312010000100006.

Vermeule, Adrian. *Law and the Limits of Reason*. New York: Oxford University Press, 2008. https://doi.org/10.1093/acprof:oso/9780195383768.001.0001.

Vieira, Fabíola Sulpino. *Direito à Saúde no Brasil: Seus contornos, judicialização e a necessidade da macrojustiça*. Texto para discussão 2547. Brasília: Instituto de Pesquisa Econômica Aplicada, 2020. https://www.ipea.gov.br/portal/index.php?option=com_content&view=article&id=35360.

Vieira, Fabiola Sulpino, Sergio Francisco Piola and Rodrigo Pucci de Sá e Benevides. *Vinculação Orçamentária do Gasto em Saúde no Brasil: Resultados e argumentos a seu favor*. Texto para discussão 2516. Brasília: Instituto de Pesquisa Econômica Aplicada, 2019. https://www.ipea.gov.br/portal/index.php?option=com_content&view=article&id=35119.

Vieira, Fabiola Sulpino and Paola Zucchi. "Distortions to national drug policy caused by lawsuits in Brazil." *Revista de saúde pública* 41(2) (April 2007): 214–222. https://doi.org/10.1590/S0034-89102007000200007.

Von Bogdandy, Armin et al., eds. *Transformative Constitutionalism in Latin America: The Emergence of the New Ius Commune*. Oxford: Oxford University Press, 2017.

Voorhoeve, Alex, Tessa T. T. Edejer, Lydia Kapiriri, Ole F. Norheim, James Snowden, Olivier Basenya, Dorjsuren Bayarsaikhan et al. Three case studies in making fair choices on the path to universal health coverage. *Health and Human Rights Journal* 18(2) (December 2016): 11–22. https://www.hhrjournal.org/2016/11/three-case-studies-in-making-fair-choices-on-the-path-to-universal-health-coverage/.

Wang, Daniel Wei Liang. "Courts and health care rationing: The case of the Brazilian Federal Supreme Court." *Health Economics, Policy and Law* 8(1) (January 2013): 75–93. https://doi.org/10.1017/s1744133112000291.

Wang, Daniel Wei Liang. "Social rights and the nirvana fallacy." *Public Law* (July 2018): 482–499.

Wang, Daniel Wei Liang and Octavio Luiz Motta Ferraz. "Pharmaceutical Companies vs. the State: Who is Responsible for Post-Trial Provision of Drugs in Brazil?. " *Journal of Law, Medicine and Ethics* 40(2) (Summer 2012): 188–196. https://doi.org/10.1111/j.1748-720X.2012.00657.x.

Wang, Daniel Wei Liang and Octavio Luiza Motta Ferraz. "Reaching out to the needy? Access to Justice and public Attorneys' Role in Right to Health Litigation in the City of Sao Paulo." *Sur – International Journal on Human Rights* 10(18) (June 2013): 159–179. https://sur.conectas.org/en/reaching-out-to-the-needy/.

Wang, Daniel Wei Liang, Denise Franco, Fernanda Terrazas, Mariana Vilella and Natália Pires. "Judiciário e fornecimento de insulinas análogas pelo sistema público de saúde: direitos, ciência e políticas públicas." *Casoteca Direito GV, Produção de casos* 2011. http://direitosp.fgv.br/casoteca/judiciario-fornecimento-de-insulinas-analogas-pelo-sistema-publico-de-saude-direitos-cienci.

Wang, Daniel Wei Liang and Benedict Rumbold. "Priority setting and judicial accountability: The case of England." In: *Philosophical Foundations of Medical Law*, edited by Andelka M. Philips, Thana C. de Campos and Jonathan Herring, 185–196. Oxford: Oxford University Press, 2020. https://doi.org/10.1093/oso/9780198796558.001.0001.

Wang, Daniel Wei Liang, Fernanda Terrazas and Ana Luiza Chieffi. "Incorporating drugs Through litigation: The case of the state of Sao Paulo." *Annual Meeting of the Law and Society Association*, 2012.

Wang, Daniel Wei Liang, Natália Pires de Vasconcelos, Vanessa Elias de Oliveira and Fernanda Vargas Terrazas. "The impact of health care judicialization in the City of São Paulo: Public expenditure and Federal organization." *Revista de administração pública* 48(5) (September/October 2014): 1191–1206. https://doi.org/10.1590/0034-76121666.

Wang, Daniel Wei Liang, Natália Pires de Vasconcelos, Mathieu J. P. Poirier, Ana Chieffi, Cauê Mônaco, Lathika Sritharan, Susan Rogers Van Katwyk and Steven J. Hoffman. "Health technology assessment and judicial deference to priority-setting decisions in healthcare: Quasi-experimental analysis of right-to-health litigation in Brazil." *Social Science and Medicine* 265 (November 2020). https://doi.org/10.1016/j.socscimed.2020.113401.

Watkins, David A., Dean T. Jamison, Anne Mills, Rifat Atun, Kristen Danforth, Amanda Glassman, Susan Horton et al. "Universal health coverage and essential packages of care." In: *Disease Control Priorities: Improving Health and Reducing Poverty*, edited by Dean T. Jamison, Hellen Gelband, Susan Horton, Prabhat Jha and Charles N. Ramanan Laxminarayan Mock and Rachel Nugent, 43–68. Washington, DC: The World Bank, 2017. http://hdl.handle.net/10986/28877.

Watt, I. and V. Entwistle. "What are the implications of the child B Case for the debate on health care policies?" In: *Sense and Sensibility in Health Care*, edited by Marshall Marinker, 142–157. London: BMJ, 1996.

Weightman, Alison, Simon Ellis, Adrienne Cullum, Lesley Sander and Ruth Turley, eds. *Grading Evidence and Recommendations for Public Health Interventions: Developing and Piloting a Framework.* London: Health Development Agency, 2005. http://orca.cf.ac.uk/id/eprint/69810.

Widrig, Daniel and Brigitte Tag. "HTA and its legal issues: A framework for identifying legal issues in health technology assessment." *International Journal of Technology*

Assessment in Health Care 30(6) (December 2014): 587–594. http://doi.org/10.1017/S0266462314000683.

Wilking, Nils and Bengt Jönsson. *A Pan-European Comparison regarding Patient Access to Cancer Drugs*. Stockholm: Karolinska Institutet in collaboration with Stockholm School of Economics, 2005.

Wilkinson, Thomas, Mark J. Sculpher, Karl Claxton, Paul Revill, Andrew Briggs, John A. Cairns, Yot Teerawattananon et al. "The international decision support initiative reference case for economic evaluation: An aid to thought." *Value in Health* 19(8) (December 2016): 921–928. https://doi.org/10.1016/j.jval.2016.04.015.

Wiseman, Virginia, Craig Mitton, Mary M. Doyle-Waters, Tom Drake, Lesong Conteh, Anthony T. Newall, Obinna Onwujekwe and Stephan Jan. "Using economic evidence to set healthcare priorities in low-income and lower-middle-income countries: A systematic review of methodological frameworks." *Health Economics* 25(S1) (February 2016): 140–161. https://doi.org/10.1002/hec.3299.

Wootton, David. *Bad Medicine: Doctors Doing Harm Since Hippocrates*. Oxford: Oxford University Press, 2007.

World Health Organization. *The World Health Report: Health Systems Financing: The Path to Universal Coverage*. Geneva: World Health Organization, 2010. https://apps.who.int/iris/handle/10665/44371.

World Health Organization. *Positioning Health in the Post-2015 Development Agenda*. WHO Discussion Paper, October 2012.

World Health Organization. *Research for Universal Health Coverage*. The World Health Report. Geneva: World Health Organization, 2013. https://apps.who.int/iris/handle/10665/85761.

World Health Organization. *Access to New Medicines in Europe: Technical Review of Policy Initiatives and Opportunities for Collaboration and Research*. Copenhagen: WHO Regional Office for Europe, 2015. https://apps.who.int/iris/handle/10665/159405.

World Health Organization. "World Health Day 2018 – Key messages for World Health Day 2018." https://www.who.int/campaigns/world-health-day/2018/key-messages/en/.

World Health Organization and Bank World. *Monitoring Progress Towards Universal Health Coverage at Country and Global Levels*. Geneva: World Health Organization, 2014. https://apps.who.int/iris/handle/10665/112824.

World Health Organization and Bank World. *Tracking Universal Health Coverage: 2017 Global Monitoring Report*. Geneva: World Health Organization, 2017. http://hdl.handle.net/10986/29042.

World Health Organization Media Centre. "World Health Assembly concludes: Adopts key resolutions affecting global public health." May 25, 2005. https://www.who.int/mediacentre/news/releases/2005/pr_wha06/en/.

Xavier, Christabelle-Ann. "Judicialização da Saúde: Perspectiva Crítica sobre os Gastos da União para o Cumprimento das Ordens Judiciais." In: *Dilemas do fenômeno da Judicialização da saúde* Vol. 2 of *Coletânea Direito e Saúde*, edited by Alethele de Oliveira Santos and Luciana Tolêdo Lopes, 52–61. Brasília: CONASS, 2018. https://www.conasems.org.br/orientacao_ao_gestor/coletanea-direito-a-saude-volume-2-dilemas-do-fenomeno-da-judicializacao/.

Yamin, Alicia Ely. "Taking the right to health seriously: Implications for health systems, courts, and achieving universal health coverage." *Human Rights Quarterly* 39(2) (May 2017): 341–368. https://doi.org/10.1353/hrq.2017.0021.

Yamin, Alicia Ely and Ariel Frisancho. "Human-rights-based approaches to health in Latin America." *The Lancet* 385(9975) (April 4, 2015): e26–e29. https://doi.org/10.1016/S0140-6736(14)61280-0.

Yamin, Alicia Ely and Siri Gloppen, eds. *Litigating Health Rights: Can Courts Bring More Justice to Health?* Cambridge, MA: Harvard University Press, 2011.

Yamin, Alicia Ely and Allan Maleche. "Realizing Universal Health Coverage in East Africa: The relevance of human rights." *BMC International Health and Human Rights* 17 (August 3, 2017). https://doi.org/10.1186/s12914-017-0128-0.

Yamin, Alicia Ely and Ole Frithjof Norheim. "Taking equality seriously: Applying human rights frameworks to priority setting in health." *Human Rights Quarterly* 36(2) (May 2014): 296–324. https://doi.org/10.1353/hrq.2014.0027.

Yamin, Alicia Ely and Oscar Parra-Vera. "How do courts set health policy? The case of the Colombian Constitutional Court." *PLOS Medicine* 6(2) (2009): e1000032. https://doi.org/10.1371/journal.pmed.1000032.

Yamin, Alicia Ely, Oscar Parra-Vera and Camila Gianella. "Colombia judicial protection of the right to health: An elusive promise?. " In: *Litigating Health Rights: Can Courts Bring More Justice to Health?*, edited by Alicia Yamin and Siri Gloppen, 103–131. Cambridge, MA: Harvard University Press, 2011.

Young, Katharine G. "A typology of economic and social rights adjudication: Exploring the catalytic function of judicial review." *International Journal of Constitutional Law* 8(3) (July 1, 2010): 385–420. https://doi.org/10.1093/icon/moq029.

Young, Katherine G. *Constituting Economic and Social Rights.* Oxford: Oxford University Press, 2012. https://doi.org/10.1093/acprof:oso/9780199641932.001.0001.

Yowell, Paul. "Empirical research in rights-based judicial review of legislation." In: *Current Problems in the Protection of Human Rights–Perspectives from Germany and the UK*, edited by Katja S. Ziegler and Peter M. Huber, 155–188. Oxford: Hart, 2012.

Index